THE
FOUR FUNDAMENTAL
CONCEPTS OF
PSYCHO-ANALYSIS

By the same author
ÉCRITS: A SELECTION

JACQUES LACAN

THE
FOUR FUNDAMENTAL
CONCEPTS OF
PSYCHO-ANALYSIS

Edited by

JACQUES-ALAIN MILLER

Translated from the French by

ALAN SHERIDAN

W · W · NORTON & COMPANY · INC ·

NEW YORK

Published simultaneously in Canada by George J. McLeod
Limited, Toronto. Printed in the United States of America.

French title: Le Seminaire de Jacques Lacan, Livre XI, 'Les
quartre concepts fondamentaux de la psychanalyse' (Éditions du
Seuil, 1973)

Copyright © Éditions du Seuil   1973
Translation © Alan Sheridan   1977
First American Edition, 1978

Library of Congress Cataloging in Publication Data

Lacan, Jacques, 1901–
    The Four fundamental concepts of psycho-analysis.
    Translation of Les quatre concepts fondamentaux de la
psychanalyse, originally published as v. 11 of the author's Le
seminaire de Jacques Lacan
    Includes Index
    1. Psychoanalysis—Addresses, essays, lectures.
I. Title.
BF173.L146213   1978   150'.19'5   77-12108
ISBN 0–393–01170–4

1 2 3 4 5 6 7 8 9 0

CONTENTS

v

CONTENTS

PREFACE TO THE
ENGLISH-LANGUAGE EDITION

When the space of a lapsus no longer carries any meaning (or interpretation), then only is one sure that one is in the unconscious. *One knows.*

But one has only to be aware of the fact to find oneself outside it. There is no friendship there, in that space that supports this unconscious.

All I can do is tell the truth. No, that isn't so—I have missed it. There is no truth that, in passing through awareness, does not lie.

But one runs after it all the same.

There is a way of sorting out this muddle that is satisfactory for other than formal reasons (symmetry, for example). Like satisfaction, it is acquired only with use, with the use of an individual—who, in psycho-analysis (psych = fiction of), is called an analysand. And, as a matter of simple fact, there is no shortage of analysands in our lands. That is a fact of human reality—what man calls reality.

It should be noted that psycho-analysis has, since it has ex-sisted, changed. Invented by a solitary, an incontestable theoretician of the unconscious (which is not what one imagines it to be—the unconscious, I would say, is real), it is now practised in couples. To be fair, the solitary was the first to set the example. Not without abusing his disciples (for they were disciples only because he knew not what he did).

This conveys the idea he had of psycho-analysis—a plague—except that it proved to be anodyne in the land where he brought it; the public adopted/adapted it quite painlessly.

Now, a little late in the day, I add my pinch of salt: a fact of hystory, or hysteria: that of my colleagues, as it happens, a case of no importance, but one in which I happened to find myself implicated for concerning myself with someone who introduced me to them as having imposed on myself Freud, the Beloved of Mathesis.

I would have preferred to forget that: but one does not forget what the public constantly reminds you of.

So one must take account of the analyst in psycho-analytic treatment. He would have no social standing, I imagine, if Freud had not opened up the way for him—Freud, I say, to call him by his name. For no one can call anyone an analyst and Freud did not do so. Handing out rings to initiates is not to call by a name. Hence my proposition that the analyst hystorizes only from himself: a patent fact. Even if he is confirmed in doing so by a hierarchy.

What hierarchy could confirm him as an analyst, give him the rubber-stamp? A certificate tells me that I was born. I repudiate this certificate: I am not a poet, but a poem. A poem that is being written, even if it looks like a subject.

There remains the question of what could drive anyone, especially after an analysis, to hystorize from himself.

It cannot come from himself, for he knows something about the analyst, now that he has liquidated, as they say, his positive transference. How could he contemplate taking up the same function?

In other words, are there cases in which you are impelled by some other reason than the wish to set yourself up, that is, to earn money, to keep those who are in your care, above all yourself, according to Jewish morality (to which Freud remained attached in this respect).

One must admit that the question (the question of another reason) is necessary to support the status of a profession newly arrived in hystory. A hystory that I do not call eternal, because its *aetas* is serious only in relation to real number, that is to say, to the serial of limit.

Why, then, should we not put this profession to the test of that truth of which the so-called unconscious function dreams, with which it dabbles? The mirage of truth, from which only lies can be expected (this is what, in polite language, we call 'resistance'), has no other term than the satisfaction that marks the end of the analysis.

Since the main aim of analysis is to give this urgently needed satisfaction, let us ask ourselves how someone can devote himself to satisfying these urgent cases.

This is an odd aspect of that love of one's neighbour upheld by the Judaic tradition. But to interpret it in Christian terms, that is to say, as Hellenic *jean-f..trerie*, what is presented to the analyst is something other than the neighbour: it is the unsorted material of a demand that has nothing to do with the meeting (of a person from Samaria fit to dictate Christic duty). The offer is prior to an urgent request that one is not sure of satisfying, unless one has weighed it.

I have therefore designated as a 'pass' that putting of the hystorization of the analysis to the test, while refraining from imposing this pass on all, because it is not a question, as it happens, of all, but of scattered, ill-assorted individuals. I have left it at the disposal of those who are prepared to run the risk of attesting at best to the lying truth.

I have done so by virtue of having produced the only conceivable idea of the object, that of the object as cause of desire, of that which is lacking.

The lack of the lack makes the real, which emerges only there, as a cork. This cork is supported by the term of the impossible —and the little we know about the real shows its antinomy to all verisimilitude.

I shall speak of Joyce, who has preoccupied me much this year, only to say that he is the simplest consequence of a refusal —such a mental refusal!—of a psycho-analysis, which, as a result, his work illustrates. But I have done no more than touch on this, in view of my embarrassment where art—an element in which Freud did not bathe without mishap—is concerned.

I would-mention that, as always, I was entangled in urgent cases as I wrote this.

I write, however, in so far as I feel I must, in order to be on a level (*au pair*) with these cases, to make a pair with them.

Paris 17.5.76   J. L.

EDITOR'S NOTE

My intention here was to be as unobtrusive as possible and to obtain from Jacques Lacan's spoken work an authentic version that would stand, in the future, for the original, which does not exist.

For the short-hand transcription, riddled as it is with inaccuracies, and lacking the speaker's gesture and intonation, cannot be regarded as the original. Nevertheless, it is the version *sine qua non*, which I have examined, word by word, and, where necessary, rectified—the expunged material amounting to less than three pages.

The most difficult matter is the invention of a system of punctuation, since all punctuation—comma, full-stop, dash, paragraph—determines meaning. But this was the price to be paid if a readable text was to be produced, and the texts of all the seminars will follow the same principles.

J.-A. M.

THE
FOUR FUNDAMENTAL
CONCEPTS OF
PSYCHO-ANALYSIS

I

EXCOMMUNICATION

Am I qualified? · The essence of comedy · What is a praxis? · Between science and religion · The hysteric and Freud's own desire

Ladies and Gentlemen,

In this series of lectures, which I have been invited to give by the École pratique des Hautes Études, I shall be talking to you about the fundamentals of psycho-analysis.

Today I should like simply to point out to you the meaning I intend to give to this title and the way I hope to justify it.

And yet, I must first introduce myself to you—despite the fact that most, though not all of you, know me already—because the circumstances are such that before dealing with this subject it might be appropriate to ask a preliminary question, namely: *am I qualified to do so?*

My qualification for speaking to you on this subject amounts to this: for ten years, I held what was called a seminar, addressed to psycho-analysts. As some of you may know, I withdrew from this role (to which I had in fact devoted my life) as a result of events occurring within what is called a psycho-analytic association, and, more specifically, within the association that had conferred this role upon me.

It might be said that my qualification to undertake the same role elsewhere is not, by that token, impugned as such. However that may be, I consider the problem deferred for the time being. And if today I am in a position to be able, let us simply say, to *further* this teaching of mine, I feel it incumbent upon me, before embarking on what for me is a new phase, to express my thanks to M. Fernand Braudel, the chairman of the section of the Hautes Études that appointed me to appear before you here. M. Braudel has informed me of his regret at being unable to be present: I would like to pay tribute to what I can only call his nobility in providing me with a means of continuing my teaching, whose style and reputation alone were known to him. Nobility is surely the right word for his welcome to someone in my position—that of a refugee otherwise reduced to silence. M. Braudel extended this welcome to me as soon as he had been alerted by the vigilance of my friend Claude Lévi-Strauss, whom I am delighted to see here today and who knows how precious for me this evidence of his interest in my work is—in work that has developed in parallel with his own.

I wish also to thank all those who on this occasion demonstrated their sympathy to such effect that M. Robert Flacelière, Director of the Ecole Normale Supérieure, was generous enough to put this auditorium at the disposal of the École des Hautes Études—and without which I should have been at a loss to welcome you in such numbers—for which I wish to express my most heartfelt thanks.

All this concerns the *base*, in the topographical and even the military sense of the word—the base for my teaching. I shall now turn to what it is about—the fundamentals of psycho-analysis.

I

As far as the fundamentals of psycho-analysis are concerned, my seminar was, from the beginning, *implicated*, so to speak. It was an element of those fundamentals, because it was a contribution, *in concreto*, to them—because it was an internal part of psycho-analytic praxis itself—because it was aimed at what is an essential of that praxis, namely, the training of psycho-analysts.

There was a time when, ironically—temporarily, perhaps, and for lack of anything better in the situation I was in—I was led to define a criterion of what psycho-analysis is, namely, the treatment handed out by psycho-analysts. Henry Ey, who is here today, will remember the article in question as it was published in a volume of the encyclopaedia he edits. And, since he is present, it is all the easier for me to recall the fury that the article aroused and the pressure exerted to get the said article withdrawn from the said encyclopaedia. As a result, M. Ey, whose sympathy for my cause is well known, was powerless to resist an operation masterminded by an editorial committee on which there were, precisely, some psycho-analysts. The article concerned will be included in a collection of a number of my essays that I am trying to put together, and you will, I think, be able to judge for yourselves whether it has lost any of its relevance. For me, this seems all the less likely given that the questions I raise in it are the very same as those that I shall be grappling with here, and which are resuscitated by the fact that here I am, in the present circumstances, still asking that very same question—*what is psycho-analysis?*

No doubt there are certain ambiguities in all this, and the question—as I pointed out in the article—still has a certain bat-like quality. To examine it in broad daylight is what I proposed to do then and, whatever position I am in, it is what I propose to do today.

The position I refer to has changed, in fact; it is not wholly inside, but whether it is outside is not known.

In reminding you of all this, I am not indulging in personal reminiscence. I think you will agree that I am having recourse neither to gossip nor to any kind of polemic if I point out here what is simply *a fact*, namely, that my teaching—specifically designated as such—has been the object of censure by a body calling itself the Executive Committee of an organization calling itself the International Psycho-analytical Association. Such censorship is of no ordinary kind, since what it amounts to is no less than a ban on this teaching—which is to be regarded as nul and void as far as any qualification to the title of psychoanalyst is concerned. And the acceptance of this ban is to be a condition of the international affiliation of the Psycho-analytical Association to which I belong.

But this is not all. It is expressly spelt out that this affiliation is to be accepted only if a guarantee is given that my teaching may *never again* be sanctioned by the Association as far as the training of analysts is concerned.

So, what it amounts to is something strictly comparable to what is elsewhere called major excommunication—although there the term is never pronounced without any possibility of repeal. The latter exists only in a religious community designated by the significant symbolic term *synagogue*, and it was precisely that which Spinoza was condemned to. On 27 July 1656—a singular bi-centenary, for it corresponds to that of Freud—Spinoza was made the object of the *kherem*, an

3

excommunication that corresponds to major excommunication, since he had to wait some time before becoming the object of the *chammata*, which consists of appending the clause of no return.

Please do not imagine that here—any more than elsewhere —I am indulging in some metaphorical game—that would be too puerile in view of the long and, God knows, serious enough terrain we have to cover. I believe—you will be able to judge for yourselves—that not only by virtue of the echoes it evokes, but by the structure it implies, this fact introduces something that is essential to our investigation of psychoanalytic praxis.

I am not saying—though it would not be inconceivable —that the psycho-analytic community is a Church. Yet the question indubitably does arise—what is it in that community that is so reminiscent of religious practice? Nor would I have stressed this point—though it is sufficiently significant to carry the musty odour of scandal—were it not that like everything I have to say today, it will be useful in what follows.

I do not mean that I am indifferent to what happens to me in such circumstances. Do not imagine that for me—any more, I suppose, than for the intercessor whose precedent I have not hesitated to evoke—this is material for comedy. It is no laughing matter. Nevertheless, I should like to let you know *en passant* that something of the order of a vast comic dimension in all this has not wholly escaped me. What I am referring to here is not at the level of what I have called excommunication. It has to do with the situation I was in for two years, that of knowing that I was—at the hands of precisely those who, in relation to me, were colleagues or even pupils—the object of what is called *a deal*.

For what was at stake was the extent to which the concessions made with respect to the validity of my teaching could be traded off with the other side of the deal, namely, the international affiliation of the Association. I do not wish to forgo this opportunity—we shall return to it later—of indicating that the situation can be experienced at the level of the comic dimension proper.

This can be fully appreciated, I think, only by a psychoanalyst.

4

No doubt, being the object of a deal is not a rare situation for an individual—contrary to all the verbiage about human dignity, not to mention the Rights of Man. Each of us at any moment and at any level may be traded off—without the notion of exchange we can have no serious insight into the social structure. The kind of exchange involved here is the exchange of individuals, that is, of those social supports which, in a different context, are known as 'subjects', with all their supposed sacred rights to autonomy. It is a well known fact that politics is a matter of trading—wholesale, in lots, in this context—the same subjects, who are now called citizens, in hundreds of thousands. There was nothing particularly exceptional, then, about my situation, except that being traded by those whom I referred to just now as colleagues, and even pupils, is sometimes, if seen from the outside, called by a different name.

But if the truth of the subject, even when he is in the position of master, does not reside in himself, but, as analysis shows, in an object that is, of its nature, concealed, to bring this object out into the light of day is really and truly the essence of comedy.

This dimension of the situation is worth pointing out, I think, especially in the position from which I can testify to it, because, after all, on such an occasion, it might be treated, with undue restraint, a sort of false modesty, as someone who had experienced it from the outside might do. From the inside, I can tell you that this dimension is quite legitimate, that it may be experienced from the analytic point of view, and even, from the moment it is perceived, in a way that overcomes it —namely, from the point of view of humour, which, here, is simply the recognition of the comic.

This remark is not without relevance to my subject—the fundamentals of psycho-analysis—for *fundamentum* has more than one meaning, and I do not need to remind you that in the Kabbala it designates one of the modes of divine manifestation, which, in this register, is strictly identified with the *pudendum*. All the same, it would be extraordinary if, in an analytic discourse, we were to stop at the *pudendum*. In this context, no doubt, the fundamentals would take the form of the *bottom* parts, were it not that those parts were already to some extent exposed.

5

Some people, on the outside, may be surprised that certain of my analysands, some of whom were still under analysis, should have taken part, a very active part, in this deal. And they may ask themselves how such a thing is possible were it not that, at the level of the relation between your analysands and yourselves, there is some discord that puts in question the very value of analysis. Well, it is precisely by setting out from something that may provide grounds for scandal that we will be able to grasp in a more precise way what is called the *training analysis*—that praxis, or that stage of praxis, which has been completely ignored in all published work on psychoanalysis—and throw some light on its aims, its limits and its effects.

This is no longer a question of *pudendum*. It is a question of knowing what may, what must, be expected of psycho-analysis, and the extent to which it may prove a hindrance, or even a failure.

That is why I thought I was under an obligation to spare you no details, but to present you with a *fact*, as an object, whose outlines, and whose possible manipulation, I hope you will see more clearly, to present it at the very outset of what I now have to say when, before you, I ask the question—*What are the fundamentals*, in the broad sense of the term, *of psychoanalysis?* Which amounts to saying—What grounds it as praxis?

2

What is a praxis? I doubt whether this term may be regarded as inappropriate to psycho-analysis. It is the broadest term to designate a concerted human action, whatever it may be, which places man in a position to treat the real by the symbolic. The fact that in doing so he encounters the imaginary to a greater or lesser degree is only of secondary importance here.

This definition of praxis, then, is very extensive. We are not going to set out in search of our psycho-analysis, like Diogenes in search of man, in the various, very diversified fields of praxis. Rather we shall take our psycho-analysis with us, and it will direct us at once towards some fairly well located, specifiable points of praxis.

Without even introducing by any kind of transition the two

terms between which I wish to hold the question—and not at all in an ironic way—I posit first that, if I am here, in such a large auditorium, in such a place, and with such an audience, it is to ask myself *whether psycho-analysis is a science,* and to examine the question with you.

The other reference, the religious one, I already mentioned a little while ago, specifying that I am speaking of religion in the true sense of the term—not of a desiccated, methodologized religion, pushed back into the distant past of a primitive form of thought, but of religion as we see it practised in a still living, very vital way. Psycho-analysis, whether or not it is worthy of being included in one of these two registers, may even enlighten us as to what we should understand by science, and even by religion.

I would like at once to avoid a misunderstanding. In any case, someone will say, psycho-analysis is a form of research. Well, allow me to say quite clearly—in particular to the public authorities for whom this search has seemed, for some time now, to serve as a shibboleth for any number of things —that I am a bit suspicious of this term research. Personally, I have never regarded myself as a researcher. As Picasso once said, to the shocked surprise of those around him—*1 do not seek, I find.*

Indeed, there are in the field of so-called scientific research two domains that can quite easily be recognized, that in which one seeks, and that in which one finds.

Curiously enough, this corresponds to a fairly well defined frontier between what may and may not qualify as science. Furthermore, there is no doubt some affinity between the research that seeks and the religious register. In the religious register, the phrase is often used—*You would not seek me if you had not already found me.* The *already found* is already behind, but stricken by something like oblivion. Is it not, then, a complaisant, endless search that is then opened up?

If the search concerns us here, it is by virtue of those elements of this debate that are established at the level of what we nowadays call the human sciences. Indeed, in these human sciences, one sees emerging, as it were, beneath the feet of whoever finds, what I will call the *hermeneutic demand,* which is precisely that which seeks—which seeks the ever new and the never exhausted signification, but one threatened with being trampled under foot by him who finds.

Now, we analysts are interested in this hermeneutics, because the way of developing signification offered by hermeneutics is confused, in many minds, with what analysis calls *interpretation*. It so happens that, although this interpretation cannot in any way be conceived in the same way as the aforementioned hermeneutics, hermeneutics, on the other hand, makes ready use of interpretation. In this respect, we see, at least, a corridor of communication between psycho-analysis and the religious register. We shall come back to this in due course.

Before allowing psycho-analysis to call itself a science, therefore, we shall require a little more.

What specifies a science is having an object. It is possible to maintain that a science is specified by a definite object, at least by a certain reproducible level of operation known as *experiment*. But we must be very prudent, because this object changes, and in a very strange way, as a science develops. We cannot say that the object of modern physics is the same now as at its birth, which I would date in the seventeenth century. And is the object of modern chemistry the same as at the moment of its birth, which I would date from the time of Lavoisier?

It is possible that these remarks will force us into an at least tactical retreat, and to start again from the praxis, to ask ourselves, knowing that praxis delimits a field, whether it is at the level of this field that the modern scientist, who is not a man who knows a lot about everything, is to be specified.

I do not accept Duhem's demand that every science should refer to a unitary, or world, system—a reference that is always in fact more or less idealist, since it is a reference to the need of identification. I would even go so far as to say that we can dispense with the implicit transcendent element in the position of the positivist, which always refers to some ultimate unity of all the fields.

We will extricate ourselves from it all the more easily in view of the fact that, after all, it is disputable, and may even be regarded as false. It is in no way necessary that the tree of science should have a single trunk. I do not think that there are many of them. There are perhaps, as in the first chapter of *Genesis*, two different trunks—not that I attach in any way an ex-

ceptional importance to this myth, which is tinged to a greater
or lesser degree with obscurantism, but why shouldn't we
expect psycho-analysis to throw some light on it?

If we hold to the notion of experience, in the sense of the
field of a praxis, we see very well that it is not enough to define
a science. Indeed, this definition might be applied very well,
for example, to the mystical experience. It is even by this door
that it is regarded once again as scientific, and that we almost
arrive at the stage of thinking that we can have a scientific
apprehension of this experience. There is a sort of ambiguity
here—to subject an experience to a scientific examination
always implies that the experience has of itself a scientific sub-
sistance. But it is obvious that we cannot re-introduce the
mystical experience into science.

One further remark. Might this definition of science, based
on the field determined by a praxis, be applied to alchemy to
give it the status of a science? I was recently rereading a little
book that is not even included in Diderot's *Complete Works*, but
which certainly seems to be by him. Although chemistry was
born with Lavoisier, Diderot speaks throughout this little book,
with all the subtlety of mind we expect of him, not of chemistry,
but of alchemy. What is it that makes us say at once that,
despite the dazzling character of the stories he recounts from
ages past, alchemy, when all is said and done, is not a science?
Something, in my view, is decisive, namely, that the purity of
soul of the operator was, as such, and in a specific way, an
essential element in the matter.

This remark is not beside the point, as you may realize, since
we may be about to raise something similar concerning the
presence of the analyst in the analytic Great Work, and to
maintain that it is perhaps what our training analysis seeks. I
may even seem to have been saying the same thing myself in my
teaching recently, when I point straight out, all veils torn aside,
and in a quite overt way, towards that central point that I put
in question, namely—*what is the analyst's desire?*

3

What must there be in the analyst's desire for it to operate
in a correct way? Can this question be left outside the limits of
our field, as it is in effect in the sciences—the modern sciences

9

of the most assured type—where no one questions himself as to what there must be in the desire, for example, of the physicist?

There really must be a series of crises for an Oppenheimer to question us all as to what there is in the desire that lies at the basis of modern physics. No one pays any attention to him anyway. It is thought to be a political incident. Is this desire something of the same order as that which is required of the adept of alchemy?

In any case, the analyst's desire can in no way be left outside our question, for the simple reason that the problem of the training of the analyst poses it. And the training analysis has no other purpose than to bring the analyst to the point I designate in my algebra as the analyst's desire.

Here, again, I must for the moment leave the question open. You may feel that I am leading you, little by little, to some such question as—Is agriculture a science? Some people will say yes, some people no. I offer this example only to suggest to you that you should make some distinction between agriculture defined by an object and agriculture defined, if you'll forgive me, by a field—between agriculture and agronomy. This enables me to bring out one definite dimension—we are at the abc stage, but, after all, we can't help it—that of *formula making*.

Is that enough to define the conditions of a science? I don't think so. A false science, just like a true science, may be expressed in formulae. The question is not so simple, then, when psycho-analysis, as a supposed science, appears to have such problematic features.

What are the formulae in psycho-analysis concerned with? What motivates and modulates this 'sliding-away' (*glissement*) of the object? Are there psycho-analytic concepts that we are now in possession of? How are we to understand the almost religious maintenance of the terms proposed by Freud to structure the analytic experience? Was Freud really the first, and did he really remain the only theoretician of this supposed science to have introduced fundamental concepts? Were this so, it would be very unusual in the history of the sciences. Without this trunk, this mast, this pile, where can our practice be moored? Can we even say that what we are dealing with are concepts in the strict sense? Are they concepts in the process of formation? Are they concepts in the process of development, in movement, to be revised at a later date?

I think this is a question in which we can maintain that some progress has already been made, in a direction that can only be one of work, of conquest, with a view to resolving the question as to *whether psycho-analysis is a science*. In fact, the maintenance of Freud's concepts at the centre of all theoretical discussion in that dull, tedious, forbidding chain—which is read by nobody but psycho-analysts—known as the psycho-analytic literature, does not alter the fact that analysts in general have not yet caught up with these concepts, that in this literature most of the concepts are distorted, debased, fragmented, and that those that are too difficult are quite simply ignored—that, for example, everything that has been developed around the concept of frustration is, in relation to Freud's concepts, from which it derives, clearly retrograde and pre-conceptual.

Similarly, no one is any longer concerned, with certain rare exceptions to be found among my pupils, with the ternary structure of the Oedipus complex or with the castration complex.

It is certainly no contribution to the theoretical status of psycho-analysis for a writer like Fenichel to reduce, by an enumeration of the 'main sewer' type, the accumulated material of the psycho-analytic experience to the level of platitude. Of course, a certain quantity of facts have been gathered together, and there is some point in seeing them grouped into a few chapters, but one cannot avoid the impression that, in a whole field, everything is explained in advance. Analysis is not a matter of discovering in a particular case the differential feature of the theory, and in doing so believe that one is explaining why your daughter is silent—for the point at issue is to *get her to speak*, and this effect proceeds from a type of intervention that has nothing to do with a differential feature.

Analysis consists precisely in getting her to speak. It might be said, therefore, that in the last resort, it amounts to overcoming the barrier of silence, and this is what, at one time, was called the analysis of the resistances.

The symptom is first of all the silence in the supposed speaking subject. If he speaks, he is cured of his silence, obviously. But this does not tell us anything about why he began to speak.

It merely designates for us a differential feature which, in the case of the silent girl, is, as was only to be expected, that of the hysteric.

Now, the differential feature of the hysteric is precisely this —it is in the very movement of speaking that the hysteric constitutes her desire. So it is hardly surprising that it should be through this door that Freud entered what was, in reality, the relations of desire to language and discovered the mechanisms of the unconscious.

That this relation of desire to language as such did not remain concealed from him is a feature of his genius, but this is not to say that the relation was fully elucidated—far from it—by the massive notion of the transference.

The fact that, in order to cure the hysteric of all her symptoms, the best way is to satisfy her hysteric's desire—which is for her to posit her desire in relation to us as an unsatisfied desire —leaves entirely to one side the specific question of *why* she can sustain her desire only as an unsatisfied desire. So hysteria places us, I would say, on the track of some kind of original sin in analysis. There has to be one. The truth is perhaps simply one thing, namely, the desire of Freud himself, the fact that something, in Freud, was never analysed.

I had reached precisely this point when, by a strange coincidence, I was put into the position of having to give up my seminar.

What I had to say on the Names-of-the-Father had no other purpose, in fact, than to put in question the origin, to discover by what privilege Freud's desire was able to find the entrance into the field of experience he designates as the unconscious.

It is absolutely essential that we should go back to this origin if we wish to put analysis on its feet.

In any case, such a mode of questioning the field of experience will be guided, in our next meeting, by the following reference—what conceptual status must we give to four of the terms introduced by Freud as fundamental concepts, namely, *the unconscious, repetition, the transference* and *the drive*?

We will reach our next step, at our next meeting, by considering the way in which, in my past teaching, I have situated these concepts in relation to the more general function that embraces them, and which makes it possible to show their operational value in this field, namely, the subjacent, implicit function of the signifier as such.

This year, I promised myself to break off at twenty-past two, so as to leave time for those who do not have to go on at once to other pursuits to ask questions arising from my lecture.

QUESTIONS AND ANSWERS

M. TORT: *When you relate psycho-analysis to Freud's desire and to the desire of the hysteric, might you not be accused of psychologism?*

LACAN: The reference to Freud's desire is not a psychological reference—and reference to the hysteric's desire is not a psychological reference.

I posed the following question: the functioning of 'Primitive Thinking' (*la Pensée sauvage*), which Lévi-Strauss places at the basis of the statutes of society, is *one* unconscious, but is it enough to accommodate the unconscious as such? And if it is able to do so, does it accommodate the Freudian unconscious?

It was through the hysterics that Freud learnt the way of the strictly Freudian unconscious. It was here that I brought the desire of the hysteric into play, while indicating at the same time that Freud did not stop there.

Freud's desire, however, I have placed at a higher level. I have said that the Freudian field of analytic practice remained dependent on a certain original desire, which always plays an ambiguous, but dominant role in the transmission of psycho-analysis. The problem of this desire is not psychological, any more than is the unsolved problem of Socrates' desire. There is an entire thematic area concerning the status of the subject when Socrates declares that he does not place desire in a position of original subjectivity, but in the position of an object. Well! Freud, too, is concerned with desire as an object.

15 January 1964

The Unconscious and Repetition

2

THE FREUDIAN UNCONSCIOUS
AND OURS

*Pensée sauvage · There is cause only in something that doesn't work ·
Gap, obstacle, discovery, loss · Discontinuity · Signorelli*

Because I am beginning on time today, I will start by reading a
poem which, in actual fact, has no relation to what I am about
to say, but which is related to what I said last year, in my
seminar, about the mysterious object, the most concealed object,
that of the scopic drive.

It is a short poem to be found on page 73 of *Fou d'Elsa*, which
Aragon entitles '*Contre-chant*'.

> *Vainement ton image arrive à ma rencontre*
> *Et ne m'entre où je suis qui seulement la montre*
> *Toi te tournant vers moi tu ne saurais trouver*
> *Au mur de mon regard que ton ombre rêvée*
>
> *Je suis ce malheureux comparable aux miroirs*
> *Qui peuvent réfléchir mais ne peuvent pas voir*
> *Comme eux mon œil est vide et comme eux habité*
> *De l'absence de toi qui fait sa cécité*

In vain your image comes to meet me
And does not enter me where I am who only shows it
Turning towards me you can find
On the wall of my gaze only your dreamt-of shadow.

I am that wretch comparable with mirrors
That can reflect but cannot see
Like them my eye is empty and like them inhabited
By your absence which makes them blind.

I dedicate this poem to the nostalgia that some of you may
feel for that interrupted seminar in which I developed the
theme of anxiety and the function of the *objet petit a*.

17

They will appreciate, I think, those who˙were with me last year—I apologize for being so allusive—they will appreciate the fact that Aragon—in this admirable work in which I am proud to find an echo of the tastes of our generation, so much so that I am forced to turn to friends of my own age if I am to make myself understood about this poem—follows his poem with this enigmatic line—*Thus said An-Nadjî once, as he was invited to a circumcision.*

This is the point at which those who heard my seminar last year will find a correspondence between the various forms of the *objet a* and the central symbolic function of the *minus-phi* $[(-\phi)]$—evoked here by the strange reference, which is certainly no accident, that Aragon confers on the historical connotation, if I may put it this way, of the propagation by his character, the mad poet, of this 'counter-song'.

I

There are some of you here, I know, who are being introduced to my teaching for the first time. They are being introduced to it through writings that are already dated. I would like them to know that one of the indispensable co-ordinates in appreciating the meaning of this first teaching must be found in the fact that they cannot, from their present position, imagine to what degree of contempt for, or simply *méconnaissance* of, the instrument of their work the practitioners of psycho-analysis can attain. They should know that for some years all my effort has been required in a struggle to bring to the attention of these practitioners the true value of this instrument, *speech* —to give it back its dignity, so that it does not always represent for them those words, devalued in advance, that force them to fix their gaze elsewhere, in order to find their guarantor.

Thus, for a time at least, I was thought to be obsessed with some kind of philosophy of language, even a Heideggerian one, whereas only a *propaedeutic* reference was involved. The fact that I am speaking here will not make me speak more philosophically.

But let me turn to something else, which indeed I will find easier to specify here. I am referring to something that I can only call the refusal of the concept. That is why, as I announced at the end of my first seminar, I will try to introduce you today to the major Freudian concepts—I have isolated four that seem to come within this category.

The few words on the blackboard under the heading Freudian concepts are the first two—the unconscious and repetition. The transference—I hope to approach it next time—will introduce us directly to the algorithms that I thought necessary to set out in practice, especially with a view to the implementation of the analytic technique as such. Lastly, the drive is still so difficult to approach—so neglected, one should say —that I do not think I can do more this year than touch upon it after we have dealt with the transference.

We shall see, therefore, only the essence of analysis—especially that which is profoundly problematic, though at the same time crucial, about it, namely, the function of the training analysis. It is only by going through this exposition that we may, at the end of the year—without wishing myself in any way to minimize the shifting, not to say scabrous, side of the approach to this concept—begin our examination of the drive. In this respect, our approach will provide a contrast with those who boldly venture into this terrain with incomplete and flimsy references.

The two small arrows that you see indicated on the blackboard after *The unconscious* and *Repetition* point towards the question-mark that follows. This question-mark indicates that our conception of the concept implies that the concept is always established in an approach that is not unrelated to that which is imposed on us, as a form, by infinitesimal calculus. Indeed, if the concept is modelled on an approach to the reality that the concept has been created to apprehend, it is only by a leap, a passage to the limit, that it manages to realize itself. We are then required to say in what respect—under what form of finite quantity, I would say—the conceptual elaboration known as the unconscious may be carried out. The same goes for repetition.

It is in relation to the other two terms written on the blackboard at the end of the line, *The subject* and *The real* that we will be led to give form to the question posed last time—can psychoanalysis, with all its paradoxical, odd, aporic qualities, be regarded, among us, as constituting a science, a potential science?

I shall take first the concept of the unconscious.

2

Most of you will have some idea of what I mean when I say — *the unconscious is structured like a language*. This statement refers to a field that is much more accessible to us today than at the time of Freud. I will illustrate it by something that is materialized, at what is certainly a scientific level, by the field that is explored, structured, elaborated by Claude Lévi-Strauss, and which he has pinpointed in the title of his book, *La Pensée Sauvage*.

Before any experience, before any individual deduction, even before those collective experiences that may be related only to social needs are inscribed in it, something organizes this field, inscribes its initial lines of force. This is the function that Claude Lévi-Strauss shows us to be the truth of the totemic function, and which reduces its appearance—the primary classificatory function.

Before strictly human relations are established, certain relations have already been determined. They are taken from whatever nature may offer as supports, supports that are arranged in themes of opposition. Nature provides—I must use the word—signifiers, and these signifiers organize human relations in a creative way, providing them with structures and shaping them.

The important thing, for us, is that we are seeking here —before any formation of the subject, of a subject who thinks, who situates himself in it—the level at which there is counting, things are counted, and in this counting he who counts is already included. It is only later that the subject has to recognize himself as such, recognize himself as he who counts. Remember the naïve failure of the simpleton's delighted attempt to grasp the little fellow who declares—*I have three brothers, Paul, Ernest and me*. But it is quite natural—first the three brothers, Paul, Ernest and I are counted, and then there is I at the level at which I am to reflect the first I, that is to say, the I who counts.

In our time, in the historical period that has seen the formation of a science that may be termed human, but which must be distinguished from any kind of psycho-sociology, namely, linguistics, whose model is the combinatory operation, functioning spontaneously, of itself, in a presubjective way

—it is this linguistic structure that gives its status to the unconscious. It is this structure, in any case, that assures us that there is, beneath the term unconscious, something definable, accessible and objectifiable. But when I urge psycho-analysts not to ignore this field, which provides them with a solid support for their labours, does this mean that I hope to include the concepts introduced historically by Freud under the term unconscious? No, I don't think so. The unconscious, the Freudian concept, is something different, which I would like to try to get you to grasp today.

It is certainly not enough to say that the unconscious is a dynamic concept, since this would be to substitute the most common kind of mystery for a particular mystery—in general, force is used to designate a locus of opacity. It is to the function of cause that I will refer today.

I am well aware that I am entering here on a terrain which, from the point of view of philosophical criticism, suggests a whole world of references, so many, in fact, as to make me hesitate among them—but let's take our pick. Some of you at least will remain unsatisfied if I simply point out that, in his *An attempt to introduce the concept of negative quantities into philosophy*, we can see how closely Kant comes to understanding the gap that the function of cause has always presented to any conceptual apprehension. In that essay, it is more or less stated that cause is a concept that, in the last resort, is unanalysable —impossible to understand by reason—if indeed the rule of reason, the *Vernunftsregel*, is always some *Vergleichung*, or equivalent—and that there remains essentially in the function of cause a certain *gap*, a term used by Kant in the *Prolegomena*.

I will not go so far as to remark that the problem of cause has always been an embarrassment to philosophers, and that it is not as simple as might be thought when, in Aristotle, one sees the four causes balancing one another—for I am not philosophizing here, and would not claim to carry out so heavy an undertaking with so few references. However, these references are enough to bring out the meaning of what I am insisting on. For me, cause—any modality, even if Kant inscribes it in the categories of pure reason—to be more precise, he inscribes it in the table of relations, between inherence and community —cause is not any the more rationalized for this.

Cause is to be distinguished from that which is determinate in a chain, in other words the *law*. By way of example, think of what is pictured in the law of action and reaction. There is here, one might say, a single principle. One does not go without the other. The mass of a body that is crushed on the ground is not the cause of that which it receives in return for its vital force—its mass is integrated in this force that comes back to it in order to dissolve its coherence by a return effect. There is no gap here, except perhaps at the end.

Whenever we speak of cause, on the other hand, there is always something anti-conceptual, something indefinite. The phases of the moon are the cause of tides—we know this from experience, we know that the word cause is correctly used here. Or again, miasmas are the cause of fever—that doesn't mean anything either, there is a hole, and something that oscillates in the interval. In short, there is cause only in something that doesn't work.

Well! It is at this point that I am trying to make you see by approximation that the Freudian unconscious is situated at that point, where, between cause and that which it affects, there is always something wrong. The important thing is not that the unconscious determines neurosis—of that one Freud can quite happily, like Pontius Pilot, wash his hands. Sooner or later, something would have been found, humoral determinates, for example—for Freud, it would be quite immaterial. For what the unconscious does is to show us the gap through which neurosis recreates a harmony with a real—a real that may well not be determined.

In this gap, something happens. Once this gap has been filled, is the neurosis cured? After all, the question remains open. But the neurosis becomes something else, sometimes a mere illness, a *scar*, as Freud said—the scar, not of the neurosis, but of the unconscious. I am not handling this topology very skilfully, because I do not have time—I have simply jumped into the deep end—but I think you will be able to feel guided by the terms that I have introduced when you come to read Freud's own works. Observe the point from which he sets out — *The Aetiology of the Neuroses*—and what does he find in the hole, in the split, in the gap so characteristic of cause? Something of the order of the *non-realized*.

One uses the term refusal. This is rather hasty—indeed, for some time now, one has no longer been sure what the term refusal means. At first, the unconscious is manifested to us as something that holds itself in suspense in the area, I would say, of the *unborn*. That repression should discharge something into this area is not surprising. It is the abortionist's relation to limbo.

Certainly, this dimension should be evoked in a register that has nothing unreal, or dereistic, about it, but is rather un-realized. It is always dangerous to disturb anything in that zone of shades, and perhaps it is part of the analyst's role, if the analyst is performing it properly, to be besieged—I mean *really*—by those in whom he has invoked this world of shades, without always being able to bring them up to the light of day. One can never be sure that what one says on this matter will have no harmful effect—even what I have been able to say about it over the last ten years owes some of its impact to this fact. It is not without effect that, even in a public speech, one directs one's attention at subjects, touching them at what Freud calls the navel—*the navel of the dreams*, he writes, to designate their ultimately unknown centre—which is simply, like the same anatomical navel that represents it, that gap of which I have already spoken.

There is a danger in public discourse, precisely in so far as it is addressed to those nearest—Nietzsche knew this, a certain type of discourse can be addressed only to those furthest away.

In actual fact, this dimension of the unconscious that I am evoking *had been forgotten*, as Freud had quite clearly foreseen. The unconscious had closed itself up against his message thanks to those active practitioners of orthopaedics that the analysts of the second and third generation became, busying themselves, by psychologizing analytic theory, in stitching up this gap.

Believe me, I myself never re-open it without great care.

3

Now, of course, at this stage in my life, I am in a position to introduce into the domain of cause the law of the signifier, in the locus in which this gap is produced. Nevertheless, we must, if we are to understand what it means in psycho-analysis, go back and trace the concept of the unconscious through the various stages of the process in which Freud elaborated it —since we can complete that process only by carrying it to its limits.

The Freudian unconscious has nothing to do with the so-called forms of the unconscious that preceded it, not to say accompanied it, and which still surround it today. To understand what I mean, open the Lalande dictionary. Or read the delightful list provided by Dwelshauvers in a book published some forty years ago. In it he lists ten or so forms of the unconscious that will tell nobody anything that he did not already know, and which simply designate the non-conscious, the more or less conscious, etc.—in the ever-expanding field of psychology, one finds hundreds of additional varieties.

Freud's unconscious is not at all the romantic unconscious of imaginative creation. It is not the locus of the divinities of night. This locus is no doubt not entirely unrelated to the locus towards which Freud turns his gaze—but the fact that Jung, who provides a link with the terms of the romantic unconscious, should have been repudiated by Freud, is sufficient indication that psycho-analysis is introducing something other. Similarly, we can say that the hold-all, heteroclite unconscious that Edward von Hartmann spent his life elaborating is not Freud's unconscious, but we should not be over-hasty, for Freud, in the seventh chapter of *The Interpretation of Dreams*, himself referred to it in a footnote—that is to say, we must look more closely at it if we are to discover in what way Freud's unconscious is to be distinguished from it.

To all these forms of unconscious, ever more or less linked to some obscure will regarded as primordial, to something pre-conscious, what Freud opposes is the revelation that at the level of the unconscious there is something at all points homologous with what occurs at the level of the subject—this thing speaks and functions in a way quite as elaborate as at the level of the conscious, which thus loses what seemed to be its privilege. I am well aware of the resistances that this simple remark can still provoke, though it is evident in everything that Freud wrote. Read, for example, the paragraph of that seventh chapter of *The Interpretation of Dreams*, called 'Forgetting in Dreams', concerning which Freud merely refers to the play of the signifier.

I will not content myself with this portentous reference. I have spelt out to you point by point the functioning of what was first produced for us by Freud as the phenomenon of the unconscious. In the dream, in parapraxis, in the flash of wit —what is it that strikes one first? It is the sense of impediment to be found in all of them.

Impediment, failure, split. In a spoken or written sentence something stumbles. Freud is attracted by these phenomena, and it is there that he seeks the unconscious. There, something other demands to be realized—which appears as intentional, of course, but of a strange temporality. What occurs, what is *produced*, in this gap, is presented as *the discovery*. It is in this way that the Freudian exploration first encounters what occurs in the unconscious.

This discovery is, at the same time, a solution—not necessarily a complete one, but, however incomplete it may be, it has that indefinable something that touches us, that peculiar accent that Theodor Reik has brought out so admirably—only brought out, for Freud certainly noted it before him—namely, *surprise*, that by which the subject feels himself overcome, by which he finds both more and less than he expected—but, in any case, it is, in relation to what he expected, of exceptional value.

Now, as soon as it is presented, this discovery becomes a rediscovery and, furthermore, it is always ready to steal away again, thus establishing the dimension of loss.

To resort to a metaphor, drawn from mythology, we have, in Eurydice twice lost, the most potent image we can find of the relation between Orpheus the analyst and the unconscious.

In this respect, if you will allow me to add a touch of irony, the unconscious finds itself, strictly speaking, on the opposite side to love, which, as everyone knows, is always unique; the expression 'one lost, ten to be found again' finds its best application here.

Discontinuity, then, is the essential form in which the unconscious first appears to us as a phenomenon—discontinuity, in which something is manifested as a vacillation. Now, if this discontinuity has this absolute, inaugural character, in the development of Freud's discovery, must we place it—as was later the tendency with analysts—against the background of a totality?

Is the *one* anterior to discontinuity? I do not think so, and everything that I have taught in recent years has tended to exclude this need for a closed *one*—a mirage to which is attached the reference to the enveloping psyche, a sort of double of the organism in which this false unity is thought to reside. You will grant me that the *one* that is introduced by the experience of the unconscious is the *one* of the split, of the stroke, of rupture.

At this point, there springs up a misunderstood form of the *un*, the *Un* of the *Unbewusste*. Let us say that the limit of the *Unbewusste* is the *Unbegriff*—not the non-concept, but the concept of lack.[1]

Where is the background? Is it absent? No. Rupture, split, the stroke of the opening makes absence emerge—just as the cry does not stand out against a background of silence, but on the contrary makes the silence emerge as silence.

If you keep hold of this initial structure, you will avoid giving yourself up to some partial aspect of the question of the unconscious—as, for example, that it is the subject, *qua* alienated in his history, at the level at which the syncope of discourse is joined with his desire. You will see that, more radically, it is in the dimension of a synchrony that you must situate the unconscious—at the level of a being, but in the sense that it can spread over everything, that is to say, at the level of the subject of the enunciation, in so far as, according to the sentences, according to the modes, it loses itself as much as it finds itself again, and in the sense that, in an interjection, in an imperative, in an invocation, even in a hesitation, it is always the unconscious that presents you with its enigma, and speaks—in short, at the level at which everything that blossoms in the unconscious spreads, like mycelium, as Freud says about the dream, around a central point. It is always a question of the subject *qua* indeterminate.

Oblivium is *lēvis* with the long *e*—smooth. *Oblivium* is that which effaces—effaces what? The signifier as such. Here we find again the basic structure that makes it possible, in an operatory way, for something to take on the function of barring,

---

[1] Lacan is playing on the French *un* (one) and the German negative prefix *un*, moving from 'oneness' to 'negation'. The *Unbewusste* is Freud's 'unconscious'. Lacan's gloss, on *Unbegriff* shifts the notion of 'negation' into one of 'lack' [Translator's note].

striking out another thing. This is a more primordial level, structurally speaking, than repression, of which we shall speak later. Well, this operatory element of effacement is what Freud designates, from the outset, in the function of the censor.

It is the censorship by scissors, the Russian censorship, or again the German censorship, see Heinrich Heine, at the beginning of the *Book of Germany. Herr and Frau Such-and-such have pleasure in announcing the birth of a child as beautiful as liberty*—and Dr Hoffmann, the censor, strikes out the word *liberty.* Certainly one may ask oneself what effect this word can have as a result of this strictly material censorship, but that is another problem. But it is certainly here that the dynamism of the unconscious operates in the most efficient way.

Let us turn again to an example that has never been sufficiently exploited, the first used by Freud to demonstrate his theory, namely, his forgetting, his inability to remember the word *Signorelli* after his visit to the paintings at Orvieto. Is it possible not to see emerging from the text itself, and establishing itself, not metaphor, but the reality of the disappearance, of the suppression, of the *Unterdrückung*, the passing underneath? The term *Signor, Herr*, passes underneath—the absolute master, I once said, which is in fact death, has disappeared there. Furthermore, do we not see, behind this, the emergence of that which forced Freud to find in the myths of the death of the father the regulation of his desire? After all, it is to be found in Nietzsche, who declares, in his own myth, that God is dead. And it is perhaps against the background of the same reasons. For the myth of the *God is dead*—which, personally, I feel much less sure about, as a myth of course, than most contemporary intellectuals, which is in no sense a declaration of theism, nor of faith in the resurrection—perhaps this myth is simply a shelter against the threat of castration.

If you know how to read them, you will see this threat in the apocalyptic frescos of Orvieto cathedral. If not, read Freud's conversation in the train—where only the end of sexual potency is referred to. Freud's interlocutor, a doctor—the same interlocutor in fact before whom he is unable to remember the name *Signorelli*—is describing to Freud the dramatic character that a loss of potency usually has for his patients.

Thus the unconscious is always manifested as that which vacillates in a split in the subject, from which emerges a discovery that Freud compares with desire—a desire that we will temporarily situate in the denuded metonymy of the discourse in question, where the subject surprises himself in some unexpected way.

As far as Freud and his relation to the father are concerned, let us not forget that, despite all his efforts to understand, he was forced to admit, to a woman of his acquaintance, that, for him, the question—*What does a woman want?*—remained unanswered. He never resolved this question, as we can see from what was in fact his relations with women, his uxorious character, as Jones rather delicately puts it. I would say that Freud would certainly have made a perfect impassioned idealist had he not devoted himself to the other, in the form of the hysteric.

I have decided to stop my seminar always at a particular time, at twenty-to-two. As you see, I have not managed today to deal fully with the function of the unconscious.

(*Questions and answers are missing.*)

22 January 1964

3

OF THE SUBJECT
OF CERTAINTY

Neither being, nor non-being · Finitude of desire · The elusive · The status of the unconscious is ethical · That all theory has to be revised · Freud, Cartesian · The desire of the hysteric

Last week, my introduction of the unconscious through the structure of a gap provided an opportunity for one of my listeners, Jacques-Alain Miller, to give an excellent outline of what he recognized, in my previous writings, as the structuring function of a lack, and by an audacious arch he linked this up with what, speaking of the function of desire, I have designated as *manque-à-être*, a 'want-to-be'.

Having made this synopsis, which has certainly not been without its uses, at least for those who already had some idea of my teaching, he questioned me as to my ontology.

I was able to answer him only within the limits imposed on dialogue by the time-table, and I ought to have obtained from him to begin with a more specific definition of what he means by the term ontology. Nevertheless, I hope he did not think that I found the question at all inappropriate. I would go further. It came at a particularly good point, in that when speaking of this gap one is dealing with an ontological function, by which I thought I had to introduce, it being the most essential, the function of the unconscious.

I

The gap of the unconscious may be said to be *pre-ontological*. I have stressed that all too often forgotten characteristic—forgotten in a way that is not without significance—of the first emergence of the unconscious, namely, that it does not lend itself to ontology. Indeed, what became apparent at first to Freud, to the discoverers, to those who made the first steps,

29

and what still becomes apparent to anyone in analysis who spends some time observing what truly belongs to the order to the unconscious, is that it is neither being, nor non-being, but the unrealized.

I mentioned the function of limbo. I might also have spoken of what, in the constructions of the Gnostics, are called the intermediary beings—sylphs, gnomes, and even higher forms of these ambiguous mediators. Furthermore, let us not forget that when Freud began to disturb this world, he gave voice to the line *Flectere si nequeo superos Acheronta movebo*. It seemed heavy with disturbing apprehensions when he pronounced it, but remarkably enough, its threat is completely forgotten after sixty years of experience. It is remarkable that what was thought to be an infernal opening should later have been so remarkably asepticized.

But it is also revealing that what seemed so evidently to be an opening on to a lower world, did not, with a few rare exceptions, form any serious alliance with that whole world— then so prevalent, and still so today, but to a lesser degree than in the period of Freudian discovery—of meta-psychical research, as one used to say, even of spiritist, invocatory, necromantic practice, as did the Gothic psychology of Myers, which strove to follow up the fact of telepathy.

Of course, in passing, Freud does touch on these facts, in so far as they were borne in upon him by experience. But it is clear that his theorization was moving towards a rationalist, elegant reduction. One may regard as exceptional, not to say aberrant, any concern in the analytic circle of today with what have been called—significantly enough, in order to sterilize them—the *psi* (ψ) phenomena. I am referring to such research as that of Servadio, for example.

Certainly, it is not in this direction that our experience has led us. The result of our research into the unconscious moves, on the contrary, in the direction of a certain desiccation, a reduction to a herbarium, whose sampling is limited to a register that has become a *catalogue raisonné*, a classification that would certainly like to be thought a natural one. If, in the register of a traditional psychology, stress is laid on the un-controllable, infinite character of human desire—seeing in it the mark of some divine slipper that has left its imprint on it—

what analytic experience enables us to declare is rather the limited function of desire. Desire, more than any other point in the range of human possibility, meets its limit somewhere.

We shall come back to all this, but I would point out that I said *desire*, not *pleasure*. Pleasure limits the scope of human possibility—the pleasure principle is a principle of homeostasis. Desire, on the other hand, finds its boundary, its strict relation, its limit, and it is in the relation to this limit that it is sustained as such, crossing the threshold imposed by the pleasure principle.

This repudiation, into the field of religious sentimentality, of what he called the oceanic aspiration does not stem from a personal prejudice of Freud himself. Our experience is there to reduce this aspiration to a phantasy, to provide us with firm foundations elsewhere and to relegate it to the place occupied by what Freud called, on the subject of religion, illusion.

What is ontic in the function of the unconscious is the split through which that something, whose adventure in our field seems so short, is for a moment brought into the light of day— a moment because the second stage, which is one of closing up, gives this apprehension a vanishing aspect. I will come back to this—it may be even the step that I will be able to cross now, not having been able to so far, for reasons of context.

The context is an urgent one, you know. Our technical habits have become—for reasons that will have to be analysed —so touchy about the functions of time, that in wishing to introduce distinctions so essential that they are emerging everywhere except in our discipline, it seemed that I was under an obligation to embark on a more or less defensive discussion.

It is apparent that the very level of the definition of the unconscious—to refer only to what Freud says about it, in a necessarily approximate way, being able at first to use it only in hesitant touches here and there, when discussing the primary process—that what happens there is inaccessible to contradiction, to spatio-temporal location and also to the function of time.

Now, although desire merely conveys what it maintains of an image of the past towards an ever short and limited future, Freud declares that it is nevertheless *indestructible*. Notice that in the term indestructible, it is precisely the most inconsistent reality of all that is affirmed. If indestructible desire escapes from time, to what register does it belong in the order of things? For what is a thing, if not that which endures, in an identical state, for a certain time? Is not this the place to distinguish in addition to duration, the substance of things, another mode of time—a logical time? You know that I have already touched on this theme in one of my essays.

We find here once again the rhythmic structure of this pulsation of the slit whose function I referred to last time. The appearance/disappearance takes place between two points, the initial and the terminal of this logical time—between the instant of seeing, when something of the intuition itself is always elided, not to say lost, and that elusive moment when the apprehension of the unconscious is not, in fact, concluded, when it is always a question of an 'absorption' fraught with false trails (*une récupération leurrée*).

Ontically, then, the unconscious is the elusive—but we are beginning to circumscribe it in a structure, a temporal structure, which, it can be said, has never yet been articulated as such.

2

Since Freud himself, the development of the analytic experience has shown nothing but disdain for what appears in the gap. We have not—according to the comparison that Freud uses at a particular turning-point of *The Interpretation of Dreams—fed with blood* the shades that have emerged from it.

We have concerned ourselves with other things, and I am here to show you this year in what way these displacements of interest have always been more in the direction of uncovering structures, which are badly described in analysis, and of which one speaks almost as a prophet. Too often, when reading the best theoretical work that analysts bring from their experience, one has the feeling that it has to be interpreted. I shall demonstrate this for you in due course when dealing with something that is of the most vital importance in our experience, namely, the transference, from which we see co-existing the most fragmentary and the most illuminating evidence, in total confusion.

This explains why I can proceed only step by step, for others will speak to you of what I am dealing with here—the unconscious, repetition—at the level of the transference, and say that it is all a question of that. It is quite common, for example, to hear it said that the transference is a form of repetition. I am not saying that this is untrue, or that there is not an element of repetition in the transference. I am not saying that it is not on the basis of his experience of the transference that Freud approached repetition. What I am saying is that the concept of repetition has nothing to do with the concept of the transference. Because of this confusion, I am obliged to go through this explanation at the outset, to lay down the necessary logical steps. For to follow chronology would be to encourage the ambiguities of the concept of repetition that derive from the fact that its discovery took place in the course of the first hesitant steps necessitated by the experience of the transference.

I would now like to make clear, astonishing as the formula may seem to you, that its status of being, which is so elusive, so unsubstantial, is given to the unconscious by the procedure of its discoverer.

The status of the unconscious, which, as I have shown, is so fragile on the ontic plane, is ethical. In his thirst for truth, Freud says, *Whatever it is, I must go there*, because, somewhere, this unconscious reveals itself. And he says this on the basis of his experience of what was, up to that time, for the physician, the most rejected, the most concealed, the most contained, reality, that of the hysteric, in so far as it is—in a sense, from its origin—marked by the sign of deception.

Of course, this led us to many other things in the field in which we were taken by this initial approach, by the discontinuity constituted by the fact that one man, a discoverer, Freud, said, *There is the country where I shall take my people*. For a long time, what was situated in this field appeared marked with the characteristics of its original discovery—the desire of the hysteric. But soon, as the discovery proceeded, something quite different made itself felt, something that was always formulated somewhat belatedly. This was because the theory had been forged only for the discoveries that preceded it. As a result, everything has to be revised, including the question of the desire of the hysteric. This imposes on us a sort of retroactive leap if we wish to mark here the essence of Freud's position concerning that which occurs in the field of the unconscious.

I am not being impressionistic when I say that Freud's approach here is ethical—I am not thinking of the legendary courage of the scientist who recoils before nothing. This image, like all the others, requires some modification. If I am formulating here that the status of the unconscious is ethical, and not ontic, it is precisely because Freud himself does not stress it when he gives the unconscious its status. And what I have said about the thirst for truth that animated him is a mere indication of the approaches that will enable us to ask ourselves where Freud's passion lay.

Freud shows that he is very well aware how fragile are the veils of the unconscious where this register is concerned, when he opens the last chapter of *The Interpretation of Dreams* with the dream which, of all those that are analysed in the book, is in a category of its own—a dream suspended around the most anguishing mystery, that which links a father to the corpse of his son close by, of his dead son. As he is falling asleep, the father sees rise up before him the image of the son, who says to him, *Father, can't you see I'm burning?* In fact, the son really is burning, in the next room.

What is the point, then, of sustaining the theory according to which the dream is the image of a desire with an example in which, in a sort of flamboyant reflection, it is precisely a reality which, incompletely transferred, seems here to be shaking the dreamer from his sleep? Why, if not to suggest a mystery that is simply the world of the beyond, and some secret or other shared by the father and the son who says to him, *Father, can't you see I'm burning?* What is he burning with, if not with that which we see emerging at other points designated by the Freudian topology, namely, the weight of the sins of the father, borne by the ghost in the myth of Hamlet, which Freud couples with the myth of Oedipus? The father, the Name-of-the-father, sustains the structure of desire with the structure of the law— but the inheritance of the father is that which Kierkegaard designates for us, namely, his sin.

Where does Hamlet's ghost emerge from, if not from the place from which he denounces his brother for surprising him and cutting him off in the full flower of his sins? And far from providing Hamlet with the prohibitions of the Law that would allow his desire to survive, this too ideal father is constantly being doubted.

Everything is within reach, emerging, in this example that Freud places here in order to indicate in some way that he does not exploit it, that he appreciates it, that he weighs it, savours it. It is from this most fascinating point that he deflects our attention, and embarks on a discussion concerning the forgetting of the dream, and the value of its transmission by the subject. This discussion centres entirely around a certain number of terms that need to be stressed.

The major term, in fact, is not truth. It is *Gewissheit*, certainty. Freud's method is Cartesian—in the sense that he sets out from the basis of the subject of certainty. The question is—of what can one be certain? With this aim, the first thing to be done is to overcome that which connotes anything to do with the content of the unconscious—especially when it is a question of extracting it from the experience of the dream—to overcome that which floats everywhere, that which marks, stains, spots, the text of any dream communication—*I am not sure, I doubt*.

And who would not have doubts about the transmission of the dream when, in effect, there is such an obvious gap between what was experienced and what is recounted?

Now—and it is here that Freud lays all his stress—doubt is the support of his certainty.

He goes on to explain why—this is precisely the sign, he says, that there is something to preserve. Doubt, then, is a sign of resistance.

Yet the function he gives to doubt remains ambiguous, for this something that is to be preserved may also be the something that has to be shown—since, in any case, what is shown, shows itself only under a *Verkleidung*, a disguise, and an ill-fitting one it often is. But, nevertheless, I must insist on the fact that there is a point at which the two approaches of Descartes and Freud come together, converge.

Descartes tells us—*By virtue of the fact that I doubt, I am sure that I think*, and—I would say, to stick to a formula that is no more prudent than his, but which will save us from getting caught up in the *cogito*, the *I think*—*by virtue of thinking, I am*.

Note in passing that in avoiding the *I think*, I avoid the discussion that results from the fact that this *I think*, for us, certainly cannot be detached from the fact that he can formulate it only by *saying* it to us, implicitly—a fact that he forgets. I will return to this later.

In a precisely similar way, Freud, when he doubts—for they are *his* dreams, and it is he who, at the outset, doubts—is assured that a thought is there, which is unconscious, which means that it reveals itself as absent. As soon as he comes to deal with others, it is to this place that he summons the *I think* through which the subject will reveal himself. In short, he is sure that this thought is there alone with all his *I am*, if I may put it like this, provided, and this is the leap, someone thinks in his place.

It is here that the dissymmetry between Freud and Descartes is revealed. It is not in the initial method of certainty grounded on the subject. It stems from the fact that the subject is 'at home' in this field of the unconscious. It is because Freud declares the certainty of the unconscious that the progress by which he changed the world for us was made.

For Descartes, in the initial *cogito*—the Cartesians will grant me this point, but I will develop it in the discussion—what the *I think* is directed towards, in so far as it lurches into the *I am*, is a real. But the true remains so much outside that Descartes then has to re-assure himself—of what, if not of an Other that is not deceptive, and which shall, into the bargain, guarantee by its very existence the bases of truth, guarantee him that there are in his own objective reason the necessary foundations for the very real, about whose existence he has just re-assured himself, to find the dimension of truth. I can do no more than suggest the extraordinary consequences that have stemmed from this handing back of truth into the hands of the Other, in this instance the perfect God, whose truth is the nub of the matter, since, whatever he might have meant, would always be *the* truth—even if he had said that two and two make five, it would have been true.

What does this imply, if not that we will be able to begin playing with the small algebraic letters that transform geometry into analysis, that the door is open to set theory, that we can permit ourselves everything as a hypothesis of truth?

But let us leave this—it is not our business, except in so far as we know that what begins at the level of the subject is never without consequence, on condition that we know what the term *subject* means.

Descartes did not know, except that it involved the subject of a certainty and the rejection of all previous knowledge—but we know, thanks to Freud, that the subject of the unconscious manifests itself, that it thinks before it attains certainty.

This is what we're left with. It's certainly our problem. But in any case, it is now a field to which we cannot refuse ourselves entry—at least as far as the question it poses is concerned.

3

I would now like to stress that the correlative of the subject is henceforth no longer the deceiving Other, but the deceived Other. And this is something that we are aware of in the most concrete way as soon as we enter the experience of analysis. What the subject fears most is to mislead us (*nous tromper*), to put us on a wrong track, or more simply, that we will make a mistake (*nous nous trompions*), for, after all, it is obvious, just to look at us, that we are people who could make a mistake like anybody else.

Now, this does not bother Freud because—it is precisely this that one must understand, especially when one reads the first paragraph of the chapter on forgetting in dreams—the signs intersect, one must take everything into account, one must free oneself, he says, *frei machen* oneself of the whole scale of the evaluation that is sought there, *Preisschätzung*, the evaluation of what is sure and what is not sure. The slightest indication that something is entering the field should make us regard it as of equal value as a trace in relation to the subject.

Later, in the famous case of a female homosexual, he pokes fun at those who, on the subject of his patient's dreams can say to him: *But where is this unconscious that is supposed to bring us to the truth, to a divine truth?* they ask sarcastically. *Your patient is just laughing at you, since, in analysis, she has dreams on purpose to convince you that she was returning to what was asked of her, a liking for men.* Freud sees no objection to this. *The unconscious,* he tells us, *is not the dream.* What he means is that the unconscious may operate in the direction of deception, and that this does not in any way count as an objection for him. Indeed, how could there not be truth about lying—that truth which makes it perfectly possible, contrary to the supposed paradox, to declare, *I am lying*?

It is simply that Freud, on this occasion, failed to formulate correctly what was the object both of the hysteric's desire and of the female homosexual's desire. This is why—in each case, in the case of Dora as well as in the famous case of the female homosexual—he allowed himself to be overwhelmed, and the treatment was broken off. With regard to his interpretation, he is himself still hesitant—a little too early, a little too late. Freud could not yet see—for lack of those structural reference-points that I hope to bring out for you—that the hysteric's desire—which is legible in the most obvious way in the case—is to sustain the desire of the father—and, in the case of Dora, to sustain it by procuring.

Dora's obvious complaisance in the father's adventure with the woman who is the wife of Herr K., whose attentions to herself she accepts, is precisely the game by which she must sustain the man's desire. Furthermore, the *passage à l'acte*—breaking off the relationship by striking him, as soon as Herr K. says to her not, *I am not interested in you*, but, *I am not interested in my wife*—shows that it was necessary for her that the link should be preserved with that third element that enabled her to see the desire, which in any case was unsatisfied, subsisting—both the desire of the father whom she favoured *qua* impotent and her own desire of being unable to realize herself *qua* desire of the Other.

Similarly, and this once again justifies the formula I have given, the formula that originated in the experience of the hysteric, as a means of situating it at its correct level—*man's desire is the desire of the Other*—it is in the desire of the father that the female homosexual finds another solution, that is, to defy the desire of the father. If you re-read the case, you will see the obviously provocative character of the whole behaviour of this girl who, dogging the footsteps of some *demi-mondaine* whom she had found in the town, constantly made show of the chivalrous attentions she paid the girl until one day, meeting her father—what she meets in the father's gaze is unconcern, disregard, contempt for what is happening in front of him—she immediately throws herself over the railing of a local railway bridge. Literally, she can no longer conceive, other than by destroying herself, of the function she had, that of showing the father how one is, oneself, an abstract, heroic, unique phallus, devoted to the service of a lady.

What the female homosexual does in her dream, in deceiving Freud, is still an act of defiance in relation to the father's desire: *You want me to love men, you will have as many dreams about love of men as you wish.* It is defiance in the form of derision.

I have developed this introduction in such detail so that you may distinguish the exact position of the Freudian approach to the subject—in so far as it is the subject that is concerned in the field of the unconscious. In this way, I have distinguished the function of the subject of certainty from the search for the truth.

Next time, we shall approach the concept of repetition, by asking ourselves how it should be conceived. We shall see how by means of repetition, as repetition of deception, Freud co-ordinates experience, *qua* deceiving, with a real that will henceforth be situated in the field of science, situated as that which the subject is condemned to miss, but even this miss is revelatory.

QUESTIONS AND ANSWERS

X: *Are not logical time and time-substance identical?*

LACAN: Logical time is constituted by three stages. First, *the moment of seeing*—which is not without mystery, although correctly enough defined in the psychological experience of the intellectual operation that is called *insight*. Secondly, *the stage of understanding*. Thirdly, *the moment to conclude*. This is merely a reminder.

In order to understand logical time, one must set out with the presupposition that from the outset the signifying battery is given. On this basis, two terms are to be introduced, necessitated, as we shall see, by the function of repetition—*Willkür*, chance, and *Zufall*, the arbitrary.

In this way, Freud considers, with a view to the interpretation of dreams, the consequences of the chance of transcription, and the arbitrary nature of the links made—why link this with that, rather than with something else? Freud certainly brings us here to the heart of the question posed by the modern development of the sciences, in so far as they demonstrate what we can ground on chance.

Nothing, in effect, can be grounded on chance—the calculation of chances, strategies—that does not involve at the outset a limited structuring of the situation, in terms of signifiers. When modern games theory elaborates the strategy of the two partners, each meets the other with the maximum chances of winning on condition that each reasons in the same way as the other. What is the value of an operation of this kind, if not that one's bearings are already laid down, the signifying reference-points of the problem are already marked in it and the solution will never go beyond them?

Well! As far as the unconscious is concerned, Freud reduces everything that comes within reach of his hearing to the function of pure signifiers. It is on the basis of this reduction that it operates, and that a moment to conclude may appear, says Freud—a moment when he feels he has the courage to judge and to conclude. This is part of what I have called his ethical witness.

Experience later shows that where the subject is concerned, he encounters limits, which are non-conviction, resistance, non-cure. Remembering always involves a limit. And, no doubt, it can be obtained more completely by other ways than analysis, but they are inoperant as far as cure is concerned.

It is here that we must distinguish the scope of these two directions, remembering and repetition. From the one to the other, there is no more temporal orientation than there is reversibility. It is simply that they are not commutative—to begin by remembering in order to deal with the resistances of repetition is not the same thing as to begin by repetition in order to tackle remembering.

It is this that shows us that the time-function is of a logical order here, and bound up with a signifying shaping of the real. Non-commutativity, in effect, is a category that belongs only to the register of the signifier.

This enables us to grasp by what means the order of the unconscious appears. To what does Freud refer it? What is its surety? It is what he succeeds, in a second stage, in resolving by elaborating the function of repetition. We will see later how we can formulate it by referring to Aristotle's *Physics*.

OF THE SUBJECT OF CERTAINTY

P. KAUFMANN : *Last year, you declared that anxiety is that which does not deceive. Can you link this statement with ontology and certainty?*

LACAN : For analysis, anxiety is a crucial term of reference, because in effect anxiety is that which does not deceive. But anxiety may be lacking.

In experience, it is necessary to canalize it and, if I may say so, to take it in small doses, so that one is not overcome by it. This is a difficulty similar to that of bringing the subject into contact with the real—a term that I shall try to define next time in order to dissipate the ambiguity that still persists about it in the minds of many of my pupils.

What, for the analyst, can confirm in the subject what occurs in the unconscious? In order to locate the truth—I have shown you this in studying the formations of the unconscious—Freud relies on a certain signifying scansion. What justifies this trust is a reference to the real. But to say the least, the real does not come to him easily. Take the example of the *Wolf Man*. The exceptional importance of this case in Freud's work is to show that it is in relation to the real that the level of phantasy functions. The real supports the phantasy, the phantasy protects the real. Next time, by way of elucidating this relation for you, I shall take Spinoza's cogitation, but I shall bring into play another term to replace the attribute.

29 January 1964

41

4

OF THE NETWORK
OF SIGNIFIERS

*Thoughts of the unconscious · The colophon of doubt · Subversion of the
subject · Introduction to repetition · The real is that which always
comes back to the same place*

It has been my habit to absent myself for the period of two of
my seminars in order to go to that mode of ritual rest, spent in
accordance with our customs, that we call winter sports. I am
pleased to announce that this will not be the case this year, the
lack of snow having given me an excuse to give up this
obligation.

Chance so has it that, by virtue of this fact, I can also
announce another event that I am happy to bring to the
knowledge of a wider public. It so happens that just as I was
declining the opportunity of leaving my deposit with the
travel agency, I was warmly thanked, for they had received a
booking from eight members of the *French Psycho-analytic
Association*.

I must say that it gives me all the more pleasure to bring this
event to your notice as it is what is called a truly good act, an
action of the kind to which one may well apply the words of
the Gospel, *The left hand must not know what the right hand is
doing*.

Eight of the most eminent members of the teaching section
of the *Association* are now in London to discuss ways of warding
off the effects of my teaching. This is a very praiseworthy
concern and the said *Association* is willing to make any sacrifice
for the well-being of its members, unless, perhaps, by reciprocity,
the British *Association* has defrayed the expenses of this journey,
as it is our custom to defray the travelling expenses of its members when they come and concern themselves very closely in the
functioning of our Association.

I thought I had to make this announcement so that the paeons of gratitude might hide the few signs of nervousness that have probably appeared in connection with this expedition.

I

Last time, I spoke to you about the concept of the unconscious, whose true function is precisely that of being in profound, initial, inaugural, relation with the function of the concept of the *Unbegriff*—or *Begriff* of the original *Un*, namely, the cut.

I saw a profound link between this cut and the function as such of the subject, of the subject in its constituent relation to the signifier itself.

It seems something of a new departure—and it is—that I should have referred to the subject when speaking of the unconscious. I thought I had succeeded in making you feel that all this happens in the same place, in the place of the subject, which—from the Cartesian experience reducing to a single point the ground of inaugural certainty—has taken on an Archimedic value, if indeed that really was the point of application that made possible the quite different direction that science has taken, namely, that initiated by Newton.

I have constantly stressed in my preceding statements the *pulsative* function, as it were, of the unconscious, the need to disappear that seems to be in some sense inherent in it—everything that, for a moment, appears in its slit seems to be destined, by a sort of pre-emption, to close up again upon itself, as Freud himself used this metaphor, to vanish, to disappear. At the same time, I have formulated the hope that through this may be renewed the trenchant, decisive crystallization that has already been produced in the physical sciences, but this time in a different direction that we shall call *the conjectural science of the subject*. This is less paradoxical than might at first appear.

When Freud realized that it was in the field of the dream that he had to find confirmation of what he had learnt from his experience of the hysteric, he began to move forward with truly unprecedented boldness. What does he now tell us about the unconscious? He declares that it is constituted essentially, not by what the consciousness may evoke, extend, locate, bring out of the subliminal, but by that which is, essentially, refused. And what does Freud call this? He calls it by the same term by

43

which Descartes designates what I just called his point of application—*Gedanken*, thoughts.

There are thoughts in this field of the beyond of consciousness, and it is impossible to represent these thoughts other than in the same homology of determination in which the subject of the *I think* finds himself in relation to the articulation of the *I doubt*.

Descartes apprehends his *I think* in the enunciation of the *I doubt*, not in its statement, which still bears all of this knowledge to be put in doubt. Shall I say that Freud makes one more step—which designates for us sufficiently the legitimacy of our association—when he invites us to integrate in the text of the dream what I shall call the *colophon of doubt*—the colophon, in an old text, is that small pointing hand that used to be printed, in the days when we still had a typography, in the margin. The colophon of doubt is part of the text. This indicates that Freud places his certainty, his *Gewissheit*, only in the constellation of the signifiers as they result from the recounting, the commentary, the association, even if they are later retracted. Everything provides signifying material, which is what he depends on to establish his own *Gewissheit*—for I stress that experience begins only with his method. That is why I compare it to the Cartesian method.

I am not saying that Freud introduces the subject into the world—the subject as distinct from psychical function, which is a myth, a confused nebulosity—since it was Descartes who did this. But I am saying that Freud addresses the subject in order to say to him the following, which is new—*Here, in the field of the dream, you are at home. Wo es war, soll Ich werden.*

This does not mean, as some execrable translation would have it, *Le moi doit déloger le ça* (the ego must dislodge the id). See how Freud—and in a formula worthy in resonance of the pre-Socratics—is translated in French. It is not a question of the ego in this *soll Ich werden;* the fact is that throughout Freud's work—one must, of course, recognize its proper place—the *Ich* is the complete, total locus of the network of signifiers, that is to say, the subject, *where it was*, where it has always been, the dream. The ancients recognized all kinds of things in dreams, including, on occasion, messages from the gods—and why not? The ancients made something of these messages from the gods. And, anyway—perhaps you will glimpse this in what I shall

44

say later—who knows, the gods may still speak through dreams. Personally, I don't mind either way. What concerns us is the tissue that envelops these messages, the network in which, on occasion, something is caught. Perhaps the voice of the gods makes itself heard, but it is a long time since men lent their ears to them in their original state—it is well known that the ears are made not to hear with.

But the subject is there to rediscover *where it was*—I anticipate —the real. I will justify what I have just said in a little while, but those who have been listening to me for some time know that I use, quite intentionally, the formula— *The gods belong to the field of the real.*

Where it was, the *Ich*—the subject, not psychology—the subject, must come into existence. And there is only one method of knowing that one is there, namely, to map the network. And how is a network mapped? One goes back and forth over one's ground, one crosses one's path, one cross-checks it always in the same way, and in this seventh chapter of *The Interpretation of Dreams* there is no other confirmation for one's *Gewissheit*, one's certainty, than this—*Speak of chance, gentlemen, if you like. In my experience I have observed nothing arbitrary in this field, for it is cross-checked in such a way that it escapes chance.*

I would remind those who have already attended my lectures on this subject of letter fifty-two to Fliess, which comments on the schema that later, in *The Interpretation of Dreams*, is called optical. This model represents a number of layers, permeable to something analogous to light whose refraction changes from layer to layer. This is the locus where the affair of the subject of the unconscious is played out. And it is not, says Freud, a spatial, anatomical locus, otherwise how could one conceive it in the way it is presented to us? That is, as an immense display, a special spectre, situated between perception and consciousness. You know that these two elements will later, when Freud establishes his second topography, form the perception–consciousness system, the *Wahrnehmung–Bewusstsein*, but one should not then forget the interval that separates them, in which the place of the Other is situated, in which the subject is constituted.

Well, to return to the letter to Fliess, how do the *Wahrnehmungszeichen*, the traces of perception, function? Freud deduces from his experience the need to make an absolute separation between perception and consciousness—in order for these traces of perception to pass into memory, they must first be effaced in perception, and reciprocally. He then designates a time when these *Wahrnehmungszeichen* must be constituted in simultaneity. What is this time, if not signifying synchrony? And, of course, Freud says this all the more in that he does not know that he is saying it fifty years before the linguists. But we can immediately give to these *Wahrnehmungszeichen* their true name of *signifiers*. And our reading makes it quite clear that Freud, when he comes back to this locus in *The Interpretation of Dreams*, designates still other layers, in which the traces are constituted this time by analogy. What we have here are those functions of contrast and similitude so essential in the constitution of metaphor, which is introduced by a diachrony.

I won't elaborate this point too much, because we must move on today. But I would like to say that we find in Freud's articulations a quite unambiguous indication that what is involved in this synchrony is not only a network formed by random and contiguous associations. The signifiers were able to constitute themselves in simultaneity only by virtue of a very defined structure of constituent diachrony. The diachrony is orientated by the structure. Freud shows clearly that, for us, at the level of the last layer of the unconscious, where the diaphragm functions, where the pre-relations between the primary process and that part of it that will be used at the level of the pre-conscious are established, there can be no such thing as a miracle. *It must*, he says, *have a relation with causality*.

All these indications cross-check one another and these cross-checkings assure us too that we are rediscovering Freud—though we do not know whether it is here that we shall find our Ariadne's thread, because, of course, we read it before formulating our theory of the signifier, but without being able, for the moment, to understand it. It is no doubt through the particular necessities of our experience that we have set at the heart of the structure of the unconscious the causal gap, but the fact that we have found an enigmatic, unexplained indication of it in Freud's text is for us a sign that we are progressing in the way of *his* certainty. For the subject of certainty is divided here—it is Freud who has certainty.

2

This brings us to the heart of the problem that I am raising. Is psycho-analysis, here and now, a science? What distinguishes modern science from science in its infancy, which is discussed in the *Theaetetus*, is that, when science arises, a master is always present. Freud is certainly a master. But if everything that is written as analytic literature is not mere buffoonery, it always functions as such—which poses the question as to whether this pedicle might, one day, be reduced.

Opposite his certainty, there is the subject, who, as I said just now, has been waiting there since Descartes. I dare to state as a truth that the Freudian field was possible only a certain time after the emergence of the Cartesian subject, in so far as modern science began only after Descartes made his inaugural step.

It is on this step that depends the fact that one can call upon the subject to re-enter himself in the unconscious—for, after all, it is important to know *who* one is calling. It is not the soul, either mortal or immortal, which has been with us for so long, nor some shade, some double, some phantom, nor even some supposed psycho-spherical shell, the locus of the defences and other such simplified notions. It is the subject who is called— there is only he, therefore, who can be chosen. There may be, as in the parable, many called and few chosen, but there will certainly not be any others except those who are called.

In order to understand the Freudian concepts, one must set out on the basis that it is the subject who is called—the subject of Cartesian origin. This basis gives its true function to what, in analysis, is called recollection or remembering. Recollection is not Platonic reminiscence—it is not the return of a form, an imprint, a *eidos* of beauty and good, a supreme truth, coming to us from the beyond. It is something that comes to us from the structural necessities, something humble, born at the level of the lowest encounters and of all the talking crowd that precedes us, at the level of the structure of the signifier, of the languages spoken in a stuttering, stumbling way, but which cannot elude constraints whose echoes, model, style can be found, curiously enough, in contemporary mathematics.

As you saw with the notion of cross-checking, the function of

47

return, *Wiederkehr*, is essential. It is not only *Wiederkehr* in the sense of that which has been repressed—the very constitution of the field of the unconscious is based on the *Wiederkehr*. It is there that Freud bases his certainty. But it is quite obvious that it is not from there that it comes to him. It comes to him from the fact that he recognizes the law of his own desire. He would not have been able to advance with this bet of certainty if he had not been guided in it, as his writings show, by his self-analysis.

And what is his self-analysis, if not the brilliant mapping of the law of desire suspended in the Name-of-the-father. Freud advances, sustained by a certain relation to his desire, and by his own achievement, namely, the constitution of psycho-analysis.

I shall not elaborate much more, though I always hesitate to leave this terrain. If I have insisted on it, it is to show you that the notion of hallucination, in Freud, as a process of regressive investment on perception necessarily implies that the subject must be completely subverted in it—which he is, in effect, only in extremely fleeting moments.

No doubt this leaves entirely open the question of hallucination proper, in which the subject does not believe, and in which he does not recognize himself as implicated. No doubt this is merely a mythical pin-pointing—for it is not certain that one can speak of the delusion of hallucinatory psychosis of a confusional origin, as Freud does, rather too rapidly, seeing in it the manifestation of the perceptual regression of arrested desire. But the fact that there is a mode in which Freud can conceive as possible the subversion of the subject shows clearly enough to what extent he identifies the subject with that which is originally subverted by the system of the signifier.

So let us leave this time of the unconscious and move towards the question of what repetition is. It will need more than one of our sessions.

3

What I now have to say to you is so new—though obviously supported by what I have said about the signifier—that I thought I ought to formulate for you today, without keeping any of my cards up my sleeve, what I understand by the function of repetition.

In any case, this function has nothing to do with the open or closed character of the circuits that I have just called *Wiederkehr*.

I am not saying that Freud introduced this function, but he articulated it for the first time, in the article of 1914, *Erinnern, Wiederholen und Durcharbeiten* ('Remembering, Repeating and Working-Through')—which, of all psycho-analytic texts is certainly the one that has inspired the greatest amount of stupidity—and which culminates in chapter five of *Jenseits des Lustprinzips*.

Try to read this chapter five, line by line, in some language other than French. Those who do not know German should read it in the English translation. You will find this translation —I say this in passing—quite entertaining. You will see, for example, that the translation of *instinct* for *Trieb*, and *instinctual* for *triebhaft* has so many drawbacks for the translator that, although it is maintained throughout quite uniformly—thus basing the whole edition on a complete misunderstanding, since *Trieb* and *instinct* have nothing in common—the discord becomes so impossible at one point that the implications of a sentence cannot be carried through by translating *Triebhaft* by *instinctual*. A footnote becomes necessary—*At the beginning of the next paragraph the word Trieb . . . is much more revealing of urgency than the word instinctual. Trieb* gives you a kick in the arse, my friends—quite different from so-called *instinct*. That's how psycho-analytic teaching is passed on!

Let us take a look, then, at how *Wiederholen* (repeating) is introduced. *Wiederholen* is related to *Erinnerung* (remembering). The subject in himself, the recalling of his biography, all this goes only to a certain limit, which is known as the real. If I wished to make a Spinozian formula concerning what is at issue, I would say—*cogitatio adaequata semper vitat eandem rem.* An adequate thought, *qua* thought, at the level at which we are, always avoids—if only to find itself again later in everything— the same thing. Here, the real is that which always comes back to the same place—to the place where the subject in so far as he thinks, where the *res cogitans*, does not meet it.

The whole history of Freud's discovery of repetition as function becomes clear only by pointing out in this way the relation between thought and the real. This was fine at the beginning, because one was dealing with hysterics. How convincing the

49

process of remembering was with the first hysterics! But what is at issue in this remembering could not be known at the outset —one did not know that the desire of the hysteric was the desire of the father, to be sustained in his status. It was hardly surprising that, for the benefit of him who takes the place of the father, one remembered things right down to the dregs.

I will take this opportunity to point out to you that in Freud's texts repetition is not reproduction. There is never any ambiguity on this point: *Wiederholen* is not *Reproduzieren*.

To reproduce is what one thought one could do in the optimistic days of catharsis. One had the primal scene in reproduction as today one has pictures of the great masters for 9 francs 50. But what Freud showed when he made his next steps—and it did not take him long—was that nothing can be grasped, destroyed, or burnt, except in a symbolic way, as one says, *in effigie, in absentia*.

Repetition first appears in a form that is not clear, that is not self-evident, like a reproduction, or a making present, *in act*. That is why I have placed *The Act* with a large question-mark at the bottom of the blackboard so as to indicate that, as long as we speak of the relations of repetition with the real, this act will remain on our horizon.

It is curious enough that neither Freud, nor any of his epigones, ever attempted to remember what is nevertheless within the grasp of everybody concerning the act—let us say, *human act*, if you like, since to our knowledge there is no other act but the human one. Why is an act not mere behaviour? Let us concentrate, for example, on an act that is unambiguous, the act of cutting open one's belly in certain conditions—incidentally, it's not called *hara-kiri*, but *seppuku*. Why do people do that? Because they think it annoys others, because, in the structure, it is an act that is done in honour of something. But wait. Let us not be precipitate until we know, and let us take note of this, that an act, a true act, always has an element of structure, by the fact of concerning a real that is not self-evidently caught up in it.

Wiederholen. Nothing has been more enigmatic—especially on the subject of that bipartition, of such structural importance to the whole of Freudian psychology, of the pleasure principle and the reality principle—nothing has been more enigmatic than this *Wiederholen*, which is very close, so the most prudent etymologists tell us, to the verb 'to haul' (*haler*)—hauling as on a towpath—very close to a *hauling* of the subject, who always drags his thing into a certain path that he cannot get out of.

And why, at first, did repetition appear at the level of what is called traumatic neurosis?

Contrary to all the neurophysiologists, pathologists and others, Freud made it quite clear that, although it was difficult for the subject to reproduce in dream the memory of the heavy bombing-raid, for example, from which his neurosis derives—it does not seem, when he is awake, to bother him either way. What, then, is this function of traumatic repetition if nothing —quite the reverse—seems to justify it from the point of view of the pleasure principle? To master the painful event, some-one may say—but who masters, where is the master here, to be mastered? Why speak so hastily when we do not know precisely where to situate the agency that would undertake this operation of mastery?

At the end of the series of writings of which I have given you the two essentials, Freud shows that we can conceive here of what occurs in the dreams of traumatic neurosis only at the level of the most primitive functioning—that in which it is a question of obtaining the binding of energy. So let us not presume in advance that it is a question here of some gap, some division of function such as we might find at some first infinitely more elaborate level of the real. On the contrary, we see here a point that the subject can approach only by dividing himself into a certain number of agencies. One might say what is said of the divided kingdom, that any conception of the unity of the psyche, of the supposed totalizing, synthesizing psyche, ascending towards consciousness, perishes there.

Lastly—in these first stages of the experience in which remembering is gradually substituted for itself and approaches ever nearer to a sort of focus, or centre, in which every event seems to be under an obligation to yield itself—precisely at this moment, we see manifest itself what I will also call—in inverted commas, for one must also change the meaning of the three words that I am going to say, one must change it com-pletely in order to give it its full scope—the *resistance of the subject*, which becomes at that moment repetition in act.

What I will articulate next time will show you how to appropriate to this statement the admirable fourth and fifth chapters of Aristotle's *Physics*. Aristotle turns and manipulates two terms that are absolutely resistant to his theory, which is nevertheless the most elaborate that has ever been made on the function of cause—two terms that are incorrectly translated as *chance* and *fortune*. It is a question, then, of revising the relation that Aristotle establishes between the *automaton*—and we know, at the present stage of modern mathematics, that it is the network of signifiers—and what he designates as the *tuché*—which is for us the encounter with the real.

Questions and Answers are missing.

5 February 1964

5

TUCHÉ AND AUTOMATON

Psycho-analysis is not an idealism · The real as trauma · Theory of the dream and of waking · Consciousness and representation · God is unconscious · The objet petit a *in the* fort-da

Today I shall continue the examination of the concept of repetition, as it is presented by Freud and the experience of psycho-analysis.

I wish to stress here that, at first sight, psycho-analysis seems to lead in the direction of idealism.

God knows that it has been reproached enough for this—it reduces the experience, some say, that urges us to find in the hard supports of conflict, struggle, even of the exploitation of man by man, the reasons for our deficiencies—it leads to an ontology of the tendencies, which it regards as primitive, internal, already given by the condition of the subject.

We have only to consider the course of this experience from its first steps to see, on the contrary, that it in no way allows us to accept some such aphorism as *life is a dream*. No praxis is more orientated towards that which, at the heart of experience, is the kernel of the real than psycho-analysis.

I

Where do we meet this real? For what we have in the discovery of psycho-analysis is an encounter, an essential encounter—an appointment to which we are always called with a real that eludes us. That is why I have put on the blackboard a few words that are for us, today, a reference-point of what we wish to propose.

First, the *tuché*, which we have borrowed, as I told you last time, from Aristotle, who uses it in his search for cause. We have translated it as *the encounter with the real*. The real is beyond the *automaton*, the return, the coming-back, the insistence of the

53

signs, by which we see ourselves governed by the pleasure principle. The real is that which always lies behind the automaton, and it is quite obvious, throughout Freud's research, that it is this that is the object of his concern.

If you wish to understand what is Freud's true preoccupation as the function of phantasy is revealed to him, remember the development, which is so central for us, of the *Wolf Man*. He applies himself, in a way that can almost be described as anguish, to the question—what is the first encounter, the real, that lies behind the phantasy? We feel that throughout this analysis, this real brings with it the subject, almost by force, so directing the research that, after all, we can today ask ourselves whether this fever, this presence, this desire of Freud is not that which, in his patient, might have conditioned the belated accident of his psychosis.

So there is no question of confusing with repetition either the return of the signs, or reproduction, or the modulation by the act of a sort of acted-out remembering. Repetition is something which, of its true nature, is always veiled in analysis, because of the identification of repetition with the transference in the conceptualization of analysts. Now, this really is the point at which a distinction should be made.

The relation to the real that is to be found in the transference was expressed by Freud when he declared that nothing can be apprehended *in effigie, in absentia*—and yet is not the transference given to us as effigy and as relation to absence? We can succeed in unravelling this ambiguity of the reality involved in the transference only on the basis of the function of the real in repetition.

What is repeated, in fact, is always something that occurs —the expression tells us quite a lot about its relation to the *tuché—as if by chance*. This is something that we analysts never allow ourselves to be taken in by, on principle. At least, we always point out that we must not be taken in when the subject tells us that something happened to him that day that prevented him from realizing his wish to come to the session. Things must not be taken at the level at which the subject puts them—in as much as what we are dealing with is precisely this obstacle, this hitch, that we find at every moment. It is this mode of apprehension above all that governs the new deciphering that we have given of the subject's relations to that which makes his condition.

The function of the *tuché*, of the real as encounter—the encounter in so far as it may be missed, in so far as it is essentially the missed encounter—first presented itself in the history of psycho-analysis in a form that was in itself already enough to arouse our attention, that of the trauma.

Is it not remarkable that, at the origin of the analytic experience, the real should have presented itself in the form of that which is *unassimilable* in it—in the form of the trauma, determining all that follows, and imposing on it an apparently accidental origin? We are now at the heart of what may enable us to understand the radical character of the conflictual notion introduced by the opposition of the pleasure principle and the reality principle—which is why we cannot conceive the reality principle as having, by virtue of its ascendancy, the last word.

In effect, the trauma is conceived as having necessarily been marked by the subjectifying homeostasis that orientates the whole functioning defined by the pleasure principle. Our experience then presents us with a problem, which derives from the fact that, at the very heart of the primary processes, we see preserved the insistence of the trauma in making us aware of its existence. The trauma reappears, in effect, frequently unveiled. How can the dream, the bearer of the subject's desire, produce that which makes the trauma emerge repeatedly—if not its very face, at least the screen that shows us that it is still there behind?

Let us conclude that the reality system, however far it is developed, leaves an essential part of what belongs to the real a prisoner in the toils of the pleasure principle.

It is this that we have to investigate, this reality, one might say, whose presence is supposed to be required by us, if the motive force of development, as it is represented for us by someone like Melanie Klein, for example, is not reducible to a formula like the one I used earlier, namely, *life is a dream*.

To this requirement correspond those radical points in the real that I call encounters, and which enable us to conceive reality as *unterlegt*, *untertragen*, which, with the superb ambiguity of the French language, appear to be translated by the same word—*souffrance*.[1] Reality is in abeyance there, awaiting attention. And *Zwang*, constraint, which Freud defines by *Wiederholung*, governs the very diversions of the primary process.

The primary process—which is simply what I have tried to define for you in my last few lectures in the form of the unconscious—must, once again, be apprehended in its experience of rupture, between perception and consciousness, in that nontemporal locus, I said, which forces us to posit what Freud calls, in homage to Fechner, *die Idee einer anderer Lokalität*, the idea of another locality, another space, another scene, *the between perception and consciousness*.

2

We can, at any moment, apprehend this primary process.

The other day, I was awoken from a short nap by knocking at my door just before I actually awoke. With this impatient knocking I had already formed a dream, a dream that manifested to me something other than this knocking. And when I awake, it is in so far as I reconstitute my entire representation around this knocking—this perception—that I am aware of it. I know that I am there, at what time I went to sleep, and why I went to sleep. When the knocking occurs, not in my perception, but in my consciousness, it is because my consciousness reconstitutes itself around this representation—that I know that I am waking up, that I am *knocked up*.

But here I must question myself as to what I am at that moment—at the moment, so immediately before and so separate, which is that in which I began to dream under the effect of the knocking which is, to all appearances, what woke me.[2]

---

[1] In French, the phrase '*en souffrance*' means 'in suspense', 'in abeyance', 'awaiting attention', 'pending'. It is this sense that translates the German word. '*Souffrance*' also means 'pain', of course. Hence the ambiguity referred to by Lacan. [Tr.].

[2] There follows a passage in which Lacan comments on the use in French of the 'pleonastic *ne*', that is, the '*ne*' used without the usually accompanying '*pas*', '*que*' or '*jamais*', etc. Since the passage includes examples of this use in French, it is strictly untranslatable. I therefore give it below in the original:

'Je suis, que je sache, *avant que je ne me réveille*—ce *ne* dit explétif, déjà dans tel de mes écrits désigné, est le mode même de présence de ce *je suis* d'avant le réveil. Il n'est point explétif, il est plutôt l'expression de mon impléance,

Observe what I am directing you towards—towards the symmetry of that structure that makes me, after the awakening knock, able to sustain myself, apparently only in a relation with my representation, which, apparently, makes of me only consciousness. A sort of involuted reflection—in my consciousness, it is only my representation that I recover possession of.

Is that all? Freud has told us often enough that he would have to go back to the function of consciousness, but he never did. Perhaps we shall see better what is at issue, by apprehending what is there that motivates the emergence of the represented reality, namely the phenomenon, distance, the gap itself that constitutes awakening.

To make things quite clear, let us return to the dream —which is also made up entirely of noise—that I left you time to look up in *The Interpretation of Dreams*. You will remember the unfortunate father who went to rest in the room next to the one in which his dead child lay—leaving the child in the care, we are told, of another old man—and who is awoken by something. By what? It is not only the reality, the shock, the knocking, a noise made to recall him to the real, but this expresses, in his dream, the quasi-identity of what is happening, the very reality of an overturned candle setting light to the bed in which his child lies.

Such an example hardly seems to confirm Freud's thesis in the *Traumdeutung*—that the dream is the realization of a desire.

What we see emerging here, almost for the first time, in the *Traumdeutung*, is a function of the dream of an apparently secondary kind—in this case, the dream satisfies only the need to prolong sleep. What, then, does Freud mean by placing, at this point, this particular dream, stressing that it is in itself full confirmation of his thesis regarding dreams?

If the function of the dream is to prolong sleep, if the dream, after all, may come so near to the reality that causes it, can we not say that it might correspond to this reality without emerging

---

chaque fois qu'elle a à se manifester. La langue, la langue française le définit bien dans l'acte de son emploi. *Aurez-vous fini avant qu'il ne vienne?* — cela m'importe que vous ayez fini, à Dieu ne plaise qu'il vînt avant. *Passerez-vous, avant qu'il vienne?* — car, déjà, quand il viendra, vous ne serez plus là.'

from sleep? After all, there is such a thing as somnambulistic activity. The question that arises, and which indeed all Freud's previous indications allow us here to produce, is—*What is it that wakes the sleeper?* Is it not, *in* the dream, another reality? —the reality that Freud describes thus—*Dass das Kind an seinem Bette steht,* that the child is near his bed, *ihn am Arme fasst,* takes him by the arm and whispers to him reproachfully, *und ihm vorwurfsvoll zuraunt: Vater, siehst du denn nicht,* Father, can't you see, *dass ich verbrenne,* that I am burning?

Is there not more reality in this message than in the noise by which the father also identifies the strange reality of what is happening in the room next door. Is not the missed reality that caused the death of the child expressed in these words? Freud himself does not tell us that we must recognize in this sentence what perpetuates for the father those words forever separated from the dead child that were said to him, perhaps, Freud supposes, because of the fever—but who knows, perhaps these words perpetuate the remorse felt by the father that the man he has put at his son's bedside to watch over him may not be up to his task: *die Besorgnis dass der greise Wächter seiner Aufgabe nicht gewachsen sein dürfte,* he may not be up to his job, in fact, he has gone to sleep.

Does not this sentence, said in relation to fever, suggest to you what, in one of my recent lectures, I called the cause of fever? And is not the action, apparently so urgent, of preventing what is happening in the next room also perhaps felt as being in any case too late now, in relation to what is at issue, in the psychical reality manifested in the words spoken? Is not the dream essentially, one might say, an act of homage to the missed reality—the reality that can no longer produce itself except by repeating itself endlessly, in some never attained awakening? What encounter can there be henceforth with that forever inert being—even now being devoured by the flames—if not the encounter that occurs precisely at the moment when, by accident, as if by chance, the flames come to meet him? Where is the reality in this accident, if not that it repeats something actually more fatal *by means of* reality, a reality in which the person who was supposed to be watching over the body still remains asleep, even when the father re-emerges after having woken up?

Thus the encounter, forever missed, has occurred between dream and awakening, between the person who is still asleep and whose dream we will not know and the person who has dreamt merely in order not to wake up.

If Freud, amazed, sees in this the confirmation of his theory of desire, it is certainly a sign that the dream is not a phantasy fulfilling a wish.

For it is not that, in the dream, he persuades himself that the son is still alive. But the terrible vision of the dead son taking the father by the arm designates a beyond that makes itself heard in the dream. Desire manifests itself in the dream by the loss expressed in an image at the most cruel point of the object. It is only in the dream that this truly unique encounter can occur. Only a rite, an endlessly repeated act, can commemorate this not very memorable encounter—for no one can say what the death of a child is, except the father *qua* father, that is to say, no conscious being.

For the true formula of atheism is not *God is dead*—even by basing the origin of the function of the father upon his murder, Freud protects the father—the true formula of atheism is *God is unconscious*.

The awakening shows us the waking state of the subject's consciousness in the representation of what has happened —the unfortunate accident in reality, against which one can do no more than take steps! But what, then, was this accident? When everybody is asleep, including the person who wished to take a little rest, the person who was unable to maintain his vigil and the person of whom some well intentioned individual, standing at his bedside, must have said, *He looks just as if he is asleep*, when we know only one thing about him, and that is that, in this entirely sleeping world, only the voice is heard, *Father, can't you see I'm burning?* This sentence is itself a firebrand—of itself it brings fire where it falls—and one cannot see what is burning, for the flames blind us to the fact that the fire bears on the *Unterlegt*, on the *Untertragen*, on the real.

This is certainly what brings us to recognizing in this detached sentence from the dream of the grief-stricken father the counterpart of what will be, once he is awake, his consciousness, and to ask ourselves what is the correlative, in the dream, of the representation. This question is all the more striking in that, here, we see the dream really as the counterpart of the representation; it is the imagery of the dream and it is an opportunity for us to stress what Freud, when he speaks of the unconscious, designates as that which essentially determines it, the *Vorstellungsrepräsentanz*. This means not, as it has been mistranslated, the representative representative (*le représentant représentatif*), but that which takes the place of the representation (*le tenant-lieu de la représentation*). We shall see its function later.

I hope I have helped you to grasp what is nodal in the encounter, *qua* encounter forever missed, and which really sustains, in Freud's text, what seems to him, in his dream, absolutely exemplary.

The place of the real, which stretches from the trauma to the phantasy—in so far as the phantasy is never anything more than the screen that conceals something quite primary, something determinant in the function of repetition—this is what we must now examine. This, indeed, is what, for us, explains both the ambiguity of the function of awakening and of the function of the real in this awakening. The real may be represented by the accident, the noise, the small element of reality, which is evidence that we are not dreaming. But, on the other hand, this reality is not so small, for what wakes us is the other reality hidden behind the lack of that which takes the place of representation—this, says Freud is the *Trieb*.

But be careful! We have not yet said what this *Trieb* is —and if, for lack of representation, it is not there, what is this *Trieb*? We may have to consider it as being only *Trieb* to come.

How can we fail to see that awakening works in two directions—and that the awakening that re-situates us in a constituted and represented reality carries out two tasks? The real has to be sought beyond the dream—in what the dream has enveloped, hidden from us, behind the lack of representation of which there is only one representative. This is the real that governs our activities more than any other and it is psychoanalysis that designates it for us.

3

Thus Freud finds himself providing the solution to the problem which, for the most acute of the questioners of the soul before him—Kierkegaard—had already been centred on repetition.

I would ask you to re-read Kierkegaard's essay on *Repetition*, so dazzling in its lightness and ironic play, so truly Mozartian in the way, so reminiscent of *Don Giovanni*, it abolishes the mirages of love. With great acuteness, and in a quite unanswerable way, Kierkegaard stresses the feature that, in his love, the young man—whose portrait Kierkegaard paints for us with a mixture of emotion and derision—addresses only to himself through the medium of memory. Really, is there not something here more profound than La Rochefoucauld's remark that few would experience love if they had not had its ways and means explained to them? Yes, but who began it? And does not everything essentially begin by deceiving the first to whom the enchantment of love was addressed—who has passed off this enchantment as the exaltation of the other, by making himself the prisoner of this exaltation, of this breathlessness which, with the other, has created the most false of demands, that of narcissistic satisfaction, the ego ideal whether it is or the ego that regards itself as the ideal?

Freud is not dealing with any repetition residing in the natural, no return of need, any more than is Kierkegaard. The return of need is directed towards consumption placed at the service of appetite. Repetition demands the new. It is turned towards the ludic, which finds its dimension in this new —Freud also tells us this in the chapter I referred to last time.

Whatever, in repetition, is varied, modulated, is merely alienation of its meaning. The adult, and even the more advanced child, demands something new in his activities, in his games. But this 'sliding-away' (*glissement*) conceals what is the true secret of the ludic, namely, the most radical diversity constituted by repetition in itself. It can be seen in the child, in his first movement, at the moment when he is formed as a human being, manifesting himself as an insistence that the story should always be the same, that its recounted realization should be ritualized, that is to say, textually the same. This requirement of a distinct consistency in the details of its telling signifies that the realization of the signifier will never be able to be careful enough in its memorization to succeed in designating the primacy of the significance as such. To develop it by varying the significations is, therefore, it would seem, to elude it. This variation makes one forget the aim of the significance by transforming its act into a game, and giving it certain outlets that go some way to satisfying the pleasure principle.

When Freud grasps the repetition involved in the game played by his grandson, in the reiterated *fort-da*, he may indeed point out that the child makes up for the effect of his mother's disappearance by making himself the agent of it—but, this phenomenon is of secondary importance. Wallon stresses that the child does not immediately watch the door through which his mother has disappeared, thus indicating that he expects to see her return through it, but that his vigilance was aroused earlier, at the very point she left him, at the point she moved away from him. The ever-open gap introduced by the absence indicated remains the cause of a centrifugal tracing in which that which falls is not the other *qua* face in which the subject is projected, but that cotton-reel linked to itself by the thread that it holds—in which is expressed that which, of itself, detaches itself in this trial, self-mutilation on the basis of which the order of significance will be put in perspective. For the game of the cotton-reel is the subject's answer to what the mother's absence has created on the frontier of his domain—the edge of his cradle—namely, a *ditch*, around which one can only play at jumping.

This reel is not the mother reduced to a little ball by some magical game worthy of the Jivaros—it is a small part of the subject that detaches itself from him while still remaining his, still retained. This is the place to say, in imitation of Aristotle, that man thinks with his object. It is with his object that the child leaps the frontiers of his domain, transformed into a well, and begins the incantation. If it is true that the signifier is the first mark of the subject, how can we fail to recognize here —from the very fact that this game is accompanied by one of the first oppositions to appear—that it is in the object to which the opposition is applied in act, the reel, that we must designate the subject. To this object we will later give the name it bears in the Lacanian algebra—the *petit a*.

The activity as a whole symbolizes repetition, but not at all that of some need that might demand the return of the mother, and which would be expressed quite simply in a cry. It is the repetition of the mother's departure as cause of a *Spaltung* in the subject—overcome by the alternating game, *fort-da*, which is a *here or there*, and whose aim, in its alternation, is simply that of being the *fort* of a *da*, and the *da* of a *fort*. It is aimed at what, essentially, is not there, *qua* represented—for it is the game itself that is the *Repräsentanz* of the *Vorstellung*. What will become of the *Vorstellung* when, once again, this *Repräsentanz* of the mother—in her outline made up of the brush-strokes and gouaches of desire—will be lacking?

I, too, have seen with my own eyes, opened by maternal divination, the child, traumatized by the fact that I was going away despite the appeal, precociously adumbrated in his voice, and henceforth more renewed for months at a time—long after, having picked up this child—I have seen it let his head fall on my shoulder and drop off to sleep, sleep alone being capable of giving him access to the living signifier that I had become since the date of the trauma.

You will see that this sketch that I have given you today of the function of the *tuché* will be essential for us in rectifying what is the duty of the analyst in the interpretation of the transference.

Let me just stress today that it is not in vain that analysis posits itself as modulating in a more radical way this relation of man to the world that has always been regarded as knowledge.

If knowledge is so often, in theoretical writings, related to something similar to the relation between ontogenesis and phylogenesis—it is as the result of a confusion, and we shall show next time that the very originality of psycho-analysis lies in the fact that it does not centre psychological ontogenesis on supposed *stages*—which have literally no discoverable foundation in development observable in biological terms. If development is entirely animated by accident, by the obstacle of the *tuché*, it is in so far as the *tuché* brings us back to the same point at which pre-Socratic philosophy sought to motivate the world itself.

It required a *clinamen*, an inclination, at some point. When Democritus tried to designate it, presenting himself as already the adversary of a pure function of negativity in order to introduce thought into it, he says, *It is not the μηδέν that is essential,* and adds—thus showing you that from what one of my pupils called the archaic stage of philosophy, the manipulation of words was used just as in the time of Heidegger —*it is not an μηδέν, but a δεν,* which, in Greek, is a coined word. He did not say *ἔν,* let alone *ὄν.* What, then, did he say? He said, answering the question I asked today, that of idealism, *Nothing, perhaps?*—not *perhaps nothing,* but *not nothing.*

QUESTIONS AND ANSWERS

F. DOLTO: *I don't see how, in describing the formation of intelligence up to the age of three or four, one can do without stages. I think that as far as the defence phantasies and the phantasies of the castration veil are concerned, and also the threats of mutilation, one needs to refer to the stages.*

LACAN: The description of the stages, *which go to form the libido,* must not be referred to some natural process of pseudomaturation, which always remains opaque. The stages are organized around the fear of castration. The copulatory fact of the introduction of sexuality is traumatizing—this is a snag of some size—and it has an organizing function for development.

The fear of castration is like a thread that perforates all the stages of development. It orientates the relations that are anterior to its actual appearance—weaning, toilet training, etc. It crystallizes each of these moments in a dialectic that has as its centre a bad encounter. If the stages are consistent, it is in accordance with their possible registration in terms of bad encounters.

The central bad encounter is at the level of the sexual. This does not mean that the stages assume a sexual taint that is diffused on the basis of the fear of castration. On the contrary, it is because this empathy is not produced that one speaks of trauma and primal scene.

12 February 1964

OF THE GAZE AS
Objet Petit a

6

THE SPLIT BETWEEN THE EYE
AND THE GAZE

The split of the subject · The facticity of the trauma · Maurice Merleau-Ponty · The philosophical tradition · Mimicry · The all-seer · In the dream, it shows

To continue.

Wiederholung—let me remind you once again of the etymological reference that I gave you, *holen* (to haul), of its connotation of something tiring, exhausting.

To haul, to draw. To draw what? Perhaps, playing on the ambiguity of the word in French, to draw lots (*tirer au sort*). This *Zwang*, this compulsion, would then direct us towards the obligatory card—if there is only one card in the pack, I can't draw another.

The character of a set, in the mathematical sense of the term, possessed by the play of signifiers, and which opposes it for example to the indefiniteness of the whole number, enables us to conceive a schema in which the function of the obligatory card is immediately applicable. If the subject is the subject of the signifier—determined by it—one may imagine the synchronic network as it appears in the diachrony of preferential effects. This is not a question, you understand, of unpredictable statistical effects—it is the very structure of the network that implies the returns. Through the elucidation of what we call strategies, this is the figure that Aristotle's *automaton* assumes for us. Furthermore, it is by *automatisme* that we sometimes translate into French the *Zwang* of the *Wiederholungszwang*, the compulsion to repeat.

I

Later, I shall give you the facts that suggest that at certain moments of that infantile monologue, imprudently termed egocentric, there are strictly syntactical games to be observed. These games belong to the field that we call pre-conscious, but make, one might say, the bed of the unconscious reserve—to be understood in the sense of an Indian reserve—within the social network.

Syntax, of course, is pre-conscious. But what eludes the subject is the fact that his syntax is in relation with the unconscious reserve. When the subject tells his story, something acts, in a latent way, that governs this syntax and makes it more and more condensed. Condensed in relation to what? In relation to what Freud, at the beginning of his description of psychical resistance, calls a nucleus.

To say that this nucleus refers to something traumatic is no more than an approximation. We must distinguish between the resistance of the subject and that first resistance of discourse, when the discourse proceeds towards the condensation around the nucleus. For the expression *resistance of the subject* too much implies the existence of a supposed ego and it is not certain whether—at the approach of this nucleus—it is something that we can justifiably call an ego.

The nucleus must be designated as belonging to the real— the real in so far as the identity of perception is its rule. At most, it is grounded on what Freud indicates as a sort of deduction, which assures us that we are in perception by means of the sense of reality that authenticates it. What does this mean, if not that, as far as the subject is concerned, this is called awakening?

Although, last time, it was around the dream in chapter seven of *The Interpretation of Dreams* that I approached the whole question of repetition, it was because the choice of this dream —so enclosed, so doubly and triply enclosed as it is, since it is not analysed—is very revealing here, occurring as it does at the moment when Freud is dealing with the process of the dream in its last resort. Is the reality that determines the awakening the slight noise against which the empire of the dream and of desire is maintained? Is it not rather something else? Is it not that which is expressed in the depths of the anxiety of this dream—namely, the most intimate aspects of the relation between the father and the son, which emerges, not so much in that death as in the fact that it is beyond, in the sense of destiny?

Between what occurs as if by chance, when everybody is asleep—the candle that overturns and the sheets that catch fire, the meaningless event, the accident, the piece of bad luck—and the element of poignancy, however veiled, in the words *Father, can't you see I'm burning*—there is the same relation to what we were dealing with in repetition. It is what, for us, is represented in the term neurosis of destiny or neurosis of failure. What is missed is not adaptation, but *tuché*, the encounter.

Aristotle's formula—that the *tuché* is defined by being able to come to us only from a being capable of choice, *proairesis*, that the *tuché*, good or bad fortune, cannot come to us from an inanimate object, a child or an animal—is controverted here. The very accident of this exemplary dream depicts this. Certainly, Aristotle marks the extreme limit of that point that stops it on the edge of the extravagant forms of sexual behaviour, which he can only describe as *teriotes*, monstrosities.

The enclosed aspect of the relation between the accident, which is repeated, and the veiled meaning, which is the true reality and leads us towards the drive—confirms for us that the demystification of that artefact of treatment known as the transference does not consist in reducing it to what is called the actuality of the situation. The direction indicated in this reduction to the actuality of the session, or the series of sessions, is not even of propedeutic value. The correct concept of repetition must be obtained in another direction, which we cannot confuse with the effects of the transference taken as a whole. Our next problem, when we approach the function of the transference, will be to grasp how the transference may lead us to the heart of repetition.

That is why it is necessary to ground this repetition first of all in the very split that occurs in the subject in relation to the encounter. This split constitutes the characteristic dimension of analytic discovery and experience; it enables us to apprehend the real, in its dialectical effects, as originally unwelcome. It is precisely through this that the real finds itself, in the subject, to a very great degree the accomplice of the drive—which we shall come to last, because only by following this way will we be able to conceive from what it returns.

For, after all, why is the primal scene so traumatic? Why is it always too early or too late? Why does the subject take either too much pleasure in it—at least, this is how at first we conceived the traumatizing causality of the obsessional neurotic —or too little, as in the case of the hysteric? Why doesn't it arouse the subject immediately, if it is true that he is so profoundly libidinal? Why is the fact here *dustuchia*? Why is the supposed maturation of the pseudo-instincts shot through, transfixed with the *tychic*, I would say—from the word *tuché*?

For the moment, it is our horizon that seems factitious in the fundamental relation to sexuality. In analytic experience, it is a question of setting out from the fact that the primal scene is traumatic; it is not sexual empathy that sustains the modulations of the analysable, but a factitious fact. A factitious fact, like that which appears in the scene so fiercely tracked down in the experience of the Wolf Man—the strangeness of the disappearance and reappearance of the penis.

Last time, I wanted to point out where the split in the subject lay. This split, after awakening, persists—between the return to the real, the representation of the world that has at last fallen back on its feet, arms raised, *what a terrible thing, what has happened, how horrible, how stupid, what an idiot he was to fall asleep* —and the consciousness re-weaving itself, which knows it is living through all this as through a nightmare, but which, all the same, keeps a grip on itself, *it is I who am living through all this, I have no need to pinch myself to known that I am not dreaming.* The fact remains that this split is still there only as representing the more profound split, which is situated between that which refers to the subject in the machinery of the dream, the image of the approaching child, his face full of reproach and, on the other hand, that which causes it and into which he sinks, the invocation, the voice of the child, the solicitation of the gaze —*Father can't you see . . .*

2

It is there that—free as I am to pursue, in the path in which I am leading you, the way that seems best to me—threading my curved needle through the tapestry, I jump on to the side on which is posed the question that offers itself as a crossroads, between us and all those who try to conceive of the way of the subject.

In so far as it is a search for truth, is this way to be forged in our style of adventure, with its trauma seen as a reflection of facticity? Or is it to be located where tradition has always placed it, at the level of the dialectic of truth and appearance, grasped at the outset of perception in its fundamentally ideic, in a way aesthetic, and accentuated character as visual centring?

It is not mere chance—belonging to the order of the pure *tychic*—if this very week I have received a copy of the newly published, posthumous work of my friend Maurice Merleau-Ponty, *Le Visible et l'invisible*.

Here is expressed, embodied, what made the alternation of our dialogue, and I remember so clearly the Congrès de Bonneval where his intervention revealed the nature of his path, a path that had broken off at one point of the *oeuvre*, which left it nevertheless in a state of completion, prefigured in the work of piety that we owe to Claude Lefort, to whom I would like to pay homage here for the kind of perfection which, in a long and difficult transcription, he seems to me to have achieved.

This work, *Le Visible et l'invisible*, may indicate for us the moment of arrival of the philosophical tradition—the tradition that begins with Plato with the promulgation of the idea, of which one may say that, setting out from an aesthetic world, it is determined by an end given to being as sovereign good, thus attaining a beauty that is also its limit. And it is not by chance that Maurice Merleau-Ponty recognized its guide in the eye.

In this work, which is both an end and a beginning, you will find both a recapitulation and a step forward in the path of what had first been formulated in Merleau-Ponty's *La Phénoménologie de la perception*. In this work, one finds a recapitulation of the regulatory function of form, invoked in opposition to that which, as philosophical thinking progressed, had been taken to that extreme of vertigo expressed in the term idealism—how could the 'lining' that representation then became be joined to that which it is supposed to cover? *La Phénoménologie* brings us back, then, to the regulation of form, which is governed, not only by the subject's eye, but by his expectations, his movement, his grip, his muscular and visceral emotion—in short, his constitutive presence, directed in what is called his total intentionality.

Maurice Merleau-Ponty now makes the next step by forcing

the limits of this very phenomenology. You will see that the ways through which he will lead you are not only of the order of visual phenomenology, since they set out to rediscover—this is the essential point—the dependence of the visible on that which places us under the eye of the seer. But this is going too far, for that eye is only the metaphor of something that I would prefer to call the seer's 'shoot' (*pousse*)—something prior to his eye. What we have to circumscribe, by means of the path he indicates for us, is the pre-existence of a gaze—I see only from one point, but in my existence I am looked at from all sides.

It is no doubt this *seeing*, to which I am subjected in an original way, that must lead us to the aims of this work, to that ontological turning back, the bases of which are no doubt to be found in a more primitive institution of form.

Precisely this gives me an opportunity to reply to someone that, of course, I have my ontology—why not?—like everyone else, however naïve or elaborate it may be. But, certainly, what I try to outline in my discourse—which, although it re-interprets that of Freud, is nevertheless centred essentially on the particularity of the experience it describes—makes no claim to cover the entire field of experience. Even this between-the-two that opens up for us the apprehension of the unconscious is of concern to us only in as much as it is designated for us, through the instructions Freud left us, as that of which the subject has to take possession. I will only add that the maintenance of this aspect of Freudianism, which is often described as naturalism, seems to be indispensable, for it is one of the few attempts, if not the only one, to embody psychical reality without substantifying it.

In the field offered us by Maurice Merleau-Ponty, more or less polarized indeed by the threads of our experience, the scopic field, the ontological status, is presented by its most factitious, not to say most outworn, effects. But it is not between the invisible and the visible that we have to pass. The split that concerns us is not the distance that derives from the fact that there are forms imposed by the world towards which the intentionality of phenomenological experience directs us—hence the limits that we encounter in the experience of the visible. The gaze is presented to us only in the form of a strange contingency, symbolic of what we find on the horizon, as the thrust of our experience, namely, the lack that constitutes castration anxiety.

The eye and the gaze—this is for us the split in which the drive is manifested at the level of the scopic field.

3

In our relation to things, in so far as this relation is constituted by the way of vision, and ordered in the figures of representation, something slips, passes, is transmitted, from stage to stage, and is always to some degree eluded in it—that is what we call the gaze.

You can be made aware of this in more than one way. Let me describe it, at its extreme point, by one of the enigmas that the reference to nature presents us with. It is a question of nothing less than the phenomenon known as mimicry.

A lot has been said about this subject and a great deal that is absurd—for example, that the phenomenon of mimicry can be explained in terms of adaptation. I do not think this is the case. I need only refer you, among others, to a short work that many of you may already know, Roger Caillois' *Méduse et compagnie*, in which the reference to adaptation is criticized in a particularly perspicacious way. On the one hand, in order to be effective, the determining mutation of mimicry, in the insect, for example, may take place only at once and at the outset. On the other hand, its supposed selective effects are annihilated by the observation that one finds in the stomach of birds, predators in particular, as many insects supposedly protected by mimicry as insects that are not.

But, in any case, the problem does not lie there. The most radical problem of mimicry is to know whether we must attribute it to some formative power of the very organism that shows us its manifestations. For this to be legitimate, we would have to be able to conceive by what circuits this force might find itself in a position to control, not only the very form of the imitated body, but its relation to the environment, from which is has to be distinguished or, on the contrary, in which it has to merge. In short, as Caillois reminds us very pertinently, on the subject of such mimetic manifestations, and especially of the manifestation that may remind us of the function of the eyes, that is, the *ocelli*, it is a question of understanding whether they

73

impress—it is a fact that they have this effect on the predator or on the supposed victim that looks at them—whether they impress by their resemblance to eyes, or whether, on the contrary, the eyes are fascinating only by virtue of their relation to the form of the *ocelli*. In other words, must we not distinguish between the function of the eye and that of the gaze?

This distinctive example, chosen as such—for its location, for its facticity, for its exceptional character—is for us simply a small manifestation of the function to be isolated, the function, let us say the word, of *the stain*. This example is valuable in marking the pre-existence to the seen of a given-to-be-seen.

There is no need for us to refer to some supposition of the existence of a universal seer. If the function of the stain is recognized in its autonomy and identified with that of the gaze, we can seek its track, its thread, its trace, at every stage of the constitution of the world, in the scopic field. We will then realize that the function of the stain and of the gaze is both that which governs the gaze most secretly and that which always escapes from the grasp of that form of vision that is satisfied with itself in imagining itself as consciousness.

That in which the consciousness may turn back upon itself —grasp itself, like Valéry's Young Parque, *as seeing oneself seeing oneself*—represents mere sleight of hand. An avoidance of the function of the gaze is at work there.

This much we can map of this topology, which last time we worked out for ourselves on the basis of that which appears from the position of the subject when he accedes to the imaginary forms offered him by the dream, as opposed to those of the waking state.

Similarly, in that order, which is particularly satisfying for the subject, connoted in psycho-analytic experience by the term narcissism—in which I have striven to reintroduce the essential structure it derives from its reference to the specular image—in the satisfaction, not to say self-satisfaction, that diffuses from it, which gives the subject a pretext for such a profound *méconnaissance*—and does its empire not extend as far as this reference of the philosophical tradition represented by plenitude encountered by the subject in the mode of contemplation—can we not also grasp that which has been eluded, namely, the function of the gaze? I mean, and Maurice

Merleau-Ponty points this out, that we are beings who are looked at, in the spectacle of the world. That which makes us consciousness institutes us by the same token as *speculum mundi*. Is there no satisfaction in being under that gaze of which, following Merleau-Ponty, I spoke just now, that gaze that circumscribes us, and which in the first instance makes us beings who are looked at, but without showing this?

The spectacle of the world, in this sense, appears to us as all-seeing. This is the phantasy to be found in the Platonic perspective of an absolute being to whom is transferred the quality of being all-seeing. At the very level of the phenomenal experience of contemplation, this all-seeing aspect is to be found in the satisfaction of a woman who knows that she is being looked at, on condition that one does not show her that one knows that she knows.

The world is all-seeing, but it is not exhibitionistic—it does not provoke our gaze. When it begins to provoke it, the feeling of strangeness begins too.

What does this mean, if not that, in the so-called waking state, there is an elision of the gaze, and an elision of the fact that not only does it look, *it* also *shows*. In the field of the dream, on the other hand, what characterizes the images is that *it shows*.

It shows—but here, too, some form of 'sliding away' of the subject is apparent. Look up some description of a dream, any one—not only the one I referred to last time, in which, after all, what I am going to say may remain enigmatic, but any dream—place it in its co-ordinates, and you will see that this *it shows* is well to the fore. So much is it to the fore, with the characteristics in which it is co-ordinated—namely, the absence of horizon, the enclosure, of that which is contemplated in the waking state, and, also, the character of emergence, of contrast, of stain, of its images, the intensification of their colours—that, in the final resort, our position in the dream is profoundly that of someone who does not see. The subject does not see where it is leading, he follows. He may even on occasion detach himself, tell himself that it is a dream, but in no case will he be able to apprehend himself in the dream in the way in which, in the Cartesian *cogito*, he apprehends himself as thought. He may say to himself, *It's only a dream*. But he does not apprehend himself as someone who says to himself—*After all, I am the consciousness of this dream.*

In a dream, he is a butterfly. What does this mean? It means that he sees the butterfly in his reality as gaze. What are so many figures, so many shapes, so many colours, if not this gratuitous *showing*, in which is marked for us the primal nature of the essence of the gaze. Good heavens, it is a butterfly that is not very different from the one that terrorized the Wolf Man —and Maurice Merleau-Ponty is well aware of the importance of it and refers us to it in a footnote to his text. When Choang-tsu wakes up, he may ask himself whether it is not the butterfly who dreams that he is Choang-tsu. Indeed, he is right, and doubly so, first because it proves he is not mad, he does not regard himself as absolutely identical with Choang-tsu and, secondly, because he does not fully understand how right he is. In fact, it is when he was the butterfly that he apprehended one of the roots of his identity—that he was, and is, in his essence, that butterfly who paints himself with his own colours —and it is because of this that, in the last resort, he is Choang-tsu.

This is proved by the fact that, when he is the butterfly, the idea does not occur to him to wonder whether, when he is Choang-tsu awake, he is not the butterfly that he is dreaming of being. This is because, when dreaming of being the butterfly, he will no doubt have to bear witness later that he represented himself as a butterfly. But this does not mean that he is captivated by the butterfly—he is a captive butterfly, but captured by nothing, for, in the dream, he is a butterfly for nobody. It is when he is awake that he is Choang-tsu for others, and is caught in their butterfly net.

This is why the butterfly may—if the subject is not Choang-tsu, but the Wolf Man—inspire in him the phobic terror of recognizing that the beating of little wings is not so very far from the beating of causation, of the primal stripe marking his being for the first time with the grid of desire.

Next time, I propose to introduce you to the essence of scopic satisfaction. The gaze may contain in itself the *objet a* of the Lacanian algebra where the subject falls, and what specifies the scopic field and engenders the satisfaction proper to it is the fact that, for structural reasons, the fall of the subject always remains unperceived, for it is reduced to zero. In so far as the gaze, *qua objet a*, may come to symbolize this central lack expressed in the phenomenon of castration, and in so far as it is an *objet a* reduced, of its nature, to a punctiform, evanescent function, it leaves the subject in ignorance as to what there is beyond the appearance, an ignorance so characteristic of all progress in thought that occurs in the way constituted by philosophical research.

QUESTIONS AND ANSWERS

X. AUDOUARD: *To what extent is it necessary, in analysis, to let the subject know that one is looking at him, that is to say, that one is situated as the person who is observing in the subject the process of looking at oneself?*

LACAN: I shall take up again what I have said above, adding that my discourse here has two aims, one of concern to analysts, the other to those who have come here in order to discover whether psycho-analysis is a science.

Psycho-analysis is neither a *Weltanschauung*, nor a philosophy that claims to provide the key to the universe. It is governed by a particular aim, which is historically defined by the elaboration of the notion of the subject. It poses this notion in a new way, by leading the subject back to his signifying dependence.

To go from perception to science is a perspective that seems to be self-evident, in so far as the subject has no better testing ground for the apprehension of being. This way is the same one that Aristotle follows, taking as his starting-point the pre-Socratics. But it is a way that analytic experience must rectify, because it avoids the abyss of castration. We see this, for example, in the fact that the *tuché* does not enter, except in a punctiform way, into theogony and genesis.

I am trying here to grasp how the *tuché* is represented in visual apprehension. I shall show that it is at the level that I call the stain that the *tychic* point in the scopic function is found. This means that the level of reciprocity between the gaze and the gazed at is, for the subject, more open than any other to alibi. That is why we should try to avoid, by our interventions in the session, allowing the subject to establish himself on this level. On the contrary, we should cut him off from this point of ultimate gaze, which is illusory.

77

The obstacle you point out is certainly there to illustrate the fact that we take a great deal of care. We do not say to the patient, at every end and turn, *Now, now! What a face you're making!*, or, *The top button of your waistcoat is undone.* It is not, after all, for nothing that analysis is not carried out face to face. The split between gaze and vision will enable us, you will see, to add the scopic drive to the list of the drives. If we know how to read it, we shall see that Freud already places this drive to the fore in *Triebe und Triebschicksale* ('Instincts and their Vicissitudes'), and shows that it is not homologous with the others. Indeed, it is this drive that most completely eludes the term castration.

19 February 1964

7

ANAMORPHOSIS

Of the foundation of consciousness · The privilege of the gaze as objet a ·
The optics of the blind · The phallus in the picture

> *Vainement ton image arrive à ma rencontre*
> *Et ne m'entre où je suis qui seulement la montre*
> *Toi te tournant vers moi tu ne saurais trouver*
> *Au mur de mon regard que ton ombre rêvée*
>
> *Je suis ce malheureux comparable aux miroirs*
> *Qui peuvent réfléchir mais ne peuvent pas voir*
> *Comme eux mon oeil est vide et comme eux habité*
> *De l'absence de toi qui fait sa cécité*[1]

You may remember that, in one of my earlier lectures, I began by quoting the poem, *Contrechant,* from Aragon's *Le Fou d'Elsa.* I did not realize at the time that I would be developing the subject of the gaze to such an extent. I was diverted into doing so by the way in which I presented the concept of repetition in Freud.

We cannot deny that it is within the explanation of repetition that this digression on the scopic function is situated —no doubt by Maurice Merleau-Ponty's recently published work, *Le Visible et l'invisible.* Moreover, it seemed to me that, if an encounter were to be found there, it was a happy one, one destined to stress, as I shall try to do today, how, in the perspective of the unconscious, we can situate consciousness.

You know that some shadow, or, to use another term, some 'resist'—in the sense one speaks of 'resist' in the dying of material—marks the fact of consciousness in Freud's very discourse.

But, before taking things up again at the point we left them last time, I must first clear up a misunderstanding that appears

---

[1] For a translation of the poem, see page 17.

to have arisen in the minds of certain members of the audience concerning a term I used last time. Some of you seem to have been perplexed by a word that is simple enough, and which I commented on, namely, the *tychic*. Apparently, it sounded to some of you like a sneeze. Yet I made it quite clear that it was the adjective formed from *tuché* just as *psychique* (psychical) is the adjective corresponding to *psuché* (psyche). I used this analogy at the heart of the experience of repetition quite intentionally, because for any conception of the psychical development as elucidated by psycho-analysis, the fact of the tychic is central. It is in relation to the eye, in relation to the *eutuchia* or the *dustuchia*, the happy encounter and the unhappy encounter, that my lecture today will be ordered.

I

I saw myself seeing myself, young Parque says somewhere. Certainly, this statement has rich and complex implications in relation to the theme developed in *La Jeune Parque*, that of femininity—but we haven't got there yet. We are dealing with the philosopher, who apprehends something that is one of the essential correlates of consciousness in its relation to representation, and which is designated as *I see myself seeing myself*. What evidence can we really attach to this formula? How is it that it remains, in fact, correlative with that fundamental mode to which we referred in the Cartesian *cogito*, by which the subject apprehends himself as thought?

What isolates this apprehension of thought by itself is a sort of doubt, which has been called methodological doubt, which concerns whatever might give support to thought in representation. How is it, then, that the *I see myself seeing myself* remains its envelope and base, and, perhaps more than one thinks, grounds its certainty? For, *I warm myself by warming myself* is a reference to the body as body—I feel that sensation of warmth which, from some point inside me, is diffused and locates me as body. Whereas in the *I see myself seeing myself*, there is no such sensation of being absorbed by vision.

Furthermore, the phenomenologists have succeeded in articulating with precision, and in the most disconcerting way, that it is quite clear that I see *outside*, that perception is not in me, that it is on the objects that it apprehends. And yet I apprehend the world in a perception that seems to concern the immanence of the *I see myself seeing myself*. The privilege of the subject seems to be established here from that bipolar reflexive relation by which, as soon as I perceive, my representations belong to me.

This is how the world is struck with a presumption of idealization, of the suspicion of yielding me only my representations. Serious practice does not really weigh very heavy, but, on the other hand, the philosopher, the idealist, is placed there, as much in confrontation with himself as in confrontation with those who are listening to him, in an embarrassing position. How can one deny that nothing of the world appears to me except in my representations? This is the irreducible method of Bishop Berkeley, about whose subjective position much might be said—including something that may have eluded you in passing, namely, this *belong to me* aspect of representations, so reminiscent of property. When carried to the limit, the process of this meditation, of this reflecting reflection, goes so far as to reduce the subject apprehended by the Cartesian meditation to a power of annihilation.

The mode of my presence in the world is the subject in so far as by reducing itself solely to this certainty of being a subject, it becomes active annihilation. In fact, the process of the philosophical meditation throws the subject towards the transforming historical action, and, around this point, orders the configured modes of active self-consciousness through its metamorphoses in history. As for the meditation on being that reaches its culmination in the thought of Heidegger, it restores to being itself that power of annihilation—or at least poses the question of how it may be related to it.

This is also the point to which Maurice Merleau-Ponty leads us. But, if you refer to his text, you will see that it is at this point that he chooses to withdraw, in order to propose a return to the sources of intuition concerning the visible and the invisible, to come back to that which is prior to all reflection, thetic or non-thetic, in order to locate the emergence of vision itself. For him, it is a question of restoring—for, he tells us, it can only be a question of a reconstruction or a restoration, not of a path traversed in the opposite direction—of reconstituting the way by which, not from the body, but from something that he calls the flesh of the world, the original point of vision was able to emerge. It would seem that in this way one sees, in this unfinished work, the emergence of something like the search for an unnamed substance from which I, the seer, extract myself. From the toils (*rets*), or rays (*rais*), if you prefer, of an iridescence of which I am at first a part, I emerge as eye, assuming, in a way, emergence from what I would like to call the function of *seeingness* (*voyure*).

A wild odour emanates from it, providing a glimpse on the horizon of the hunt of Artemis—whose touch seems to be associated at this moment of tragic failure in which we lost him who speaks.

Yet is this really the way he wished to take? The traces that remain of the part to come from his meditation permits us to doubt it. The reference-points that are provided in it, more particularly for the strictly psycho-analytic unconscious, allow us to perceive that he may have been directed towards some search, original in relation to the philosophical tradition, towards that new dimension of meditation on the subject that analysis enables us to trace.

Personally, I cannot but be struck by certain of these notes, which are for me less enigmatic than they may seem to other readers, because they correspond very exactly to the schemata —with one of them, in particular—that I shall be dealing with here. Read, for example, the note concerning what he calls the turning inside-out of the finger of a glove, in as much as it seems to appear there—note the way in which the leather envelops the fur in a winter glove—that consciousness, in its illusion of *seeing itself seeing itself*, finds its basis in the inside-out structure of the gaze.

2

But what is the gaze?

I shall set out from this first point of annihilation in which is marked, in the field of the reduction of the subject, a break— which warns us of the need to introduce another reference, that which analysis assumes in reducing the privileges of the consciousness.

Psycho-analysis regards the consciousness as irremediably limited, and institutes it as a principle, not only of idealization, but of *méconnaissance*, as—using a term that takes on new value by being referred to a visible domain—*scotoma*. The term was introduced into the psycho-analytic vocabulary by the French School. Is it simply a metaphor? We find here once again the ambiguity that affects anything that is inscribed in the register of the scopic drive.

For us, consciousness matters only in its relation to what, for propaedeutic reasons, I have tried to show you in the fiction of the incomplete text—on the basis of which it is a question of recentring the subject as speaking in the very lacunae of that in which, at first sight, it presents itself as speaking. But I am stating here only the relation of the pre-conscious to the un-conscious. The dynamic that is attached to the consciousness as such, the attention the subject brings to his own text, remains up to this point, as Freud has stressed, outside theory and, strictly speaking, not yet articulated.

It is here that I propose that the interest the subject takes in his own split is bound up with that which determines it —namely, a privileged object, which has emerged from some primal separation, from some self-mutilation induced by the very approach of the real, whose name, in our algebra, is the *objet a*.

In the scopic relation, the object on which depends the phantasy from which the subject is suspended in an essential vacillation is the gaze. Its privilege—and also that by which the subject for so long has been misunderstood as being in its dependence—derives from its very structure.

Let us schematize at once what we mean. From the moment that this gaze appears, the subject tries to adapt himself to it, he becomes that punctiform object, that point of vanishing being with which the subject confuses his own failure. Furthermore, of all the objects in which the subject may recognize his de-pendence in the register of desire, the gaze is specified as un-apprehensible. That is why it is, more than any other object, misunderstood (*méconnu*), and it is perhaps for this reason, too, that the subject manages, fortunately, to symbolize his own vanishing and punctiform bar (*trait*) in the illusion of the con-sciousness of *seeing oneself see oneself*, in which the gaze is elided.

If, then, the gaze is that underside of consciousness, how shall we try to imagine it?

83

The expression is not inapt, for we can give body to the gaze. Sartre, in one of the most brilliant passages of *L'Être et le Néant*, brings it into function in the dimension of the existence of others. Others would remain suspended in the same, partially de-realizing, conditions that are, in Sartre's definition, those of objectivity, were it not for the gaze. The gaze, as conceived by Sartre, is the gaze by which I am surprised—surprised in so far as it changes all the perspectives, the lines of force, of my world, orders it, from the point of nothingness where I am, in a sort of radiated reticulation of the organisms. As the locus of the relation between me, the annihilating subject, and that which surrounds me, the gaze seems to possess such a privilege that it goes so far as to have me scotomized, I who look, the eye of him who sees me as object. In so far as I am under the gaze, Sartre writes, I no longer see the eye that looks at me and, if I see the eye, the gaze disappears.

Is this a correct phenomenological analysis? No. It is not true that, when I am under the gaze, when I solicit a gaze, when I obtain it, I do not see it as a gaze. Painters, above all, have grasped this gaze as such in the mask and I have only to remind you of Goya, for example, for you to realize this.

The gaze sees itself—to be precise, the gaze of which Sartre speaks, the gaze that surprises me and reduces me to shame, since this is the feeling he regards as the most dominant. The gaze I encounter—you can find this in Sartre's own writing —is, not a seen gaze, but a gaze imagined by me in the field of the Other.

If you turn to Sartre's own text, you will see that, far from speaking of the emergence of this gaze as of something that concerns the organ of sight, he refers to the sound of rustling leaves, suddenly heard while out hunting, to a footstep heard in a corridor. And when are these sounds heard? At the moment when he has presented himself in the action of looking through a keyhole. A gaze surprises him in the function of voyeur, disturbs him, overwhelms him and reduces him to a feeling of shame. The gaze in question is certainly the presence of others as such. But does this mean that originally it is in the relation of subject to subject, in the function of the existence of others as looking at me, that we apprehend what the gaze really is? Is it not clear that the gaze intervenes here only in as much as it is not the annihilating subject, correlative of the world of objectivity, who feels himself surprised, but the subject sustaining himself in a function of desire?

Is it not precisely because desire is established here in the domain of seeing that we can make it vanish?

3

We can apprehend this privilege of the gaze in the function of desire, by pouring ourselves, as it were, along the veins through which the domain of vision has been integrated into the field of desire.

It is not for nothing that it was at the very period when the Cartesian meditation inaugurated in all its purity the function of the subject that the dimension of optics that I shall distinguish here by calling 'geometral' or 'flat' (as opposed to perspective) optics was developed.

I shall illustrate for you, by one object among others, what seems to me exemplary in a function that so curiously attracted so much reflection at the time.

One reference, for those who would like to carry further what I tried to convey to you today, is Baltrušaitis' book, *Anamorphoses*.

In my seminar, I have made great use of the function of anamorphosis, in so far as it is an exemplary structure. What does a simple, non-cylindrical anamorphosis consist of? Suppose there is a portrait on this flat piece of paper that I am holding. By chance, you see the blackboard, in an oblique position in relation to the piece of paper. Suppose that, by means of a series of ideal threads or lines, I reproduce on the oblique surface each point of the image drawn on my sheet of paper. You can easily imagine what the result would be—you would obtain a figure enlarged and distorted according to the lines of what may be called a perspective. One supposes that —if I take away that which has helped in the construction, namely, the image placed in my own visual field—the impression I will retain, while remaining in that place, will be more or less the same. At least, I will recognize the general outlines of the image—at best, I will have an identical impression.

I will now pass around something that dates from a hundred years earlier, from 1533, a reproduction of a painting that, I think, you all know—Hans Holbein's *The Ambassadors*. It will serve to refresh the memories of those who know the picture well. Those who do not should examine it attentively. I shall come back to it shortly.

Vision is ordered according to a mode that may generally be called the function of images. This function is defined by a point-by-point correspondence of two unities in space. Whatever optical intermediaries may be used to establish their relation, whether their image is virtual, or real, the point-by-point correspondence is essential. That which is of the mode of the image in the field of vision is therefore reducible to the simple schema that enables us to establish anamorphosis, that is to say, to the relation of an image, in so far as it is linked to a surface, with a certain point that we shall call the 'geometral' point. Anything that is determined by this method, in which the straight line plays its role of being the path of light, can be called an image.

Art is mingled with science here. Leonardo da Vinci is both a scientist, on account of his dioptric constructions, and an artist. Vitruvius's treatise on architecture is not far away. It is in Vignola and in Alberti that we find the progressive interrogation of the geometral laws of perspective, and it is around research on perspective that is centred a privileged interest for the domain of vision—whose relation with the institution of the Cartesian subject, which is itself a sort of geometral point, a point of perspective, we cannot fail to see. And, around the geometral perspective, the picture—this is a very important function to which we shall return—is organized in a way that is quite new in the history of painting.

I should now like to refer you to Diderot. The *Lettre sur les aveugles à l'usage de ceux qui voient* (Letter on the Blind for the use of those who see) will show you that this construction allows that which concerns vision to escape totally. For the geometral space of vision—even if we include those imaginary parts in the virtual space of the mirror, of which, as you know, I have spoken at length—is perfectly reconstructible, imaginable, by a blind man.

What is at issue in geometral perspective is simply the mapping of space, not sight. The blind man may perfectly well conceive that the field of space that he knows, and which he knows as real, may be perceived at a distance, and as a simultaneous act. For him, it is a question of apprehending a temporal function, instantaneity. In Descartes, dioptrics, the action of the eyes, is represented as the conjugated action of two sticks. The geometral dimension of vision does not exhaust, therefore, far from it, what the field of vision as such offers us as the original subjectifying relation.

This is why it is so important to acknowledge the inverted use of perspective in the structure of anamorphosis.

It was Dürer himself who invented the apparatus to establish perspective. Dürer's 'lucinda' is comparable to what, a little while ago, I placed between that blackboard and myself, namely, a certain image, or more exactly a canvas, a treliss that will be traversed by straight lines—which are not necessarily rays, but also threads—which will link each point that I have to see in the world to a point at which the canvas will, by this line, be traversed.

It was to establish a correct perspective image, therefore, that the *lucinda* was introduced. If I reverse its use, I will have the pleasure of obtaining not the restoration of the world that lies at the end, but the distortion, on another surface, of the image that I would have obtained on the first, and I will dwell, as on some delicious game, on this method that makes anything appear at will in a particular stretching.

I would ask you to believe that such an enchantment took place in its time. Baltrusaïtis' book will tell you of the furious polemics that these practices gave rise to, and which culminated in works of considerable length. The convent of the Minims, now destroyed, which once stood near the rue des Tournelles, carried on the very long wall of one of its galleries and representing as if by chance St John at Patmos a picture that had to be looked at through a hole, so that its distorting value could be appreciated to its full extent.

Distortion may lend itself—this was not the case for this particular fresco—to all the paranoiac ambiguities, and every possible use has been made of it, from Arcimboldi to Salvador Dali. I will go so far as to say that this fascination complements what geometral researches into perspective allow to escape from vision.

How is it that nobody has ever thought of connecting this

with . . . the effect of an erection? Imagine a tattoo traced on the sexual organ *ad hoc* in the state of repose and assuming its, if I may say so, developed form in another state.

How can we not see here, immanent in the geometral dimension—a partial dimension in the field of the gaze, a dimension that has nothing to do with vision as such—something symbolic of the function of the lack, of the appearance of the phallic ghost?

Now, in *The Ambassadors*—I hope everyone has had time now to look at the reproduction—what do you see? What is this strange, suspended, oblique object in the foreground in front of these two figures?

The two figures are frozen, stiffened in their showy adornments. Between them is a series of objects that represent in the painting of the period the symbols of *vanitas*. At the same period, Cornelius Agrippa wrote his *De Vanitate scientiarum*, aimed as much at the arts as the sciences, and these objects are all symbolic of the sciences and arts as they were grouped at the time in the *trivium* and *quadrivium*. What, then, before this display of the domain of appearance in all its most fascinating forms, is this object, which from some angles appears to be flying through the air, at others to be tilted? You cannot know—for you turn away, thus escaping the fascination of the picture.

Begin by walking out of the room in which no doubt it has long held your attention. It is then that, turning round as you leave—as the author of the *Anamorphoses* describes it—you apprehend in this form . . . What? A skull.

This is not how it is presented at first—that figure, which the author compares to a cuttlebone and which for me suggests rather that loaf composed of two books which Dali was once pleased to place on the head of an old woman, chosen deliberately for her wretched, filthy appearance and, indeed, because she seems to be unaware of the fact, or, again, Dali's soft watches, whose signification is obviously less phallic than that of the object depicted in a flying position in the foreground of this picture.

All this shows that at the very heart of the period in which the subject emerged and geometral optics was an object of research, Holbein makes visible for us here something that is simply the subject as annihilated—annihilated in the form that is, strictly speaking, the imaged embodiment of the *minus-phi* $[(-\phi)]$ of castration, which for us, centres the whole organization of the desires through the framework of the fundamental drives.

But it is further still that we must seek the function of vision. We shall then see emerging on the basis of vision, not the phallic symbol, the anamorphic ghost, but the gaze as such, in its pulsatile, dazzling and spread out function, as it is in this picture.

This picture is simply what any picture is, a trap for the gaze. In any picture, it is precisely in seeking the gaze in each of its points that you will see it disappear. I shall try to develop this further next time.

QUESTIONS AND ANSWERS

F. WAHL: *You have explained that the original apprehension of the gaze in the gaze of others, as described by Sartre, was not the fundamental experience of the gaze. I would like you to explain in greater detail what you have already sketched for us, the apprehension of the gaze in the direction of desire.*

LACAN: If one does not stress the dialectic of desire one does not understand why the gaze of others should disorganize the field of perception. It is because the subject in question is not that of the reflexive consciousness, but that of desire. One thinks it is a question of the geometral eye-point, whereas it is a question of a quite different eye—that which flies in the foreground of *The Ambassadors*.

WAHL: *But I don't understand how others will reappear in your discourse . . .*

LACAN: Look, the main thing is that I don't come a cropper!

WAHL: *I would also like to say that, when you speak of the subject and of the real, one is tempted, on first hearing, to consider the terms in themselves. But gradually one realizes that they are to be understood in their relation to one another, and that they have a topological definition —subject and real are to be situated on either side of the split, in the resistance of the phantasy. The real is, in a way, an experience of resistance.*

LACAN: My discourse proceeds, in the following way: each term is sustained only in its topological relation with the others, and the subject of the *cogito* is treated in exactly the same way.

WAHL: *Is topology for you a method of discovery or of exposition?*

LACAN: It is the mapping of the topology proper to our experience as analysts, which may later be taken in a metaphysical perspective. I think Merleau-Ponty was moving in this direction—see the second part of the book, his reference to the *Wolf Man* and to the finger of a glove.

P. KAUFMANN: *You have provided us with a typical structure of the gaze, but you have said nothing of the dilation of light.*

LACAN: I said that the gaze was not the eye, except in that flying form in which Holbein has the cheek to show me my own soft watch . . . Next time, I will talk about embodied light.

26 February 1964

8

THE LINE AND LIGHT

Desire and the picture · The story of a sardine can · The screen · Mimi-cry · The organ · You never look at me from the place I see you

The function of the eye may lead someone who is trying to enlighten you to distant explorations. When, for example, did the function of the organ and, to begin with, its very presence, appear in the evolution of living beings?

The relation of the subject with the organ is at the heart of our experience. Among all the organs with which we deal, the

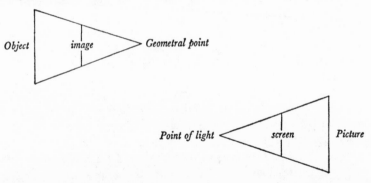

breast, the faeces, etc., there is the eye, and it is striking to see that it goes back as far as the species that represent the appearance of life. You no doubt eat oysters, innocently enough, without knowing that at this level in the animal kingdom the eye has already appeared. Such discoveries teach us, it should be said, all manner of things. Yet we must choose from among these things those that are most relative to our search.

Last time, I think I said enough to enable you to grasp the interest of this small, very simple triangular schema that I have reproduced at the top of the blackboard.

It is there simply to remind you in three terms of the optics used in this operational montage that bears witness to the inverted use of perspective, which came to dominate the technique of painting, in particular, between the end of the fifteenth and the end of the seventeenth centuries. Anamorphosis shows us that it is not a question in painting of a realistic reproduction of the things of space—a term about which one could have many reservations.

The little schema also allows me to remark that certain optics allow that which concerns vision to escape. Such optics are within the grasp of the blind. I have already referred you to Diderot's *Lettre*, which shows to what extent the blind man is capable of taking account of, reconstructing, imagining, speaking about everything that vision yields to us of space. No doubt, on this possibility, Diderot constructs a permanent equivocation with metaphysical implications, but this ambiguity animates his text and gives it its mordant character.

For us, the geometral dimension enables us to glimpse how the subject who concerns us is caught, manipulated, captured, in the field of vision.

In Holbein's picture I showed you at once—without hiding any more than usual—the singular object floating in the foreground, which is there to be looked at, in order to catch, I would almost say, *to catch in its trap*, the observer, that is to say, us. It is, in short, an obvious way, no doubt an exceptional one, and one due to some moment of reflection on the part of the painter, of showing us that, as subjects, we are literally called into the picture, and represented here as caught. For the secret of this picture, whose implications I have pointed out to you, the kinships with the *vanitas*, the way this fascinating picture presents, between the two splendidly dressed and immobile figures, everything that recalls, in the perspective of the period, the vanity of the arts and sciences—the secret of this picture is given at the moment when, moving slightly away, little by little, to the left, then turning around, we see what the magical floating object signifies. It reflects our own nothingness, in the figure of the death's head. It is a use, therefore, of the geometral dimension of vision in order to capture the subject, an obvious relation with desire which, nevertheless, remains enigmatic.

What is the desire which is caught, fixed in the picture, but

which also urges the artist to put something into operation?
And what is that something? This is the path along which we
shall try to move today.

I

In this matter of the visible, everything is a trap, and in a
strange way—as is very well shown by Maurice Merleau-Ponty
in the title of one of the chapters of *Le Visible et l'invisible*—
entrelacs (interlacing, intertwining). There is not a single one of
the divisions, a single one of the double sides that the function
of vision presents, that is not manifested to us as a labyrinth. As
we begin to distinguish its various fields, we always perceive
more and more the extent to which they intersect.

In the domain that I have called that of the geometral, it
seems at first that it is light that gives us, as it were, the thread.
In effect, you saw this thread last time linking us to each point
of the object and, in the place where it crosses the network in
the form of a screen on which we are going to map the image,
functioning quite definitely as a thread. Now, the light is
propagated, as one says, in a straight line, this much is certain.
It would seem, then, that it is light that gives us the thread.

Yet, reflect that this thread has no need of light—all that is
needed is a stretched thread. This is why the blind man would
be able to follow all our demonstrations, providing we took
some trouble in their presentation. We would get him, for
example, to finger an object of a certain height, then follow the
stretched thread. We would teach him to distinguish, by the
sense of touch in his finger-ends, on a surface, a certain configuration that reproduces the mapping of the images—in
the same way that we imagine, in pure optics, the variously
proportioned and fundamentally homological relations, the
correspondences from one point to another in space, which
always, in the end, amounts to situating two points on a single
thread. This construction does not, therefore, particularly
enable us to apprehend what is provided by light.

How can we try to apprehend that which seems to elude us
in this way in the optical structuring of space? It is always on
this question that the traditional argument bears. Philosophers,
going back from Alain, the last to have concerned himself with
it, and quite brilliantly, to Kant, and even to Plato, all expatiate

on the supposed deceptiveness of perception—and, at the same time, they all find themselves once again masters of the exercise, by stressing the fact that perception finds the object where it is, and that the appearance of the cube as a parallelogram is precisely, owing to the rupture of space that underlies our very perception, what makes us perceive it as a cube. The whole trick, the hey presto!, of the classic dialectic around perception, derives from the fact that it deals with geometral vision, that is to say, with vision in so far as it is situated in a space that is not in its essence the visual.

The essence of the relation between appearance and being, which the philosopher, conquering the field of vision, so easily masters, lies elsewhere. It is not in the straight line, but in the point of light—the point of irradiation, the play of light, fire, the source from which reflections pour forth. Light may travel in a straight line, but it is refracted, diffused, it floods, it fills— the eye is a sort of bowl—it flows over, too, it necessitates, around the ocular bowl, a whole series of organs, mechanisms, defences. The iris reacts not only to distance, but also to light, and it has to protect what takes place at the bottom of the bowl, which might, in certain circumstances, be damaged by it. The eyelid, too, when confronted with too bright a light, first blinks, that is, it screws itself up in a well-known grimace.

Furthermore, it is not that the eye has to be photo-sensitive —we know this. The whole surface of the tegument—no doubt for various reasons that are not visual—may be photo-sensitive, and this dimension can in no way be reduced to the functioning of vision. There is a certain adumbration of photo-sensitive organs in the pigmentary spots. In the eye, the pigment functions fully, in a way, of course, that the phenomenon shows to be infinitely complex. It functions within the cones, for example, in the form of a rhodopsin. It also functions inside the various layers of the retina. This pigment comes and goes in functions that are not all, nor always immediately discoverable and clear, but which suggest the depth, the complexity and, at the same time, the unity of the mechanisms concerned with light.

The relation of the subject with that which is strictly concerned with light seems, then, to be already somewhat ambiguous. Indeed, you see this on the schema of the two triangles, which are inverted at the same time as they must be placed one upon the other. What you have here is the first example of this functioning of interlacing, intersection, chiasma, which I pointed out above, and which structures the whole of this domain.

In order to give you some idea of the question posed by this relation between the subject and light, in order to show you that its place is something other than the place of the geometral point defined by geometric optics, I will now tell you a little story.

It's a true story. I was in my early twenties or thereabouts— and at that time, of course, being a young intellectual, I wanted desperately to get away, see something different, throw myself into something practical, something physical, in the country say, or at the sea. One day, I was on a small boat, with a few people from a family of fishermen in a small port. At that time, Brittany was not industrialized as it is now. There were no trawlers. The fisherman went out in his frail craft at his own risk. It was this risk, this danger, that I loved to share. But it wasn't all danger and excitement—there were also fine days. One day, then, as we were waiting for the moment to pull in the nets, an individual known as Petit-Jean, that's what we called him—like all his family, he died very young from tuberculosis, which at that time was a constant threat to the whole of that social class—this Petit-Jean pointed out to me something floating on the surface of the waves. It was a small can, a sardine can. It floated there in the sun, a witness to the canning industry, which we, in fact, were supposed to supply. It glittered in the sun. And Petit-Jean said to me— *You see that can? Do you see it? Well, it doesn't see you!*

He found this incident highly amusing—I less so. I thought about it. Why did I find it less amusing than he? It's an interesting question.

To begin with, if what Petit-Jean said to me, namely, that the can did not see me, had any meaning, it was because in a sense, it was looking at me, all the same. It was looking at me at the level of the point of light, the point at which everything that looks at me is situated—and I am not speaking metaphorically.

The point of this little story, as it had occurred to my partner, the fact that he found it so funny and I less so, derives from the fact that, if I am told a story like that one, it is because I, at that moment—as I appeared to those fellows who were earning their livings with great difficulty, in the struggle with what for them was a pitiless nature—looked like nothing on earth. In short, I was rather out of place in the picture. And it was because I felt this that I was not terribly amused at hearing myself addressed in this humorous, ironical way.

I am taking the structure at the level of the subject here, and it reflects something that is already to be found in the natural relation that the eye inscribes with regard to light. I am not simply that punctiform being located at the geometral point from which the perspective is grasped. No doubt, in the depths of my eye, the picture is painted. The picture, certainly, is in my eye. But I am not in the picture.

That which is light looks at me, and by means of that light in the depths of my eye, something is painted—something that is not simply a constructed relation, the object on which the philosopher lingers—but something that is an impression, the shimmering of a surface that is not, in advance, situated for me in its distance. This is something that introduces what was elided in the geometral relation—the depth of field, with all its ambiguity and variability, which is in no way mastered by me. It is rather it that grasps me, solicits me at every moment, and makes of the landscape something other than a landscape, something other than what I have called the picture.

The correlative of the picture, to be situated in the same place as it, that is to say, outside, is the point of gaze, while that which forms the mediation from the one to the other, that which is between the two, is something of another nature than geometral, optical space, something that plays an exactly reverse role, which operates, not because it can be traversed, but on the contrary because it is opaque—I mean the screen.

In what is presented to me as space of light, that which is gaze is always a play of light and opacity. It is always that gleam of light—it lay at the heart of my little story—it is always this which prevents me, at each point, from being a screen, from making the light appear as an iridescence that overflows it. In short, the point of gaze always participates in the ambiguity of the jewel.

And if I am anything in the picture, it is always in the form of the screen, which I earlier called the stain, the spot.

2

This is the relation of the subject with the domain of vision. The word subject must not be understood here in the usual sense of the word, in the subjective sense—this relation is not an idealist relation. This overview, which I call the subject, and which I regard as giving consistency to the picture, is not simply a representative overview.

There are many ways of being wrong about this function of the subject in the domain of the spectacle.

Certainly, there are plenty of examples in *La Phénoménologie de la perception* of what happens behind the retina. Merleau-Ponty cleverly extracts from a mass of writing some very remarkable facts, showing, for example, that simply the fact of masking, by means of a screen, part of a field functioning as a source of composite colours—produced, for example, by two wheels, two screens, which, one revolving behind the other, must compose a certain tone of light—that this intervention alone reveals in a quite different way the composition in question. Indeed, here we grasp the purely subjective function, in the ordinary sense of the word, the note of central mechanism that intervenes, for the play of light arranged in the experiment, all the elements of which we know, is distinct from what is perceived by the subject.

Perceiving the effects of reflection of a field or a colour is quite different—it does have a subjective side to it, but one arranged quite differently. Let us, for example, place a yellow field beside a blue field—by receiving the light reflected on the yellow field, the blue field will undergo some change. But, certainly, everything that is colour is merely subjective—there is no objective correlative in the spectrum to enable us to attach the quality of colour to the wavelength, or to the relevant frequency at this level of light vibration. There is something objective here, but it is situated differently.

Is that all there is to it? Is that what I am talking about when I speak of the relation between the subject and what I have called the picture? Certainly not.

The relation between the subject and the picture has been

approached by certain philosophers, but they have, if I may say so, missed the point. Read the book by Raymond Ruyer called *Néo-finalisme*, and see how, in order to situate perception in a teleological perspective, he is forced to situate the subject in an absolute overview. There is no need, except in the most abstract way, to posit the subject in absolute overview, when, in the example he gives, it is merely a question of getting us to grasp what the perception of a draught-board is—a draught-board belongs essentially to that geometral optics that I was careful to distinguish at the outset. We are here in space *partes extra partes*, which always provides such an objection to the apprehension to the object. In this direction, the thing is irreducible.

Yet there is a phenomenal domain—infinitely more extended than the privileged points at which it appears—that enables us to apprehend, in its true nature, the subject in absolute overview. Even if we cannot give it being, it is nonetheless necessary. There are facts that can be articulated only in the phenomenal dimension of the overview by which I situate myself in the picture as stain—these are the facts of mimicry.

This is not the place to go into all the more or less complex problems posed by the question of mimicry. I would refer you to the specialized works on the subject—they are not only fascinating in themselves, but they provide ample material for reflexion. I shall content myself with stressing what has not, perhaps, been sufficiently brought out. To begin with, I shall ask a question—how important is the function of adaptation in mimicry?

In certain phenomena of mimicry one may speak perhaps of an adaptive or adapted coloration and realize, for example—as Cuénot has shown, probably with some relevance in certain cases—that coloration, in so far as it is adapted completely, is simply a way of defending oneself against light. In an environment in which, because of what is immediately around, the colour green predominates, as at the bottom of a pool containing green plants, an animalcule—there are innumerable ones that might serve as examples—becomes green for as long as the light may do it harm. It becomes green, therefore, in order to reflect the light *qua* green, thus protecting itself, by adaptation, from its effects.

But, in mimicry, we are dealing with something quite different. Let us take an example chosen almost at random—it is not a privileged case—that of the small crustacean known as *caprella*, to which is added the adjective *acanthifera*. When such a crustacean settles in the midst of those animals, scarcely animals, known as briozoaires, what does it imitate? It imitates what, in that quasi-plant animal known as the briozoaires, is a stain—at a particular phase of the briozoaires, an intestinal loop forms a stain, at another phase, there functions something like a coloured centre. It is to this stain shape that the crustacean adapts itself. It becomes a stain, it becomes a picture, it is inscribed in the picture. This, strictly speaking, is the origin of mimicry. And, on this basis, the fundamental dimensions of the inscription of the subject in the picture appear infinitely more justified than a more hesitant guess might suggest at first sight.

I have already referred to what Caillois says about this in his little book *Méduse et compagnie*, with that unquestionable penetration that is sometimes found in the non-specialist—his very distance may enable him to grasp certain implications in what the specialist has merely stated.

Certain scientists claim to see in the register of coloration merely more or less successful facts of adaptation. But the facts show that practically nothing that can be called adaptation—in the sense in which the term is usually understood, that is to say, as behaviour bound up with the needs of survival—practically nothing of this is to be found in mimicry, which, in most cases, proves to be inoperant, or operating strictly in the opposite direction from that which the adaptive result might be presumed to demand. On the other hand, Caillois brings out the three headings that are in effect the major dimensions in which the mimetic activity is deployed—travesty, camouflage, intimidation.

Indeed, it is in this domain that the dimension by which the subject is to be inserted in the picture is presented. Mimicry reveals something in so far as it is distinct from what might be called an *itself* that is behind. The effect of mimicry is camouflage, in the strictly technical sense. It is not a question of harmonizing with the background but, against a mottled background, of becoming mottled—exactly like the technique of camouflage practised in human warfare.

In the case of travesty, a certain sexual finality is intended. Nature shows us that this sexual aim is produced by all kinds of effects that are essentially disguise, masquerade. A level is constituted here quite distinct from the sexual aim itself, which is found to play an essential role in it, and which must not be distinguished too hastily as being that of deception. The function of the lure, in this instance, is something else, something before which we should suspend judgement before we have properly measured its effects.

Finally, the phenomenon known as intimidation also involves this over-valuation that the subject always tries to attain in his appearance. Here too, we should not be too hasty in introducing some kind of inter-subjectivity. Whenever we are dealing with imitation, we should be very careful not to think too quickly of the other who is being imitated. To imitate is no doubt to reproduce an image. But at bottom, it is, for the subject, to be inserted in a function whose exercise grasps it. It is here that we should pause for a moment.

Let us now see what the unconscious function as such tells us, in so far as it is the field which, for us, offers itself to the conquest of the subject.

3

In this direction, a remark of Caillois' should guide us. Caillois assures us that the facts of mimicry are similar, at the animal level, to what, in the human being is manifested as art, or painting. The only objection one might make to this is that it seems to indicate, for René Caillois, that the notion of painting is itself so clear that one can refer to it in order to explain something else.

What is painting? It is obviously not for nothing that we have referred to as picture the function in which the subject has to map himself as such. But when a human subject is engaged in making a picture of himself, in putting into operation that something that has as its centre the gaze, what is taking place? In the picture, the artist, we are told by some, wishes to be a subject, and the art of painting is to be distinguished from all others in that, in the work, it is as subject, as gaze, that the artist intends to impose himself on us. To this, others reply by stressing the object-like side of the art product. In both

these directions, something more or less appropriate is manifested, which certainly does not exhaust the question.

I shall advance the following thesis—certainly, in the picture,
something of the gaze is always manifested. The painter knows
this very well—his morality, his search, his quest, his practice
is that he should sustain and vary the selection of a certain
kind of gaze. Looking at pictures, even those most lacking in
what is usually called the gaze, and which is constituted by a
pair of eyes, pictures in which any representation of the human
figure is absent, like a landscape by a Dutch or a Flemish
painter, you will see in the end, as in filigree, something so
specific to each of the painters that you will feel the presence of
the gaze. But this is merely an object of research, and perhaps
merely illusion.

The function of the picture—in relation to the person to
whom the painter, literally, offers his picture to be seen—has a
relation with the gaze. This relation is not, as it might at first
seem, that of being a trap for the gaze. It might be thought
that, like the actor, the painter wishes to be looked at. I do not
think so. I think there is a relation with the gaze of the spectator,
but that it is more complex. The painter gives something to the
person who must stand in front of his painting which, in part,
at least, of the painting, might be summed up thus—*You want
to see? Well, take a look at this!* He gives something for the eye
to feed on, but he invites the person to whom this picture is
presented to lay down his gaze there as one lays down one's
weapons. This is the pacifying, Apollonian effect of painting.
Something is given not so much to the gaze as to the eye, something that involves the abandonment, the *laying down*, of the
gaze.

The problem is that a whole side of painting—expressionism
—is separated from this field. Expressionist painting, and this
is its distinguishing feature, provides something by way of a
certain satisfaction—in the sense in which Freud uses the term
in relation to the drive—of a certain satisfaction of what is
demanded by the gaze.

In other words, we must now pose the question as to the
exact status of the eye as organ. The function, it is said, creates
the organ. This is quite absurd—function does not even
explain the organ. Whatever appears in the organism as an

organ is always presented with a large multiplicity of functions. In the eye, it is clear that various functions come together. The discriminatory function is isolated to the maximum degree at the level of the *fovea*, the chosen point of distinct vision. Something quite different occurs over the rest of the surface of the retina, incorrectly distinguished by specialists as the locus of the scotopic function. But here, too, chiasma is to be found, since it is this last field, supposedly created to perceive things in diminished lighting, which provides the maximum possibility of perceiving the effects of light. If you wish to see a star of the fifth or six size, do not look straight at it—this is known as the Arago phenomenon. You will be able to see it only if you fix your eye to one side.

These functions of the eye do not exhaust the character of the organ in so far as it emerges on the couch, and in so far as the eye determines there what every organ determines, namely, duties. What is wrong about the reference to instinct, a reference that is so confused, is that one does not realize that instinct is the way in which an organism has of extricating itself in the best possible way from an organ. There are many examples, in the animal kingdom, of cases in which the organism succumbs to an excess, a hyper-development of an organ. The supposed function of instinct in the relation between organism and organ certainly seems to have been defined as a kind of morality. We are astonished by the so-called pre-adaptations of instinct. The extraordinary thing is that the organism can do anything with its organ at all.

In my reference to the unconscious, I am dealing with the relation to the organ. It is not a question of the relation to sexuality, or even to the sex, if it is possible to give any specific reference to this term. It is a question rather of the relation to the phallus, in as much as it is lacking in the real that might be attained in the sexual goal.

It is in as much as, at the heart of the experience of the unconscious, we are dealing with that organ—determined in the subject by the inadequacy organized in the castration complex —that we can grasp to what extent the eye is caught up in a similar dialectic.

From the outset, we see, in the dialectic of the eye and the gaze, that there is no coincidence, but, on the contrary, a lure.

When, in love, I solicit a look, what is profoundly unsatisfying and always missing is that—*You never look at me from the place from which I see you.*

Conversely, *what I look at is never what I wish to see.* And the relation that I mentioned earlier, between the painter and the spectator, is a play, a play of *trompe-l'œil*, whatever one says. There is no reference here to what is incorrectly called figurative, if by this you mean some reference or other to a subjacent reality.

In the classical tale of Zeuxis and Parrhasios, Zeuxis has the advantage of having made grapes that attracted the birds. The stress is placed not on the fact that these grapes were in any way perfect grapes, but on the fact that even the eye of the birds was taken in by them. This is proved by the fact that his friend Parrhasios triumphs over him for having painted on the wall a veil, a veil so lifelike that Zeuxis, turning towards him said, *Well, and now show us what you have painted behind it.* By this he showed that what was at issue was certainly deceiving the eye *(tromper l'œil).* A triumph of the gaze over the eye.

Next time, we shall return to this function of the eye and the gaze.

QUESTIONS AND ANSWERS

M. SAFOUAN: *In the contemplation of the picture, if I have understood you correctly, the eye seeks relaxation from the gaze?*

LACAN: I shall take up here the dialectic of appearance and its beyond, in saying that, if beyond appearance there is nothing in itself, there is the gaze. It is in this relation that the eye as organ is situated.

SAFOUAN: *Beyond the appearance, is there a lack, or the gaze?*

LACAN: At the level of the scopic dimension, in so far as the drive operates there, is to be found the same function of the *objet a* as can be mapped in all the other dimensions.

The *objet a* is something from which the subject, in order to constitute itself, has separated itself off as organ. This serves as a symbol of the lack, that is to say, of the phallus, not as such, but in so far as it is lacking. It must, therefore, be an object that is, firstly, separable and, secondly, that has some relation to the lack. I'll explain at once what I mean.

At the oral level, it is the nothing, in so far as that from which the subject was weaned is no longer anything for him. In anorexia nervosa, what the child eats is the nothing. This will enable you to grasp obliquely how the object of weaning may come to function at the level of castration, as privation.

The anal level is the locus of metaphor—one object for another, give the faeces in place of the phallus. This shows you why the anal drive is the domain of oblativity, of the gift. Where one is caught short, where one cannot, as a result of the lack, give what is to be given, one can always give something else. That is why, in his morality, man is inscribed at the anal level. And this is especially true of the materialist.

At the scopic level, we are no longer at the level of demand, but of desire, of the desire of the Other. It is the same at the level of the invocatory drive, which is the closest to the experience of the unconscious.

Generally speaking, the relation between the gaze and what one wishes to see involves a lure. The subject is presented as other than he is, and what one shows him is not what he wishes to see. It is in this way that the eye may function as *objet a*, that is to say, at the level of the lack $(-\phi)$.

4 March 1964

9

WHAT IS A PICTURE?

Being and its semblance · *The lure of the screen* · Dompte-regard *and* trompe-l'œil[1] · *The backward glance* · *Gesture and touch* · Le donner-à-voir *and* invidia[2]

Today, then, I must keep to the wager to which I committed myself in choosing the terrain in which the *objet a* is most evanescent in its function of symbolizing the central lack of desire, which I have always indicated in a univocal way by the algorithm $(-\phi)$.

I don't know whether you can see the blackboard, but as usual I have marked out a few reference-points. *The* objet a *in the field of the visible is the gaze.* After which, enclosed in a chain bracket, I have written:

$$\left\{ \begin{array}{l} in\ nature \\ as = (-\phi) \end{array} \right.$$

We can grasp in effect something which, already in nature, appropriates the gaze to the function to which it may be put in the symbolic relation in man.

Below this, I have drawn the two triangular systems that I have already introduced—the first is that which, in the geometral field, puts in our place the subject of the representation, and the second is that which turns *me* into a picture. On the right-hand line is situated, then, the apex of the first triangle, the point of the geometral subject, and it is on that line that I,

---

[1] The sense of the verb *dompter* is 'to tame', 'to subdue'. The reference, then, is to a situation in which the gaze is tamed by some object, such as a picture. Lacan has invented the phrase *dompte-regard* as a counterpart to the notion of *trompe-l'œil*, which has of course passed into the English language [Tr.].

[2] *Donner-à-voir* means literally 'to give to be seen' and, therefore, 'to offer to the view'. The Latin *invidia*, translated as 'envy', derives, as Lacan points out, from *videre*, to see.

too, turn myself into a picture under the gaze, which is inscribed at the apex of the second triangle. The two triangles are here superimposed, as in fact they are in the functioning of the scopic register.

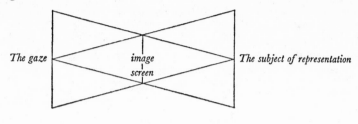

I

I must, to begin with, insist on the following: in the scopic field, the gaze is outside, I am looked at, that is to say, I am a picture.

This is the function that is found at the heart of the institution of the subject in the visible. What determines me, at the most profound level, in the visible, is the gaze that is outside. It is through the gaze that I enter light and it is from the gaze that I receive its effects. Hence it comes about that the gaze is the instrument through which light is embodied and through which—if you will allow me to use a word, as I often do, in a fragmented form—I am *photo-graphed*.

What is at issue here is not the philosophical problem of representation. From that point of view, when I am presented with a representation, I assure myself that I know quite a lot about it, I assure myself as a consciousness that knows that it is only representation, and that there is, beyond, the thing, the thing itself. Behind the phenomenon, there is the noumenon, for example. I may not be able to do anything about it, because my *transcendental categories*, as Kant would say, do just as they please and force me to take the thing in their way. But, then, that's all right, really—everything works out for the best.

In my opinion, it is not in this dialectic between the surface and that which is beyond that things are suspended. For my part, I set out from the fact that there is something that establishes a fracture, a bi-partition, a splitting of the being to which the being accommodates itself, even in the natural world.

This fact is observable in the variously modulated scale of what may be included, ultimately, under the general heading of mimicry. It is this that comes into play, quite obviously, both in sexual union and in the struggle to the death. In both situations, the being breaks up, in an extraordinary way, between its being and its semblance, between itself and that paper tiger it shows to the other. In the case of display, usually on the part of the male animal, or in the case of grimacing swelling by which the animal enters the play of combat in the form of intimidation, the being gives of himself, or receives from the other, something that is like a mask, a double, an envelope, a thrown-off skin, thrown off in order to cover the frame of a shield. It is through this separated form of himself that the being comes into play in his effects of life and death, and it might be said that it is with the help of this doubling of the other, or of oneself, that is realized the conjunction from which proceeds the renewal of beings in reproduction.

The lure plays an essential function therefore. It is not something else that seizes us at the very level of clinical experience, when, in relation to what one might imagine of the attraction to the other pole as conjoining masculine and feminine, we apprehend the prevalence of that which is presented as *travesty*. It is no doubt through the mediation of masks that the masculine and the feminine meet in the most acute, most intense way.

Only the subject—the human subject, the subject of the desire that is the essence of man—is not, unlike the animal, entirely caught up in this imaginary capture. He maps himself in it. How? In so far as he isolates the function of the screen and plays with it. Man, in effect, knows how to play with the mask as that beyond which there is the gaze. The screen is here the locus of mediation.

Last time, I alluded to the reference given by Maurice Merleau-Ponty in *La Phénoménologie de la perception* in which, from well-chosen examples based on the experiments of Gelb and Goldstein, one can already see, simply at the perceptual level, how the screen re-establishes things, in their status as real. If, by being isolated, an effect of lighting dominates us, if, for example, a beam of light directing our gaze so captivates us that it appears as a milky cone and prevents us from seeing what it illuminates, the mere fact of introducing into this field a small screen, which cuts into that which is illuminated without being seen, makes the milky light retreat, as it were, into the shadow, and allows the object it concealed to emerge.

At the perceptual level, this is the phenomenon of a relation that is to be taken in a more essential function, namely, that in its relation to desire, reality appears only as marginal.

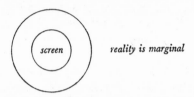

This is certainly one of the features that scarcely seems to have been noticed in pictorial creation. Yet rediscovering in the picture what is, strictly speaking, composition, the lines dividing the surfaces created by the painter, vanishing traces, lines of force, frames (*bâtis*) in which the image finds its status is a fascinating game—but I am astonished that in one very remarkable book they are called *frameworks* (*charpentes*). For this term eliminates their principal effect. By a sort of irony, on the back of this book, there nevertheless figures, as being more exemplary than any other, a picture by Rouault on which is traced a circular line to enable us to grasp the main point.

Indeed, there is something whose absence can always be observed in a picture—which is not the case in perception. This is the central field, where the separating power of the eye is exercised to the maximum in vision. In every picture, this central field cannot but be absent, and replaced by a hole—a reflection, in short, of the pupil behind which is situated the gaze. Consequently, and in as much as the picture enters into a relation to desire, the place of a central screen is always marked, which is precisely that by which, in front of the picture, I am elided as subject of the geometral plane.

This is why the picture does not come into play in the field of representation. Its end and effect are elsewhere.

2

In the scopic field, everything is articulated between two terms that act in an antinomic way—on the side of things, there is the gaze, that is to say, things look at me, and yet I see them. This is how one should understand those words, so strongly stressed, in the Gospel, *They have eyes that they might not see.* That they might not see what? Precisely, that things are looking at them.

This is why I have introduced painting into our field of exploration by the narrow door offered by us by Roger Caillois —everyone noticed last time that I made a slip of the tongue in calling him René, heaven knows why—in observing that mimicry is no doubt the equivalent of the function which, in man, is exercised in painting.

This is not the occasion to begin a psycho-analysis of the painter, which is always such a tricky matter, and which always produces a shocked reaction on the part of the listener. Nor is it a question of art criticism, and yet someone who is close to me, and whose views count for a great deal with me, told me that he was very troubled when I embarked on something very like art criticism. Of course, that is the danger, and I shall try to avoid any such confusion.

If one considers all the modulations imposed on painting by the variations of the subjectifying structure that have occurred in history, it is clear that no formula can possibly embrace those aims, those ruses, those infinitely varied tricks. Indeed, you saw clearly enough last time that after declaring that there is in painting a certain *dompte-regard*, a taming of the gaze, that is to say, that he who looks is always led by the painting to lay down his gaze, I immediately introduced the corrective that it is nevertheless in a quite direct appeal to the gaze that expression-ism is situated. For those who remain unconvinced, I will explain what I mean. I am thinking of the work of such painters as Munch, James Ensor, Kubin, or even of that painting which, curiously enough, one might situate in a geographical way as laying siege to that which in our time is concentrated in paint-ing in Paris. When will we see the limits of this siege lifted? That, if I am to believe the painter André Masson, with whom I was talking recently, is the most immediate question. Well!

To point out references like these, is not to enter into the shifting, historical game of criticism, which tries to grasp what is the function of painting at a particular moment, for a particular author at a particular time. For me, it is at the radical principle of the function of this fine art that I am trying to place myself.

To begin with, I would stress that it is in setting out from painting that Maurice Merleau-Ponty was particularly led to overthrow the relation, which has always been made by thought, between the eye and the mind. What he has shown in a quite admirable way, beginning with what he calls, with Cézanne himself, *those little blues, those little browns, those little whites,* those touches that fall like rain from the painter's brush, is that the function of the painter is something quite different from the organization of the field of representation in which the philosopher held us in our status as subjects.

And what is that? Where does that get us? It already gives form and embodiment to the field in which the psycho-analyst has advanced since Freud, with what, in Freud, is crazy daring, and what, in those who follow him, soon becomes imprudence.

Freud always stressed with infinite respect that he did not intend to settle the question of what it was in artistic creation that gave it its true value. When he is dealing with painters and poets, there is a point at which his appreciation stops. He cannot say, he does not know, what, for everybody, for those who look or hear, is the value of artistic creation. Nevertheless, when he studies Leonardo, let us say, roughly speaking, that he tries to find the function that the artist's original phantasy played in his creation—his relation to those two mothers Freud sees represented in the painting in the Louvre or in the cartoon in London, by that double body, branching at the level of the waist, which seems to blossom from the entwined legs at the base. Is it in this direction that we must look?

Or should we see the principle of artistic creation in the fact that it seems to extract—remember how I translated *Vorstellungsrepräsentanz*—that something that stands for representation? Was it to this that I was leading you when I made a distinction between the picture and representation?

Certainly not—except in very rare works, except in a painting that sometimes emerges, a dream painting, so rare that it can scarcely be situated in the function of painting. Indeed, perhaps this is the limit at which we would have to designate what is called psychopathological art.

That which is the creation of the painter is structured in a quite different way. Precisely to the extent that we restore the point of view of structure in the libidinal relation, perhaps the time has come when we may question to advantage—because our new algorithms allow us to articulate the answer better —what is involved in artistic creation. For me, it is a question of creation as Freud designated it, that is to say, as sublimation, and of the value it assumes in a social field.

In a way that is at once vague and precise, and which concerns only the success of the work, Freud declares that if a creation of desire, which is pure at the level of the painter, takes on commercial value—a gratification that may, all the same, be termed secondary—it is because its effect has something profitable for society, for that part of society that comes under its influence. Broadly speaking, one can say that the work calms people, comforts them, by showing them that at least some of them can live from the exploitation of their desire. But for this to satisfy them so much, there must also be that other effect, namely, that *their* desire to contemplate finds some satisfaction in it. It elevates the mind, as one says, that is to say, it encourages renunciation. Don't you see that there is something here that indicates the function I called *dompte-regard*?

As I said last time, *dompte-regard* is also presented in the form of *trompe-l'œil*. In this sense, I appear to be moving in the opposite direction from tradition, which situates its function as being very distinct from that of painting. Yet I did not hesitate to end my last talk by observing, in the opposition of the works of Zeuxis and Parrhasios, the ambiguity of two levels, that of the natural function of the lure and that of *trompe-l'œil*.

If the birds rushed to the surface on which Zeuxis had deposited his dabs of colour, taking the picture for edible grapes, let us observe that the success of such an undertaking does not imply in the least that the grapes were admirably reproduced, like those we can see in the basket held by Caravaggio's *Bacchus* in the Uffizi. If the grapes had been painted in this way, it is not very likely that the birds would have been deceived, for why should the birds see grapes portrayed with such extraordinary verisimilitude? There would have to be something more reduced, something closer to the sign, in something representing grapes for the birds. But the opposite example of Parrhasios makes it clear that if one wishes to deceive a man, what one presents to him is the painting of a veil, that is to say, something that incites him to ask what is behind it.

It is here that this little story becomes useful in showing us why Plato protests against the illusion of painting. The point is not that painting gives an illusory equivalence to the object, even if Plato seems to be saying this. The point is that the *trompe-l'œil* of painting pretends to be something other than what it is.

What is it that attracts and satisfies us in *trompe-l'œil*? When is it that it captures our attention and delights us? At the moment when, by a mere shift of our gaze, we are able to realize that the representation does not move with the gaze and that it is merely a *trompe-l'œil*. For it appears at that moment as something other than it seemed, or rather it now seems to be that something else. The picture does not compete with appearance, it competes with what Plato designates for us beyond appearance as being the Idea. It is because the picture is the appearance that says it is that which gives the appearance that Plato attacks painting, as if it were an activity competing with his own.

This other thing is the *petit a*, around which there revolves a combat of which *trompe-l'œil* is the soul.

If one tries to represent the position of the painter concretely in history, one realizes that he is the source of something that may pass into the real and on which, at all times, one might say, one takes a lease. The painter, it is said, no longer depends on aristocratic patrons. But the situation is not fundamentally changed with the advent of the picture dealer. He, too, is a patron, and a patron of the same stamp. Before the aristocratic patron, it was the religious institution, with the holy image, that gave artists a living. The artist always has some financial body behind him and it is always a question of the *objet a*, or rather a question of reducing it—which may, at a certain level, strike you as being rather mythical—to an *a* with which—this is true in the last resort—it is the painter as creator who sets up a dialogue.

But it is much more instructive to see how the *a* functions in its social repercussions.

Icons—the Christ in triumph in the vault at Daphnis or the admirable Byzantine mosaics—undoubtedly have the effect of holding us under their gaze. We might stop there, but were we to do so we would not really grasp the motive that made the painter set about making this icon, or the motive it satisfies in being presented to us. It is something to do with the gaze, of of course, but there is more to it than that. What makes the value of the icon is that the god it represents is also looking at it. It is intended to please God. At this level, the artist is operating on the sacrificial plane—he is playing with those things, in this case images, that may arouse the desire of God.

Indeed, God is the creator of certain images—we see this in *Genesis*, with the *Zelem Elohim*. And iconoclastic thought itself still preserves this when it declares there is a god that does not care for this. He is certainly alone in this. But I do not want to go too far today in a direction that would take us right to the heart of one of the most essential elements of the province of the Names-of-the-Father: a certain pact may be signed beyond every image. Where we are, the image remains a go-between with the divinity—if Javeh forbids the Jews to make idols, it is because they give pleasure to the other gods. In a certain register it is not God who is not anthropomorphic, it is man who is begged not to be so. But that's enough of that.

Let us pass now to the next stage, which I shall call *communal*. Let us go to the great hall of the Doges' Palace in which are painted all kinds of battles, such as the battle of Lepanto, etc. The social function, which was already emerging at the religious level, is now becoming clear. Who comes here? Those who form what Retz calls '*les peuples*', the audiences. And what do the audiences see in these vast compositions. They see the gaze of those persons who, when the audience are not there, deliberate in this hall. Behind the picture, it is their gaze that is there.

You see, one can say that there are always lots of gazes behind. Nothing new is introduced in this respect by the epoch that André Malraux distinguishes as the modern, that which comes to be dominated by what he calls '*the incomparable monster*', namely, the gaze of the painter, which claims to impose itself as being the only gaze. There always was a gaze behind. But

—this is the most subtle point—where does this gaze come from?

3

We now come back to the *little blues, little whites, little browns* of Cézanne, or again to the delightful example that Maurice Merleau-Ponty gives in passing in his *Signes,* namely, that strange slow-motion film in which one sees Matisse painting. The important point is that Matisse himself was overwhelmed by the film. Maurice Merleau-Ponty draws attention to the paradox of this gesture which, enlarged by the distension of time, enables us to imagine the most perfect deliberation in each of these brush strokes. This is an illusion, he says. What occurs as these strokes, which go to make up the miracle of the picture, fall like rain from the painter's brush is not choice, but something else. Can we not try to formulate what this something else is?

Should not the question be brought closer to what I called the rain of the brush? If a bird were to paint would it not be by letting fall its feathers, a snake by casting off its scales, a tree by letting fall its leaves? What it amounts to is the first act in the laying down of the gaze. A sovereign act, no doubt, since it passes into something that is materialized and which, from this sovereignty, will render obsolete, excluded, inoperant, whatever, coming from elsewhere, will be presented before this product.

Let us not forget that the painter's brushstroke is something in which a movement is terminated. We are faced here with something that gives a new and different meaning to the term regression—we are faced with the element of motive in the sense of response, in so far as it produces, behind it, its own stimulus.

There, that by which the original temporality in which the relation to the other is situated as distinct is here, in the scopic dimension, that of the terminal moment. That which in the identificatory dialectic of the signifier and the spoken will be projected forward as haste, is here, on the contrary, the end, that which, at the outset of any new intelligence, will be called the moment of seeing.

This terminal moment is that which enables us to distinguish between a gesture and an act. It is by means of the gesture that the brushstroke is applied to the canvas. And so true is it that the gesture is always present there that there can be no doubt that the picture is first felt by us, as the terms *impression* or *impressionism* imply, as having more affinity with the gesture than with any other type of movement. All action represented in a picture appears to us as a battle scene, that is to say, as something theatrical, necessarily created for the gesture. And, again, it is this insertion in the gesture that means that one cannot turn it upside down—whether or not it is figurative. If you turn a transparency around, you realize at once if it is being shown to you with the left in the place of the right. The direction of the gesture of the hand indicates sufficiently this lateral symmetry.

What we see here, then, is that the gaze operates in a certain descent, a descent of desire, no doubt. But how can we express this? The subject is not completely aware of it—he operates by remote control. Modifying the formula I have of desire as unconscious—*man's desire is the desire of the Other*—I would say that it is a question of a sort of desire *on the part of* the Other, at the end of which is the *showing* (*le donner-à-voir*).

How could this *showing* satisfy something, if there is not some appetite of the eye on the part of the person looking? This appetite of the eye that must be fed produces the hypnotic value of painting. For me, this value is to be sought on a much less elevated plane than might be supposed, namely, in that which is the true function of the organ of the eye, the eye filled with voracity, the evil eye.

It is striking, when one thinks of the universality of the function of the evil eye, that there is no trace anywhere of a good eye, of an eye that blesses. What can this mean, except that the eye carries with it the fatal function of being in itself endowed—if you will allow me to play on several registers at once—with a power to separate. But this power to separate goes much further than distinct vision. The powers that are attributed to it, of drying up the milk of an animal on which it falls—a belief as widespread in our time as in any other, and in the most civilized countries—of bringing with it disease or misfortune—where can we better picture this power than in *invidia*?

Invidia comes from *videre*. The most exemplary *invidia*, for us analysts, is the one I found long ago in Augustine, in which he sums up his entire fate, namely, that of the little child seeing his brother at his mother's breast, looking at him *amare conspectu*, with a bitter look, which seems to tear him to pieces and has on himself the effect of a poison.

In order to understand what *invidia* is in its function as gaze it must not be confused with jealousy. What the small child, or whoever, *envies* is not at all necessarily what he might want —*avoir envie*, as one improperly puts it. Who can say that the child who looks at his younger brother still needs to be at the breast? Everyone knows that envy is usually aroused by the possession of goods which would be of no use to the person who is envious of them, and about the true nature of which he does not have the least idea.

Such is true envy—the envy that makes the subject pale before the image of a completeness closed upon itself, before the idea that the *petit a*, the separated *a* from which he is hanging, may be for another the possession that gives satisfaction, *Befriedigung*.

It is to this register of the eye as made desperate by the gaze that we must go if we are to grasp the taming, civilizing and fascinating power of the function of the picture. The profound relation between the *a* and desire will serve as an example when I introduce the subject of the transference.

QUESTIONS AND ANSWERS

M. TORT: *Could you say more about the relation you posited between gesture and the moment of seeing?*

LACAN: What is a gesture? A threatening gesture, for example? It is not a blow that is interrupted. It is certainly something that is done in order to be arrested and suspended.

I may carry it to its logical conclusion later, but, as a threatening gesture it is inscribed behind.

It is this very special temporality, which I have defined by the term arrest and which creates its signification behind it, that makes the distinction between the gesture and the act.

What is very remarkable in the Peking Opera—I don't know whether you saw them on their recent visit—is the way fighting is depicted. One fights as one has always fought since time immemorial, much more with gestures than with blows.

Of course, the spectacle itself is content with an absolute dominance of gestures. In these ballets, no two people ever touch one another, they move in different spaces in which are spread out whole series of gestures, which, in traditional combat, nevertheless have the value of weapons, in the sense that they may well be effective as instruments of intimidation. Everyone knows that primitive peoples go into battle with grimacing, horrible masks and terrifying gestures. You mustn't imagine that this is over and done with! When fighting the Japanese, the American marines were taught to make as many grimaces as they. Our more recent weapons might also be regarded as gestures. Let us hope that they will remain such!

The authenticity of what emerges in painting is diminished in us human beings by the fact that we have to get our colours where they're to be found, that is to say, in the shit. If I referred to birds who might let fall their feathers, it is because *we* do not have these feathers. The creator will never participate in anything other than the creation of a small dirty deposit, a succession of small dirty deposits juxtaposed. It is through this dimension that we are in scopic creation—the gesture as displayed movement.

Does this explanation satisfy you? Was that the question you asked me?

TORT: *No, I wanted you to say more about that temporality to which you already referred once, and which presupposes, it seems to me, references that you have made elsewhere to logical time.*

LACAN: Look, what I noticed there was the suture, the pseudo-identification, that exists between what I called the time of terminal arrest of the gesture and what, in another dialectic that I called the dialectic of identificatory haste, I put as the first time, namely, the moment of seeing. The two overlap, but they are certainly not identical, since one is initial and the other is terminal.

I would like to say more about something for which I was not able, for lack of time, to give you the necessary indications.

This terminal time of the gaze, which completes the gesture, I place strictly in relation to what I later say about the evil eye. The gaze in itself not only terminates the movement, it freezes it. Take those dances I mentioned—they are always punctuated by a series of times of arrest in which the actors pause in a frozen attitude. What is that thrust, that time of arrest of the movement? It is simply the fascinatory effect, in that it is a question of dispossessing the evil eye of the gaze, in order to ward it off. The evil eye is the *fascinum*, it is that which has the effect of arresting movement and, literally, of killing life. At the moment the subject stops, suspending his gesture, he is mortified. The anti-life, anti-movement function of this terminal point is the *fascinum*, and it is precisely one of the dimensions in which the power of the gaze is exercised directly. The moment of seeing can intervene here only as a suture, a conjunction of the imaginary and the symbolic, and it is taken up again in a dialectic, that sort of temporal progress that is called haste, thrust, forward movement, which is concluded in the *fascinum*.

What I wish to emphasize is the total distinction between the scopic register and the invocatory, vocatory, vocational field. In the scopic field, the subject is not essentially indeterminate. The subject is strictly speaking determined by the very separation that determines the break of the *a*, that is to say, the fascinatory element introduced by the gaze. Does that satisfy you more? Completely?

TORT: *Almost.*

F. WAHL: *You have left to one side a phenomenon that is situated, like the evil eye, in the Mediterranean civilizations, and which is the prophylactic eye. It has a protective function that lasts for the duration of a journey, and which is linked, not to an arrest, but to a movement.*

LACAN: What is prophylactic about such things is, one might say, allopathic, whether it is a question of a horn, whether or not made of coral, or innumerable other things whose appearance is clearer, like the *turpicula res*, described by Varro, I think, which is quite simply a phallus. For it is in so far as all human desire is based on castration that the eye assumes its virulent, aggressive function, and not simply its luring function as in nature. One can find among these amulets forms in which a counter-eye emerges—this is homeopathic. Thus, obliquely, the so-called prophylactic function is introduced.

I was thinking that in the Bible, for example, there must be passages in which the eye confers the *baraka* or blessing. There are a few small places where I hesitated—but no. The eye may be prophylactic, but it cannot be beneficent—it is maleficent. In the Bible and even in the New Testament, there is no good eye, but there are evil eyes all over the place.

J.-A. MILLER: *On several occasions recently, you have explained that the subject cannot be located in the dimension of quantity or measure, in a Cartesian space. On the other hand, you have said that Merleau-Ponty's research converged with your own. You have even maintained that he laid down the reference-points of the unconscious . . .*

LACAN: I did not say that. I suggested that the few whiffs of the unconscious to be detected in his notes might have led him to pass, let us say, into my field. I'm not at all sure.

MILLER: *To continue. Now, if Merleau-Ponty is seeking to subvert Cartesian space, is it in order to open up the transcendental space of the relation to the Other? No, it is in order to accede either to the so-called dimension of inter-subjectivity, or to that so-called pre-objective, savage, primordial world. This leads me to ask you if* Le Visible et l'invisible *has led you to change anything in the article that you published on Merleau-Ponty in a number of* Les Temps Modernes?

LACAN: Absolutely nothing.

11 March 1964

The Transference and the Drive

IO

PRESENCE OF THE ANALYST

Problems of the transference · Obscurantism in analysis · Ablata causa · *The Other, already there · The unconscious is outside · An article in* The International Journal

So that I would not always have to be looking for a box of matches, someone gave me a very large box, as you can see. On it is written the following motto: *the art of listening is almost as important as that of saying the right thing.* This apportions our tasks. Let us hope that we will measure up to them.

Today I shall be dealing with the transference, or rather I shall approach the question, in the hope of giving you some idea of the concept, as I promised I would do in my second talk.

I

The transference is usually represented as an affect. A rather vague distinction is then made between a positive and a negative transference. It is generally assumed, not without some foundation, that the positive transference is love—though it must be said that, in the way it is used here, this term is employed in a very approximate way.

At a very early stage, Freud posed the question of the authenticity of love as it occurs in the transference. To come to the point, it is usually maintained that in these circumstances it is a sort of false love, a shadow of love. But Freud himself did not weigh down the scales in this direction—far from it. Not least among the consequences of the experience of the transference was that it led Freud to take the question of what is called true love, *eine echte Liebe,* further perhaps than it had ever been taken.

In the case of the negative transference, commentators are more prudent, more restrained, in the way they refer to it, and it is never identified with hate. They usually employ the term ambivalence, a term which, even more than the first, conceals things very well, confused things that are not always handled in a satisfactory way.

It would be truer to say that the positive transference is when you have a soft spot for the individual concerned, the analyst in this instance, and the negative transference is when you have to keep your eye on him.

There is another use of the term transference that is worth pointing out, as when one says that it structures all the particular relations with that other who is the analyst, and that the value of all the thoughts that gravitate around this relation must be connoted by a sign of particular reserve. Hence the expression—which is always added as a kind of after-thought or parenthesis, as if to convey some kind of suspicion, when used about the behaviour of a subject—*he is in full transference.* This presupposes that his entire mode of apperception has been restructured around the dominant centre of the transference.

I will not go any further because this double semantic mapping seems to me to be adequate for the moment.

We cannot, of course, remain satisfied with this, since our aim is to approach the concept of the transference.

This concept is determined by the function it has in a particular praxis. This concept directs the way in which patients are treated. Conversely, the way in which they are treated governs the concept.

It might seem to settle the question at the outset if we could decide whether or not the transference is bound up with analytic practice, whether it is a product, not to say an artefact, of analytic practice. Ida Macalpine, one of the many authors who have been led to express their opinions on the transference, has carried as far as possible the attempt to articulate the transference in this direction. Whatever her merits—she is a very stubborn person—let me say at once that I cannot, in any sense, accept this extreme position.

In any case, approaching the question in this way does not settle it. Even if we must regard the transference as a product of the analytic situation, we may say that this situation cannot create the phenomenon in its entirety, and that, in order to produce it, there must be, outside the analytic situation, possibilities already present to which it will give their perhaps unique composition.

This in no way excludes the possibility, where no analyst is in view, that there may be, properly speaking, transference effects that may be structured exactly like the gamut of transference phenomena in analysis. It is simply that, in discovering these effects, analysis will make it possible to give them an experimental model that need not necessarily be at all different from the model I shall call the natural one. So to bring out the transference in analysis, where it acquires its structural foundations, may very well be the only way of introducing the universality of the application of this concept. It should be enough, then, to open up this package in the sphere of analysis and, more especially, of the *doxa* that goes with it.

This, after all, is a truism. Nevertheless, it is a rough indication worth making as a start.

2

The aim of this introduction is to remind you that if we are to approach the fundamentals of psycho-analysis we must introduce a certain coherence into the major concepts on which it is based. Such a coherence is already to be found in the way I have approached the concept of the unconscious—which, you will remember, I was unable to separate from the presence of the analyst.

Presence of the analyst—a fine phrase that should not be reduced to the tear-jerking sermonizing, the serous inflation, the rather sticky caress to be found in a book that has appeared under this title.

The presence of the analyst is itself a manifestation of the unconscious, so that when it is manifested nowadays in certain encounters, as a refusal of the unconscious—this is a tendency, readily admitted, in some people's thinking—this very fact must be integrated into the concept of the unconscious. You have rapid access here to the formulation, which I have placed in the forefront, of a movement of the subject that opens up only to close again in a certain temporal pulsation—a pulsation I regard as being more radical than the insertion in the signifier that no doubt motivates it, but is not primary to it at the level of essence, since I have been driven to speak of essence.

I have shown, in a maieutic, eristic way, that one should see in the unconscious the effects of speech on the subject—in so far as these effects are so radically primary that they are properly what determine the status of the subject as subject. This proposition was intended to restore the Freudian unconscious to its true place. Certainly, the unconscious has always been present, it existed and acted before Freud, but it is important to stress that all the acceptations given, before Freud, to this function of the unconscious have absolutely nothing to do with the Freudian unconscious.

The primal unconscious, the unconscious as archaic function, the unconscious as veiled presence of a thought to be placed at the level of being before it is revealed, the metaphysical unconscious of Edward von Hartmann—whatever reference Freud makes to it in an *ad hominem* argument—above all the unconscious as instinct—all this has nothing to do with the Freudian unconscious, nothing at all, whatever its analytic vocabulary, its inflections, its deviations may be—nothing at all to do with our experience. I will ask analysts a straight question: *have you ever, for a single moment, the feeling that you are handling the clay of instinct?*

In my Rome report,[1] I proceeded to a new alliance with the meaning of the Freudian discovery. The unconscious is the sum of the effects of speech on a subject, at the level at which the subject constitutes himself out of the effects of the signifier. This makes it clear that, in the term *subject*—this is why I referred it back to its origin—I am not designating the living substratum needed by this phenomenon of the subject, nor any sort of substance, nor any being possessing knowledge in his *pathos*, his suffering, whether primal or secondary, nor even some incarnated logos, but the Cartesian subject, who appears at the moment when doubt is recognized as certainty—except that, through my approach, the bases of this subject prove to be wider, but, at the same time much more amenable to the certainty that eludes it. This is what the unconscious is.

There is a link between this field and the moment, Freud's

[1] 'Fonction et champ de la parole et du langage en psychanalyse', *Écrits*, Paris, Ed. du Seuil, 1966; 'The Function and Field of Speech and Language in Psycho-Analysis', *Écrits: a selection*, trans. Alan Sheridan, London, Tavistock Publications, 1977.

moment, when it is revealed. It is this link I express when I compare it with the approach of a Newton, an Einstein, a Planck, an a-cosmological approach, in the sense that all these fields are characterized by tracing in the real a new furrow in relation to the knowledge that might from all eternity be attributed to God.

Paradoxically, the difference which will most surely guarantee the survival of Freud's field, is that the Freudian field is a field which, of its nature, is lost. It is here that the presence of the psycho-analyst as witness of this loss, is irreducible.

At this level, we can get nothing more out of it—for it is a dead loss, with no gain to show, except perhaps its resumption in the function of pulsation. The loss is necessarily produced in a shaded area—which is designated by the oblique stroke with which I divide the formulae which unfold, in linear form, opposite each of the terms, unconscious, repetition, transference. This area of loss even involves, as far as these facts of analytic practice are concerned, a certain deepening of obscurantism, very characteristic of the condition of man in our times of supposed information—obscurantism which, without really knowing why, I can well believe will be regarded as incredible in the future. What I mean by obscurantism is, in particular, the function assumed by psycho-analysis in the propagation of a style that calls itself the *American way of life*, in so far as it is characterized by the revival of notions long since refuted in the field of psycho-analysis, such as the predominance of the functions of the ego.

In this sense, then, the presence of the psycho-analyst, seen in the very same perspective in which the vanity of his discourse appears, must be included in the concept of the unconscious. Psycho-analysts of today, we must take account of this slag in our operations, as we must of the *caput mortuum* of the discovery of the unconscious. It justifies the maintenance, within analysis, of a conflict situation, necessary to the very existence of analysis.

If it is true that psycho-analysis rests on a fundamental conflict, on an initial, radical drama as far as everything that might be included under the heading psychical is concerned, the innovation to which I refer, and which is called *recall of the field and function of speech and language in psychoanalytic experience*, does not claim to exhaust the possibilities of the unconscious, since it is, itself, an intervention in the conflict. This recall has an immediate implication in that it has itself a transferential effect. In any case, this is recognized by the fact that my seminar has been criticized precisely for playing, in relation to my audience, a function regarded by the orthodoxy of the psycho-analytic association as dangerous, for intervening in the transference. Now, far from denying it, I would regard this effect as radical, as constituting, indeed, this renewal of the alliance with Freud's discovery. This indicates that the cause of the unconscious—and you see that the word cause is to be taken here in its ambiguity, a cause to be sustained, but also a function of the cause at the level of the unconscious—this cause must be conceived as, fundamentally, a lost cause. And it is the only chance one has of winning it.

That is why, in the misunderstood concept of repetition, I stress the importance of the ever avoided encounter, of the missed opportunity. The function of missing lies at the centre of analytic repetition. The appointment is always missed—this is what constitutes, in comparison with *tuché*, the vanity of repetition, its constitutive occultation.

The concept of repetition brings me to the following dilemma —either I assume quite simply my implication as analyst in the eristic character of the discord of any description of my experience, or I polish up the concept at the level of something that would be impossible to objectify, if not at the level of a transcendental analysis of cause.

Cause might be formulated on the basis of the classical formula of the *ablata causa tollitur effectus*—I would have only to stress the singular of the protasis, *ablata causa*, by putting the terms of the apodosis in the plural *tolluntur effectus*—which would mean that *the effects are successful only in the absence of cause.* All the effects are subjected to the pressure of a transfactual, causal order which demands to join in their dance, but, if they held their hands tightly, as in the song, they would prevent the cause intruding in their round.

At this point, I should define unconscious cause, neither as an existent, nor as a οὐϰόν, a non-existent—as, I believe Henri Ey does, a non-existent of possibility. It is a μὴόν of the prohibition that brings to being an existent in spite of its non-advent, it is a function of the impossible on which a certainty is based.

3

This brings us to the function of the transference. For this indeterminate of pure being that has no point of access to determination, this primary position of the unconscious that is articulated as constituted by the indetermination of the subject—it is to this that the transference gives us access, in an enigmatic way. It is a Gordian knot that leads us to the following conclusion—the subject is looking for his certainty. And the certainty of the analyst himself concerning the unconscious cannot be derived from the concept of the transference.

It is striking, therefore, to observe the multiplicity, the plurality, the plurivalence even, of the conceptions of the transference that have been formulated in analysis. I do not claim to be able to provide you with an exhaustive account of them. I shall simply try to guide you through the paths of a chosen exploration.

At its emergence in the writings and teachings of Freud, a sliding-away (*glissement*), which we cannot impute to him, lies in wait for us—this consists in seeing in the concept of the transference no more than the concept of repetition itself. Let us not forget that when Freud presents it to us, he says —*what cannot be remembered is repeated in behaviour*. This behaviour, in order to reveal what it repeats, is handed over to the analyst's reconstruction.

One may go so far as to believe that the opacity of the trauma—as it was then maintained in its initial function by Freud's thought, that is to say, in my terms, its resistance to signification—is then specifically held responsible for the limits of remembering. And, after all, it is hardly surprising, given my own theorization, that I should see this as a highly significant moment in the transfer of powers from the subject to the Other, what I call the capital Other (*le grand Autre*), the locus of speech and, potentially, the locus of truth.

Is this the point at which the concept of the transference appears? It would seem so, and one often goes no further. But let us look at it more closely. In Freud, this moment is not simply the moment-limit that seems to correspond to what I designated as the moment of the closing up of the unconscious, a temporal pulsation that makes it disappear at a certain point of its statement (*énoncé*). When Freud introduces the function of the transference, he is careful to mark this moment as the cause of what we call the transference. The Other, latent or not, is, even beforehand, present in the subjective revelation, It is already there, when something has begun to yield itself from the unconscious.

The analyst's interpretation merely reflects the fact that the unconscious, if it is what I say it is, namely, a play of the signifier, has already in its formations—dreams, slips of tongue or pen, witticisms or symptoms—proceeded by interpretation. The Other, the capital Other, is already there in every opening, however fleeting it may be, of the unconscious.

What Freud shows us, from the outset, is that the transference is essentially resistant, *Übertragungswiderstand*. The transference is the means by which the communication of the unconscious is interrupted, by which the unconscious closes up again. Far from being the handing over of powers to the unconscious, the transference is, on the contrary, its closing up.

This is essential in noting the paradox that is expressed quite commonly in the fact—which may even be found in Freud's writings—that the analyst must await the transference before beginning to give his interpretation.

I want to stress this question because it is the dividing line between the correct and incorrect conception of the transference.

In analytic practice, there are many ways of conceiving the transference. They are not necessarily mutually exclusive. They may be defined at different levels. For example, although the conceptions of the relation of the subject to one or other of those agencies which, in the second stage of his *Topography*, Freud was able to define as the ego-ideal or the super-ego, are partial, this is often simply to give a lateralized view of what is essentially the relation with the capital Other.

But there are other divergences that are irreducible. There is a conception which, wherever it is formulated, can only contaminate practice—I am referring to the conception which would have the analysis of the transference proceed on the basis of an alliance with the healthy part of the subject's ego, and consists in appealing to his common sense, by way of pointing out to him the illusory character of certain of his actions in his relation with the analyst. This is a thesis that subverts what it is all about, namely the bringing to awareness of this split in the subject, realized here, in fact, in presence. To appeal to some healthy part of the subject thought to be there in the real, capable of judging with the analyst what is happening in the transference, is to misunderstand that it is precisely this part that is concerned in the transference, that it is this part that closes the door, or the window, or the shutters, or whatever—and that the beauty with whom one wishes to speak is there, behind, only too willing to open the shutters again. That is why it is at this moment that interpretation becomes decisive, for it is to the beauty one must speak.

I can do no more than suggest here the reversion involved in this schema in relation to the model one has of it in one's head. I say somewhere that *the unconscious is the discourse of the Other*. Now, the discourse of the Other that is to be realized, that of the unconscious, is not beyond the closure, it is *outside*. It is this discourse, which, through the mouth of the analyst, calls for the reopening of the shutter.

Nevertheless, there is a paradox in designating this movement of closure as the initial moment when the interpretation may assume its full force. And here is revealed the permanent conceptual crisis that exists in analysis concerning the way in which the function of the transference should be conceived.

The contradiction of its function, which causes it to be apprehended as the point of impact of the force of the interpretation by the very fact that, in relation to the unconscious, it is a moment of closure—this is why we must treat it as what it is, namely, a knot. Whether or not we treat it as a Gordian knot remains to be seen. It is a knot, and it prompts us to account for it—as I have been doing for several years—by considerations of topology. It will not be thought unnecessary, I hope, to remind you of these.

4

There is a crisis in analysis and, to show that there is nothing biased in this, I would support my view by citing a recent article that demonstrates this in the most striking way—and it is the work of no mediocre mind. It is a closely argued, very engaging article by Thomas S. Szasz—who hails from Syracuse, which fact, unfortunately, does not make him any more closely related to Archimedes, for this Syracuse is in New York State—which appeared in the latest number of *The International Journal of Psychoanalysis.*

The author was inspired to write this article by an idea in keeping with the line of investigation that inspired his earlier articles, a truly moving search for the authenticity of the analytic way.

It is quite striking that an author, who is indeed one of the most highly regarded in his circle, which is specifically that of American psycho-analysis, should regard the transference as nothing more than a defence on the part of the psycho-analyst, and should arrive at the following conclusion—*the transference is the pivot on which the entire structure of psycho-analytic treatment rests.* This is a concept that he calls *inspired*—I am always suspicious of *faux amis* in English vocabulary, so I have tried to tread warily when translating it. This *inspired*, it seemed to me, did not mean *inspiré*, but something like *officieux. It is an inspired and indispensable concept*—I quote—*yet it harbours the seeds, not only of its own destruction, but of the destruction of psycho-analysis itself.* Why? *Because it tends to place the person of the analyst beyond the reality testing of patients, colleagues, and self. This hazard must be frankly recognized. Neither professionalization, nor the 'raising of standards', nor coerced training analyses can protect us from this danger.* And here the confusion arises—*only the integrity of the analyst and of the analytic situation can safeguard from extinction the unique dialogue between analysand and analyst.*

This blind alley that Szasz has created for himself is, for him, necessitated by the very fact that he can conceive of the analysis of the transference only in terms of an assent obtained from the healthy part of the ego, that part which is capable of judging reality and of separating it from illusion.

His article begins thus, quite logically—*Transference is similar to such concepts as delusion, illusion, and phantasy.* Once the presence of the transference has been established, it is a question of agreement between the analysand and the analyst, except that here the analyst is a judge against whom there is neither appeal nor recourse, we are led to call any analysis of the transference a field of pure, uncontrolled hazard.

I have taken this article only as an extreme case, but a very revealing one, so as to encourage us to restore here a determination that should bring into play another order—that of truth. Truth is based only on the fact that speech, even when it consists of lies, appeals to it and gives rise to it. This dimension is always absent from the logical positivism that happens to dominate Szasz's analysis of the concept of transference.

My own conception of the dynamics of the unconscious has been called an intellectualization—on the grounds that I based the function of the signifier in the forefront. Is it not apparent that it is in this operational mode—in which everything makes light of the confrontation between a reality and a connotation of illusion attributed to the phenomenon of the transference— that this supposed intellectualization really resides?

Far from us having to consider two subjects, in a dual position, to discuss an objectivity that appears to have been posited there as the gravitational effect of a compression in behaviour, we must bring out the domain of possible deception. When I introduced you to the subject of Cartesian certainty as the necessary starting-point of all our speculations as to what the unconscious reveals, I pointed out the role of essential balancer played in Descartes by the Other which, it is said, must on no account be deceptive. In analysis, the danger is that this Other will be deceived. This is not the only dimension to be apprehended in the transference. But one has to admit that if there is one domain in which, in discourse, deception has some chance of success, it is certainly love that provides its model. What better way of assuring oneself, on the point on which one is mistaken, than to persuade the other of the truth of what one says! Is not this a fundamental structure of the dimension of love that the transference gives us the opportunity of depicting? In persuading the other that he has that which may complement us, we assure ourselves of being able to continue to misunderstand precisely what we lack. The circle of deception, in so far as it highlights the dimension of love at the point named—this will serve us as an exemplary door to demonstrate the trick next time.

But this is not all I have to show you, for it is not what radically causes the closure involved in the transference. What causes it, and this will be the other side of our examination of the concepts of the transference, is—to come back to the question mark inscribed in the left part, the shaded, reserved part—what I have designated by the *objet a.*

QUESTIONS AND ANSWERS

F. WAHL: *To what theory of knowledge, in the system of existing theories, might what you said in the first half of the lecture be related?*

LACAN: Since I am saying that it is the novelty of the Freudian field to provide us in experience with something that is fundamentally apprehended like that, it is hardly surprising if you cannot find a model for it in Plotinus.

Having said this, I know that, despite my refusal to follow Miller's first question on the subject of an ontology of the unconscious, I nevertheless gave you a little rope with some very precise references. I spoke of the ὄν, of the οὐκ. With the ὄν, I was referring specifically to the formulation of it given by Henri Ey, of whom it cannot be said that he is the best qualified person to speak of the unconscious—he manages to situate the unconscious somewhere in his theory of consciousness. I spoke of the μὴὄν, of the prohibition, of the says-no. This does not go very far as a strictly metaphysical indication, and I do not think that here I am transgressing the boundaries that I have laid down for myself. All the same, it does structure in a perfectly transmissible way the points on which your question bears. In the unconscious there is a corpus of knowledge (*un savoir*), which must in no way be conceived as knowledge to be completed, to be closed.

ὄν, οὐκ ὄν, μὴὄν—to use these terms is still to over-sub-stantify the unconscious. This is why I have carefully avoided them. What there is beyond, what a little while ago I called the beauty behind the shutters, this is what is in question and which I have not touched on today. It is a question of mapping out how something of the subject is, behind the screen, magnetized, magnetized to the profound degree of dissociation, of split. This is the key-point at which we must see the Gordian knot.

P. KAUFMANN: *What relation is there between what you have designated as slag and what you earlier spoke of as remainder?*

LACAN: In human destiny, the remainder is always fruitful. The slag is the extinguished remainder. Here, the term slag is used in an entirely negative way. It refers to that true regression that may occur on the plane of the theory of psychological knowledge, in so far as the analyst finds himself placed in a field in which he has no other course but to flee. He then seeks for assurances in theories that operate in the direction of an orthopaedic, conformist therapeutics, providing access for the subject to the most mythical conception of *happiness* [English in the original—Tr.]. Together with an uncritical manipulation of evolutionism, this is what sets the tone of our era. By slag, I mean here the analysts themselves, nothing more—whilst the discovery of the unconscious is still young, and it is an unprecedented opportunity for subversion.

15 April 1964

I I

ANALYSIS AND TRUTH OR
THE CLOSURE OF THE UNCONSCIOUS

Telling the truth, lying, being wrong · The I *lie and the* I *think ·*
Homunculus or $ · *The validity of psychology · Illusion and its rectifica-*
tion · The transference is the enaction of the reality of the unconscious

Last time, I introduced the concept of the transference. I did
so in a rather problematic way, from the standpoint of the
difficulties it presented to the analyst. I took the opportunity
offered me by an article published in a recent number of the
most official organ of psycho-analysis, *The International Journal
of Psycho-Analysis*, which went so far as to question the use in
analysis of the notion of transference. I now intend to return
to this article.

I

According to the author, the analyst is supposed to point out to
the patient the effects of more or less manifest discordances
that occur with regard to the reality of the analytic situation,
namely, the two real subjects who are present in it.

First, there are the cases in which the effect of discordance
is very obvious. It is illustrated, in a humourous way, by
Spitz, one of the old guard, and no fool, by way of amusing his
public. He takes as an example one of his patients, who, in a
dream that is called a transference dream—that is to say, a
dream involving the realization of erotic desires with one's
analyst, with Spitz himself, as it happens—sees him sporting a
head of luxuriant blond hair—which, for anyone who has seen
the bald pate of the character in question, and it is well enough
known to be regarded as famous, would seem to be a case in
which the analyst could quite easily show the subject just how
far the effects of the unconscious can give rise to distortion.

But when it is a question of qualifying a patient's behaviour as uncomplimentary to the analyst, You have the choice of two things, says Szasz—*the analyst's view is correct and is considered 'reality'; the patient's view is incorrect, and is considered 'transference'.* This brings us back to that at once mythical and idealizing pole that Szasz calls *the integrity of the analyst.* What can this mean, if it is not a recall to the dimension of truth?

I can only situate this article, then, in the perspective in which its author himself places it, considering him as operating not in a heuristic, but in an eristic way, manifesting, in the impasse into which his reflection has led him, the presence of a true crisis of conscience in the function of the analyst. This crisis of conscience concerns us only in an incidental way, since I have shown that a certain one-sided way of theorizing the practice of the analysis of the transference would necessarily lead to it. It is a slippery slope that I myself have been denouncing for a long time.

To bring us back to the almost phenomenological data that enable us to resituate the problem where it actually is, I showed you last time that in the relation of the one with the other that is set up in analysis, one dimension is eluded.

It is clear that this relation is established on a plane that is not reciprocal, not symmetrical. This much Szasz observes, only, quite wrongly, to deplore it—in this relation of the one with the other, there is established a search for truth in which the one is supposed to know, or at least to know more than the other. From the latter, the thought immediately arises that not only must he not make a mistake (*se trompe*), but also that he can be misled (*on peut le tromper*). The *making a mistake* (*se tromper*) is, by the same token, thrown back upon the subject. It is not simply that the subject is, in a static way, lacking, in error. It is that, in a moving way, in his discourse, he is essentially situated in the dimension of the *making a mistake* (*se tromper*).

I have found a description of this from yet another analyst. I am referring to Nunberg, who, in the *International Journal of Psycho-analysis*, published, in 1926, an article entitled *The Will of Recovery*. By *recovery*, he means not so much *guérison* (cure), as *restauration* (restoration), *retour* (return). The word is very well chosen and poses a question well worth our attention. What, in the last resort, can drive the patient to have recourse to the analyst, to ask him for something he calls health, when his symptom—so the theory says—is created in order to bring him certain satisfactions?

With a great many examples, many of them humorous, Nunberg has no difficulty in showing that one doesn't have to have gone very far in analysis to see, sometimes with great clarity, that what motivated the patient in his search for health, for balance, is precisely his unconscious aim, in its most immediate implications. What shelter, for example, does recourse to analysis have to offer him, in order to re-establish peace in his home, when some hitch has occurred in his sexual function, or some extra-marital desire! From the outset, the patient admits to a desire, in the form of a temporary suspension of his presence at home, the opposite of what he came to propose as the first aim of his analysis—not the restoration of his marriage, but a break with it.

We now find ourselves at last—in the very act of the commitment to analysis and certainly, therefore, in its first stages —in maximum contact with the profound ambiguity of any assertion on the part of the patient, and the fact that it is, of itself, double-sided. In the first instance, it is as establishing itself in, and even by, a certain lie, that we see set up the dimension of truth, in which respect it is not, strictly speaking, shaken, since the lie as such is itself posited in this dimension of truth.

2

You will see why the relation of the subject to the signifier is the reference-point that I wished to place at the forefront of a general rectification of analytic theory, for it is as primary and constitutive in the establishment of analytic experience as it is primary and constitutive in the radical function of the unconscious.

It is, no doubt, one of the effects of my teaching to limit the unconscious to what might be called its narrowest platform. But it is in relation to this point of division that I cannot err on the side of any substantiation.

I will centre things on the four-cornered schema of my graph, which purposely distinguishes the level of the enunciation (énonciation) from the level of the statement (énoncé). Its use can be illustrated from the fact that a too formal logical thinking introduces absurdities, even an antinomy of reason in the statement *I am lying*, whereas everyone knows that there is no such thing.

It is quite wrong to reply to this *I am lying*—If you say, *I am lying*, you are telling the truth, and therefore you are not lying, and so on. It is quite clear that the *I am lying*, despite its paradox, is perfectly valid. Indeed, the *I* of the enunciation is not the same as the *I* of the statement, that is to say, the shifter which, in the statement, designates him. So, from the point at which I state, it is quite possible for me to formulate in a valid way that the *I*—the *I* who, at that moment, formulates the

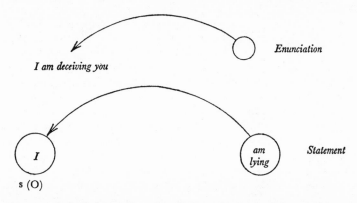

statement—is lying, that he lied a little before, that he is lying afterwards, or even, that in saying *I am lying*, he declares that he has the intention of deceiving. One does not have to go very far to illustrate this with an example—take the Jewish joke in which one Jew tells another that he is catching the train for Lemberg. *Why are you telling me you are going to Lemberg,* the other replies, *since you really are going there, and that, if you are telling me this, it is so that I shall think that you are going to Cracow?*

This division between the statement and the enunciation means that, in effect, from the *I am lying* which is at the level of the chain of the statement—the *am lying* is a signifier, forming part, in the Other, of the treasury of vocabulary in which the *I*, determined retroactively, becomes a signification, engendered at the level of the statement, of what it produces at the level of the enunciation—what results is an *I am deceiving you*. The *I am deceiving you* arises from the point at which the analyst awaits the subject, and sends back to him, according to the formula, his own message in its true signification, that is to say, in an inverted form. He says to him— *in this* I am deceiving you, *what you are sending as message is what* I *express to you, and in doing so you are telling the truth.*

In the way of deception in which the subject is venturing, the analyst is in a position to formulate this *you are telling the truth,* and my interpretation has meaning only in this dimension.

I would like to show you how this schema can help us in grasping Freud's fundamental approach, which became possible with the discovery of the unconscious—which, of

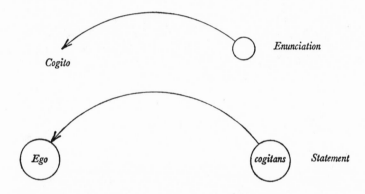

course, has always been there, at the time of Thales and at the level of the most primitive inter-human modes of relations.

Let us bring to this schema the Cartesian *I think.* Certainly, the distinction between the enunciation and the statement is what makes their sliding away (*glissement*) always possible, and their possible stumbling block. In effect, if anything is established by the *cogito,* it is the register of thought, in so far as it is extracted from an opposition to extension—a fragile status, but a sufficient status in the order of the signifying constitution. Let us say that it is by taking its place at the level of the enunciation that the *cogito* acquires its certainty. But the status of the *I think* is as reduced, as minimal, as punctual—and might be just as affected by the connotation of the *that is meaningless*—as that of the *I am lying* referred to earlier.

Perhaps the *I think,* reduced to this punctuality of being certain only of the absolute doubt concerning all signification, its own included, has a still more fragile status than that in which we were able to attack the *I am lying.*

I will now dare to define the Cartesian *I think* as participating, in its striving towards certainty, in a sort of abortion. The difference of status given to the subject by the discovered dimension of the Freudian unconscious derives from desire, which must be situated at the level of the *cogito.* Whatever animates, that which any enunciation speaks of, belongs to desire. I would remark in passing that desire, as I formulate it, in relation to what Freud contributes here, goes further.

I will pinpoint the function of the Cartesian *cogito* by the term monster or homunculus. This function is illustrated by the curve, which has not failed to occur in the history of what is called thought, which consists in taking this *I* of the *cogito* for the homunculus who has long been represented whenever one has wished to practise psychology—whenever one has wished to account for inanity or psychological discordance by the presence, inside man, of the celebrated little fellow who governs him, who is the driver, the point of synthesis, as we now say. The function of this little fellow was already denounced by pre-Socratic thought.

In my own vocabulary, on the other hand, I symbolize the subject by the barred S [$], in so far as it is constituted as secondary in relation to the signifier. In order to illustrate this, I will remind you that the thing may be presented in the simplest possible way by the single stroke. The first signifier is the notch by which it is indicated, for example, that the subject has killed *one* animal, by means of which he will not become confused in his memory when he has killed ten others. He will not have to remember which is which, and it is by means of this single stroke that he will count them.

The subject himself is marked off by the single stroke, and first he marks himself as a tatoo, the first of the signifiers. When this signifier, this *one*, is established—the reckoning is *one* one. It is at the level, not of the one, but of the *one* one, at the level of the reckoning, that the subject has to situate himself as such. In this respect, the two ones are already distinguished. Thus is marked the first split that makes the subject as such distinguish himself from the sign in relation to which, at first, he has been able to constitute himself as subject. I would now warn you

against confusing the function of the $ with the image of the
objet a, in so far as it is thus that the subject sees himself dupli-
cated—sees himself as constituted by the reflected, momentary,
precarious image of mastery, imagines himself to be a man
merely by virtue of the fact that he imagines himself.

In analytic practice, mapping the subject in relation to
reality, such as it is supposed to constitute us, and not in relation
to the signifier, amounts to falling already into the degradation
of the psychological constitution of the subject.

3

Any departure taken from the relation of the subject to a real
context may have its *raison d'être* in this or that psychologist's
experience. It may produce results, have effects, make possible
the drawing up of tables. Of course, this will always be in
contexts in which it is we who make reality—for example,
when we arrange for the subject to take tests, tests which have
been organized by us. It is the domain of validity of what is
called psychology, which has nothing to do with the level at
which we sustain the psycho-analytic experience, and which,
if I may say so, reinforces to an incredible degree the denuda-
tion of the subject.

What I have called the psychological *isolate* is not the old, or
ever young, monad traditionally set up as the centre of knowledge, for the Leibnizian monad, for example, is not isolated,
it is the centre of knowledge; it is not separable from a cos-
mology, it is, in the cosmos, the centre from which, according
to the inflections, what is contemplation or harmony takes
place. The psychological isolate comes up again in the concept
of the ego, which—by a deviation which, I think, is merely a
detour—is confused, in psycho-analytic thinking, with the
subject in distress in the relation to reality.

I would first like to stress that this way of theorizing the
operation is in flagrant contradiction, totally at variance, with
what in other respects experience leads me to stress, and which
we cannot eliminate from the analytic text, namely, the function
of the internal object.

The terms introjection or projection are always used rather
recklessly. But, certainly, even in this context of unsatisfactory
theorization, something is given to us that comes into the

foreground on all sides, namely, the function of the internal object. In the end, this function is polarized into the extremes of that good or bad object, around which, for some, revolves everything in a subject's behaviour that represents distortion, inflection, paradoxical fear, foreign body. It is thus the operating point on which, in conditions of urgency—those, for example, involving the selection of subjects for various responsible jobs, in cybernetics or management, for example, or when it is a question of training air-line pilots or train-drivers —some have pointed out that it was a question of concentrating the focusing of a rapid analysis, even of a lightning-analysis, even of the use of certain so called personality tests.

We cannot avoid posing the question of the status of this internal object. Is it an object of perception? From what angle do we approach it? Where does it come from? Following this rectification, in what would the analysis of the transference consist?

I will present you with a model, which will have to be improved a great deal later, so take it as a problematic model. The schemata centred on the function of rectifying illusion have such adhesive power that I will never be able to launch anything too prematurely that, at the very least, acts as an obstacle to them.

If the unconscious is what closes up again as soon as it has opened, in accordance with a temporal pulsation, if furthermore repetition is not simply a stereotype of behaviour, but repetition in relation to something always missed, you see here and now that the transference—as it is represented to us, as a mode of access to what is hidden in the unconscious—could only be of itself a precarious way. If the transference is only repetition, it will always be repetition of the same missed encounter. If the transference is supposed through this repetition, to restore the continuity of a history, it will do so only by reviving a relation that is, of its nature, syncopated. We see, then, that the transference, as operating mode, cannot be satisfied with being confused with the efficacity of repetition, with the restoration of what is concealed in the unconscious, even with the catharsis of the unconscious elements.

When I speak to you of the unconscious as of that which appears in the temporal pulsation, you may picture it to yourselves as a *hoop net* (*nasse*) which opens slightly at the neck and at the bottom of which the catch of fish will be found. Whereas according to the image of the *double sack* (*besace*), the unconscious is something kept in reserve, closed up inside, in which *we* have to penetrate from the outside. I therefore reverse the topology of the traditional imagery by presenting to you the following schema.

You will have to superimpose it upon the optical model I gave in my article *Remarque sur le rapport de Daniel Lagache*,[1] concerning the ideal ego and the ego ideal. You will then see that it is in the Other that the subject is constituted as ideal, that he has to regulate the completion of what comes as ego, or ideal ego—which is not the ego ideal—that is to say, to constitute himself in his imaginary reality. This schema makes

Schema of the hoop net

clear—I stress it in relation to the latest elements I have introduced around the scopic drive—that where the subject sees himself, namely, where that real, inverted image of his own body that is given in the schema of the ego is forged, it is not from there that he looks at himself.

But, certainly, it is in the space of the Other that he sees himself and the point from which he looks at himself is also in that space. Now, this is also the point from which he speaks, since in so far as he speaks, it is in the locus of the Other that he begins to constitute that truthful lie by which is initiated that which participates in desire at the level of the unconscious.

So we must consider the subject, in terms of the hoop net —especially in relation to its orifice, which constitutes its essential structure—as being inside. What matters is not what goes in there, as the Gospel has it, but what comes out.

We can conceive of the closing of the unconscious through the effect of something that plays the role of obturator—the

[1] *Écrits*, p. 647.

objet a, sucked, breathed, into the orifice of the net. You can draw an image like those great balls in which the number to be drawn in a lottery are enclosed. What is concocted in this great roulette out of the first statements of free association emerges from it in the interval in which the object is not blocking the orifice. This brutal, elementary image enables you to restore the constitutive function of the symbolic in its reciprocal contraposition. It is the subject's game of odds and evens constituted by his renewed meetings with that which in the

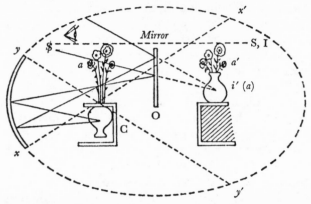

effective action of the analytic manœuvre is made present in the subject.

This schema is quite inadequate, but it is a bulldozer-schema which renders congruent the notion that the transference is both an obstacle to remembering, and a making present of the closure of the unconscious, which is the act of missing the right meeting just at the right moment.

I could illustrate all this from the variety and divergence of the definitions that analysts have given of the function of the transference. What is certain is that the transference is one thing, the therapeutic end another. Nor is the transference to be confused with a mere means. The two extremes of what has been formulated in analytic literature are situated here. How often will you read formulas that associate, for example, the transference with identification, whereas identification is merely a pause, a false termination of the analysis which is very frequently confused with its normal termination. Its relation with the transference is close, but precisely in that by which the transference has not been analysed. On the other hand, you will see the function of the transference formulated as a means of rectification from the standpoint of reality, to which everything I am saying today is opposed.

It is impossible to situate the transference correctly in any of these references. Since it is a question of reality, it is on this plane that I wish to bring my criticism to bear. Today I will leave you with an aphorism by way of introduction to what I will say next time—the transference is not the enactment (*mise en acte*) of the illusion that seems to drive us to this alienating identification that any conformity constitutes, even when it is with an ideal model, of which the analyst, in any case, cannot be the support—the transference is the enactment of the reality of the unconscious.

I have left this in suspense in the concept of the unconscious —oddly enough, it is the very thing that is more and more forgotten that I have not recalled until now. I hope, later, to be able to explain why this is so. In discussing the unconscious, I have been concerned so far to remind you of the effects of the constitutive act of the subject, because this is my primary concern here. But let us not omit what is especially stressed by Freud as being strictly consubstantial with the dimension of the unconscious, namely, sexuality. Because it has increasingly forgotten what this relation of the unconscious to the sexual means, analysis has inherited a conception of reality that no longer has anything to do with reality as situated by Freud at the level of the secondary process.

So it is by positing the transference as the enactment of the reality of the unconscious that I shall begin next time.

QUESTIONS AND ANSWERS

DR ROSOLATO: *I would like to say what thoughts have occurred to me during your seminar. First an analogy —your schema is remarkably similar to an eye. To what extent does the* petit a *play the role of a crystalline lens? To what extent does this lens play the role of a cataract? I would also like you to say more about the ego ideal and the ideal ego specifically in relation to this schema. Lastly, what do you understand by enactment?*

LACAN: *Enactment* is a promissory term. To define the

transference as enactment is necessary if it is not to be the locus of alibis, inadequate modes of operation, taken by indirect and roundabout ways that are not for that reason necessarily inoperant, and which take into account the limits of the analytic intervention. Today I have specifically pointed out false definitions that may be given of its termination, like that of Balint when he speaks of identification with the analyst. If you do not take the transference at the correct level, which, I must say, has not yet been illustrated today, but which will be the subject of the next seminar, you can never do more than grasp some of its partial effects.

As for your other remarks, well it's funny. In everything concerning topology one must always be very careful to avoid attributing it with any kind of *Gestalt* function. This does not mean that certain living forms do not give us, sometimes, the sensation of being a kind of effort of the biological to forge something that resembles the portions of those fundamental topological objects that I developed for you in my seminar on *Identification*—for example, the mitre, you will remember, is a self-intersecting surface projected into three-dimensional space. I could very easily designate for you a particular point or plane of the anatomical configuration that seems to exemplify life's touching strivings after, topological configurations.

It is certain that it is only these considerations that can provide us with the appropriate image when it is a question of something inside that is also outside. This is why such considerations are particularly necessary when it is a question of the unconscious, which I represent to you as that which is inside the subject, but which can be realized only outside, that is to say, in that locus of the Other in which alone it may assume its status. I cannot take for granted all that has been said in my previous seminars, for the good reason that part of my audience is new. So I have used the simple schema of the net, and I have simply introduced the notion of the obturator. The object is an obturator: we still do not know how. It is not that passive obturator, that cork which, by way of launching your thought on a certain scent, I wished to picture. I will give a more complete representation of it in which you may recognize certain affinities with the structure of the eye.

It is certainly very odd that the structure of the eye presents us with a general form that so easily springs to mind whenever we try to figure chronologically the relations of the subject with the world. This is probably no accident. But we should not jump at it too precipitously and apply it in too narrow a way.

However, since you have made this remark, I will take the opportunity of pointing out to you the difference between my schema and that in which Freud represents the ego as the lens through which the perception–consciousness operates on the amorphous mass of the *Unbewusstsein*. Whatever the value of Freud's schema, it is as limited in its scope as mine, in a way. But nevertheless you can see the difference—if I had wanted to put the ego somewhere, I would have written $i(a)$. Whereas for me, here, it is the a that is in question.

22 April 1964

12

SEXUALITY IN THE DEFILES
OF THE SIGNIFIER

*The reality of the unconscious is sexual · Of Chinese astronomy · Against
Jung and against hermeneutics · Desexualization of reality · The entrance into the unconscious · Anna O. and Freud's desire*

Last time, I ended with a formula which, I later realized, was
well received, which I can attribute only to the fact that it
contains promises, since, in its aphoristic form, it was not yet
developed.

I said that we would be dealing with the following proposition—*the transference is the enactment of the reality of the unconscious.* What is implied here is precisely what one tends most
to avoid in the analysis of the transference.

I

In advancing this proposition, I find myself in a problematic
position—for what have I taught about the unconscious? The
unconscious is constituted by the effects of speech on the subject, it is the dimension in which the subject is determined in
the development of the effects of speech, consequently the unconscious is structured like a language. Such a direction seems
well fitted to snatch any apprehension of the unconscious from
an orientation to reality, other than that of the constitution of the
subject. And yet this teaching has had, in its approach, an end
that I have called transferential. In order to recentre those of
my listeners with whom I was most concerned—the psycho-
analysts—in a direction conforming with analytic experience,
the very handling of the concept must, depending on the level
at which the teacher's speech is placed, take into account the
effects of the formulation on the listener. We are all such that
we, the teacher included, are in a relation to the reality of the
unconscious, which my intervention not only elucidates, but,
to a certain point engenders.

Let us look at the facts. The reality of the unconscious is sexual reality—an untenable truth. At every opportunity, Freud defended his formula, if I may say so, with tooth and nail. Why is it an untenable reality?

On the question of sex, we have, since the time when Freud articulated his discovery of the unconscious, that is to say, the 1900s, or the last years of the nineteenth century, made some scientific progress. However integrated it may be in our mental imagery, it must not be thought that the knowledge we have obtained of sex since then has always been there. We now know a little more about sex. We know that sexual division, in so far as it reigns over most living beings, is that which ensures the survival of a species.

Whether, with Plato, we place the species among the Ideas, or whether we say, with Aristotle, that it is to be found nowhere but in the individuals that support it, hardly matters here. Let us say that the species survives in the form of its individuals. Nevertheless, the survival of the horse as a species has a meaning—each horse is transitory and dies. So you see, the link between sex and death, sex and the death of the individual, is fundamental.

Existence, thanks to sexual division, rests upon copulation, accentuated in two poles that time-honoured tradition has tried to characterize as the male pole and the female pole. This is because the mainspring of reproduction is to be found there. Around this fundamental reality, there have always been grouped, harmonized, other characteristics, more or less bound up with the finality of reproduction. I can do no more than point out here, what, in the biological register, is associated with sexual differentiation, in the form of secondary sexual characteristics and functions. We know today how, in society, a whole distribution of functions in a play of alternation is grounded on this terrain. It is modern structuralism that has brought this out best, by showing that it is at the level of matrimonial alliance, as opposed to natural generation, to biological lineal descent—at the level therefore of the signifier—that the fundamental exchanges take place and it is there that we find once again that the most elementary structures of social functioning are inscribed in the terms of a combinatory.

The integration of this combinatory into sexual reality raises the question of whether it is not in this way that the signifier came into the world, into the world of man.

What would make it legitimate to maintain that it is through sexual reality that the signifier came into the world—that man learnt to think—is the recent field of discoveries that begins by a more accurate study of mitosis. There are then revealed the modes according to which the maturation of sexual cells operates, namely, the double process of reduction. What is involved, in this reduction, is the loss of a certain number of visible elements, chromosomes. This, of course, brings us to genetics. And what emerges from this genetics if not the dominant function, in the determination of certain elements of the living organism, of a combinatory that operates at certain of its stages by the expulsion of remainders?

I am not rushing into analogical speculation by referring here to the function of the *petit a*—I am simply pointing out an affinity between the enigmas of sexuality and the play of the signifier.

The only thing that I am bringing to the light of day at this point is the remark that, in fact, in history, primitive science has taken root in a mode of thinking which, playing on a combinatory, on such oppositions as those of Yin and Yang, water and fire, hot and cold, make them lead the dance—the word is chosen for its more than metaphorical implications, for their dance is based on dance ritual profoundly motivated by the sexual divisions in society.

This is not the place to embark on a lecture, even a short one, on Chinese astronomy. Amuse yourselves by opening the book by Léopold de Saussure—geniuses tend to pop up from time to time in that family. You will see there that Chinese astronomy is based on the play of the signifiers that reverberate from top to bottom in politics, the social structure, ethics, the regulation of the slightest acts, and that it is, nevertheless, a very fine astronomical science. It is true that, up to a certain point, all the reality of the heavens may be inscribed in nothing more than a vast constellation of signifiers.

To carry the thing to its limit, one might say that primitive science is a sort of sexual technique. It is not possible to say where the limit occurs, for it is certainly a science. Their perfectly valid observations show us that the Chinese had a perfectly efficient system for predicting diurnal and nocturnal variations, for example, at a very early period—which because of their signifying plotting we can date, because it is far enough away for the precession of the equinoxes to be marked in it on the figure of the heavens, and because the pole star does not appear in it in the same place as in our time. This is not a line of demarcation between experimental collation which remains valid for all and the principles that have guided it. Any more, Claude Lévi-Strauss emphasizes, than one can say that everything in primitive magic is phantasy and mystification, since an enormous collation of quite usuable experiences is contained in it.

But, nevertheless, there comes a moment, with the sexual initiation of the mechanism, when the moorings are broken. Paradoxical as it may seem, the break occurs all the later as the function of the signifier is more implicit, less mapped in this mechanism.

I will illustrate what I mean. Well after the Cartesian revolution and the Newtonian revolution, we still see, at the heart of positivist doctrine, a religious theory of the earth as a great fetish, perfectly coherent with a statement to be found in Comte, namely, that we shall never know anything about the chemical composition of the stars, that the stars will continue to be stuck to their places, that is to say—if we can see it from another perspective—purely as signifiers. Tough luck! At almost that very moment, the analysis of light enabled us to see in the stars many things at once, including their chemical composition. The break was then consummated between astronomy and astrology—which does not mean that astrology is not alive for a great many people.

2

Where is all this leading? It is leading us to the question as to whether we must regard the unconscious as a remanence of that archaic junction between thought and sexual reality. If sexuality is the reality of the unconscious—just think what this involves—the thing is so difficult of access that we may be able to elucidate it only by a consideration of history.

The solution, which, in history, has taken form in the thought of Jung, where the relation between the psychical world of the subject and reality are embodied under the term archetype, is to restore the level at which man's thought follows those aspects of the sexual experience that have been reduced by the invasion of science.

Now, Jungianism—in so far as it makes of the primitive modes of articulating the world something that survives, the kernel, he says, of the psyche itself—is necessarily accompanied by a repudiation of the term *libido*, by the neutralization of this function by recourse to a notion of psychical energy, a much more generalized notion of interest.

What we have here is not some scholastic quibble, some small difference of opinion. For what Freud intends to make present in the function of this libido is not some archaic relation, some primitive mode of access of thoughts, some world that is there like some shade of an ancient world surviving in ours. The libido is the effective presence, as such, of desire. It is what now remains to indicate desire—which is not substance, but which is there at the level of the primary process, and which governs the very mode of our approach.

I was recently rereading, in the context of an address I gave to a congress that took place in 1960, what someone else said about the unconscious. This person—it was M. Ricœur in fact —was trying to remove himself as far as possible from his own position in order to conceptualize our domain. He had certainly gone a long way to reach what, for a philosopher, is the area most difficult of access, namely, the reality of the unconscious—that the unconscious is not an ambiguity of acts, future knowledge that is already known not to be known, but lacuna, cut, rupture inscribed in a certain lack. M. Ricœur concedes that there is something of this dimension to be retained. But, philosopher that he is, he monopolizes it for himself. He calls it hermeneutics.

A lot of fuss is made nowadays of what is called hermeneutics. Hermeneutics not only objects to what I have called our analytic adventure, it objects to structuralism, as it appears in the works of Lévi-Strauss. Now, what is hermeneutics, if it is not to read, in the succession of man's mutations, the progress of the signs according to which he constitutes his history, the progress of his history—a history that may also, at the fringes, extend into less definite times? And so M. Ricœur casts into the limbo of pure contingency what the analysts at every stage are dealing with. One has to admit that, from the outside, the corporation of analysts does not give him the impression of an agreement so fundamental as to impress him. But this is no reason to leave the field to him.

I maintain that it is at the level of analysis —if we can take a few more steps forward—that the nodal point by which the pulsation of the unconscious is linked to sexual reality must be revealed. This nodal point is called desire, and the theoretical elaboration that I have pursued in recent years will show you, through each stage of clinical experience, how desire is situated in dependence on demand—which, by being articulated in signifiers, leaves a metonymic remainder that runs under it, an element that is not indeterminate, which is a condition both, absolute and unapprehensible, an element necessarily lacking, unsatisfied, impossible, misconstrued (*méconnu*), an element that is called desire. It is this that makes the junction with the field defined by Freud as that of the sexual agency at the level of the primary process.

The function of desire is a last residuum of the effect of the signifier in the subject. *Desidero* is the Freudian *cogito*. It is necessarily there that the essential of the primary process is established. Note well what Freud says of this field, in which the impulse is satisfied essentially by hallucination.

No mechanism-schema will ever be able to do justice to what is given as a regression on the reflex arc. What enters by the *sensorium* must leave by the *motorium*, and if the *motorium* does not work, it goes back. But if it goes back, how can we conceive that this constitutes a perception—if not by the image of something which, from an arrested current, makes the energy flow back in the form of a lamp which lights up, but for whom? The dimension of the third party is essential in this supposed regression. It can only be conceived in a form strictly analogical with what, the other day, I drew on the blackboard in the form of the duplicity between the subject of the statement and the subject of the enunciation. Only the presence of the desiring and sexually desiring, subject, brings us that dimension of natural metaphor from which the supposed identity of perception is decided.

Freud maintains the libido as the essential element of the

primary process. This means—contrary to how it may seem in the texts in which he tries to illustrate his theory—that in hallucination, the simplest hallucination of the simplest of needs, the hallucination of food, as it occurred in the dream of little Anna when she speaks of *tart, strawberries, eggs,* and other delicacies, there is not purely and simply a making present of the objects of a need. It is only on account of the sexualization of these objects that the hallucination of the dream is possible —for, as you will notice, little Anna only hallucinates forbidden objects. One can argue over each case, but it is absolutely essential to map the dimension of signification in every hallucination if we are to grasp what the pleasure principle means. It is from the point at which the subject desires that the connotation of reality is given in the hallucination. And if Freud contrasts the reality principle with the pleasure principle, it is precisely in so far as reality is defined as desexualized.

A lot is said in the most recent analytic theories about desexualized functions. It is said, for example, that the ego ideal rests on the investment of a desexualized libido. It seems to me very difficult to speak of a desexualized libido. But the notion that the approach of reality involves a desexualization lies at the very principle of Freud's definition of the *Zwei Prinzipien des psychischen Geschehens,* of the two principles into which psychical 'eventiality' is divided.

What does this mean? It means that in the transference we must see established the weight of sexual reality. Largely unknown and, up to a point, masked, it runs beneath what happens at the level of the analytic discourse, which is well and truly, as it takes form, that of demand—it is not for nothing that all experience leads us to throw it on to the side of the terms frustration and gratification.

I tried to draw on the blackboard the topology of the subject according to a sign that I once called the *interior 8.* This is certainly reminiscent of Euler's famous circles, except, as you will see, that Euler was concerned with a surface that could actually be made. The edge is continuous, except that at one point it does not proceed without being concealed by the surface that has previously unfolded itself. This drawing, seen from a certain perspective, may seem to represent two intersecting fields.

I have placed the libido at the point at which the lobe defined

as field of the development of the unconscious covers and conceals the other lobe, that of sexual reality. The libido, then,
would be that which belongs to both—the point of intersection,
as one says in logic. But this is precisely what it does not mean.
For this sector at which the fields appear to overlap is, if you
see the true profile of the surface, a void.

This surface belongs to another whose topology I have described to my pupils at various times, and which is called the
cross-cap, in order words, the mitre. I have not drawn it here,
but I would simply ask you to note what is its most obvious
characteristic. You can obtain it from the interior 8. Bring the
edges together two by two as they are presented here, by a
complementary surface, and close it. In a way, it plays the
same role as complement in relation to the initial 8 as a sphere

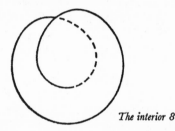

The interior 8

in relation to a circle, a sphere that would close what the circle
would already offer itself as ready to contain. Well! This surface is a Mœbius surface, and its outside continues its inside.
There is a second necessity that emerges from this figure, that
is, that it must, in order to close its curve, traverse at some point
the preceding surface, at that point, according to the line that
I have just reproduced here on the second model.

This image enables us to figure desire as a locus of junction
between the field of demand, in which the syncopes of the unconscious are made present, and sexual reality. All this depends
on a line that I will call the line of desire, linked to demand,
and by which the effects of sexuality are made present in experience.

What is this desire? Do you think it is there that I designate
the agency of the transference? Yes and no. You will see that
the thing is not so simple, if I tell you that the desire we are
concerned with here is the desire of the analyst.

3

In order not to leave you thunderstruck by an affirmation that might seem to you somewhat risky, I shall do no more than remind you how Freud sees the entrance into the unconscious.

Anna O.—let us drop this story of O. and call her by her real name, Bertha Pappenheim, one of the great names in the world of social welfare in Germany—not long ago one of my pupils brought me a small German postage stamp bearing her face, so you see she left some mark in history. It was in the case of Anna O. that the transference was discovered. Breuer was quite delighted with the smooth way the operation was going. At that time, no one would have challenged the signifier, if it had been possible to restore this word to life from the Stoic vocabulary. The more Anna provided signifiers, the more she chattered on, the better it went. It was a case of the chimney-sweeping treatment. There was no trace, in all this, of the least embarrassing thing. Look again. No sexuality, either under the microscope or in the distance.

Yet sexuality was nevertheless introduced by Breuer. Something even began to come back to him, it came back to him from himself— *You are rather preoccupied by it.* Thereupon, the dear man, somewhat alarmed, good husband that he was, decided that things had gone quite far enough—in response to which, as you know, O. displayed the magnificent and dramatic manifestations of what, in scientific language, is called *pseudo-cyesis* or, more familiarly, she blew up with what is called a nervous pregnancy.

What did she show by this? One may speculate, but one must refrain from resorting too precipitously to the language of the body. Let us say simply that the domain of sexuality shows a natural functioning of signs. At this level, they are not signifiers, for the nervous pregnancy is a symptom, and, according to the definition of the sign, something intended for someone. The signifier, being something quite different, represents a subject for another signifier.

There is a great difference to be articulated here, for, and not without cause, there is a tendency to say quite simply that it was Bertha's fault. But I would beg you to suspend your thoughts on this matter for a moment—why is it that we do not consider Bertha's pregnancy rather, according to my formula *man's desire is the desire of the Other*, as the manifestation of Breuer's desire? Why do you not go as far as to think that it was Breuer who had a desire for a child? I will give you the beginning of a proof; namely that Breuer, setting off for Italy with his wife, lost no time in giving her a child, as Ernest Jones reminds his interlocutor—a child which, from being born in these conditions, says the imperturbable Welshman, had just, at the moment when Jones was speaking, committed suicide.

Let us leave to one side what we might in fact think of a desire to which even this outcome is not indifferent. But let us observe what Freud says to Breuer—*What! The transference is the spontaneity of the said Bertha's unconscious. It's not yours, not your desire, it's the desire of the Other.* I think Freud treats Breuer as a hysteric here, since he says to him: *Your desire is the desire of the Other.* The curious thing is, he does not make him feel less guilty, but he certainly makes him feel less anxious—those who know the difference that I am making between these two levels may take this as an instance of it.

This brings us to the question of what Freud's desire decided, in diverting the whole apprehension of the transference in a direction that has now reached its final term of absurdity, to the point at which an analyst may say that the whole theory of the transference is merely a defence of the analyst.

I swing this extreme term in another direction. Indeed, I show precisely the opposite side when I say that it is the desire of the analyst. You must follow my thinking here. It's not simply a matter of turning things upside-down. With this key, read some general account of the question of the transference, written by anybody—anyone who could write a *Que sais-je?*[1] on psycho-analysis can just as easily give you a general account of the transference. So read his general account of the transference, which I designate here adequately enough, and draw your own conclusions with this in mind.

Is not the contribution that each individual, Freud apart, brings to the subject of the transference something in which his desire is perfectly legible? I could do an analysis of Abraham for you simply on the basis of his theory of part-objects. It is

[1] A popular series of cheap books that sets out to provide an introduction to a wide range of subjects.

not only a question of what the analyst wants to do with his patient in the matter. It is also a question of what his patient wants to do with him. Abraham, we might say, wanted to be a complete mother.

Then I might also amuse myself by punctuating the fringes of Ferenczi's theory with a famous song by Georgius *Je suis fils-père* ('I am son-father').

Nunberg, too, has his own intentions, and in his truly remarkable article on *Love and Transference*, he shows himself to be in the position of arbiter between the powers of life and death, in which one cannot fail to see an aspiration to the divine position.

All this may be no more than a kind of game. But it is in the course of some such story that one can isolate functions like those that I wished to reproduce here on the blackboard.

In order to conjugate the schema of the net with those I have made in response to a psychologizing theory of the psycho-analytic personality, you have only to turn the obturator I referred to earlier into a camera shutter, except that it would be a mirror. It is in this little mirror, which shuts out what is on the other side, that the subject sees emerge the game by means of which he may—according to the illusion of what is obtained in the experiment of the inverted bunch of flowers, that is to say, a real image—accommodate his own image around what appears, the *petit a*. It is in the sum of these accommodations of images that the subject must find the opportunity for an essential integration. What do we know of all this?—if it is only at the mercy of fluctuations in the history of analysis, of the commitment of the desire of each analyst, we manage to add some small detail, some corroborating observation, some incidental addition or refinement, which enables us to define the presence, at the level of desire, of each of the analysts. This was the band, as Freud put it, that he left behind to follow him.

After all, the people who followed Christ were not so brilliant. Freud was not Christ, but he was perhaps something like Viridiana.[2] The characters who are photographed, so ironically

---

[2] The allusion is to a film by Bunuel of the same name in which a group of peasants pose to be 'photographed' at a dinner-table. The characters are so arranged as to reproduce Leonardo's painting of the Last Supper.

in that film, with a small apparatus, sometimes remind me irresistibly of the group, also photographed innumerable times, of those who were Freud's apostles and epigones. Does this diminish them in any way? No more than the apostles. It is precisely at this level that they could bear the best witness. It is by virtue of a certain naivety, a certain poverty, a certain innocence that they have most instructed us. It is true that those around Socrates were more brilliant and that they teach us no less about the transference—those who remember my seminar on this subject will bear me out.

I will take this up again next time, when I will try to articulate for you the significance of the function of the analyst's desire.

QUESTIONS AND ANSWERS

J.-A. MILLER: *The question arises of the specific relation between these two discourses, the scientific discourse and the discourse of the Other, that is, the unconscious. Unlike the discourses that preceded its arrival, science is not based on the unconscious combinatory. It sets out to establish with the unconscious a relation of non-relation. It is disconnected. Yet the unconscious does not disappear, and its effects continue to be felt. Perhaps to reflect on the scientificity of analysis, which you postulate, would lead to writing a new history of scientific thought. I would like to know what you have to say about this.*

LACAN: You see the emergence of a double questioning. If we can couple psycho-analysis to the train of modern science, despite the essential effect of the analyst's desire, we have a right to ask the question of the desire that lies behind modern science. There is certainly a disconnection between scientific discourse and the conditions of the discourse of the unconscious. We see this in set theory. At a time when the combinatory is coupled to the capture of sexuality, set theory cannot emerge. How is this disconnection possible? It is at the level of desire that we will be able to find the answer.

29 April 1964

The 'photograph' is taken by one of the girls raising her skirt at the assembly—hence the reference to the 'small apparatus' [Tr.].

13

THE DECONSTRUCTION
OF THE DRIVE

I ended my last talk by pointing out the place where I had taken you with the topological schematization of a certain division, and of a perimeter involuted upon itself, which is that constituted by what is usually called, quite incorrectly, the analytic situation.

This topology is intended to give you some notion of the location of the point of disjuncture and conjuncture, of union and frontier, that can be occupied only by the desire of the analyst.

To go further, to show you how this mapping is necessitated by all the deviations, of concept and of practice, that a long experience of analysis and of its doctrinal statements enables one to accumulate, I must—for those who have not been able, for purely practical reasons, to follow my earlier seminars—put forward the fourth concept that I have proposed as essential to the analytic experience—that of drive.

I

I can only write this introduction—this *Einführung*, to use Freud's term—in the wake of Freud, in so far as this notion is absolutely new in Freud.

The term *Trieb* certainly has a long history, not only in psychology or in physiology, but in physics itself and, of course, it is no accident that Freud chose this term. But he gave to *Trieb* so specific a use, and *Trieb* is so integrated into analytic practice itself, that its past is truly concealed. Just as the past of the term unconscious weights on the use of the term in analytic theory—so, as far as *Trieb* is concerned, everyone uses it as a designation of a sort of radical given of our experience.

Sometimes, people even go so far as to invoke it against my doctrine of the unconscious, which they see as some kind of intellectualization—if they knew what I think of intelligence, they would certainly retract this criticism—as if I were ignoring what any analyst knows from experience, namely the domain of the drive. We will meet in experience something that has an irrepressible character even through repressions—indeed, if repression there must be, it is because there is something beyond that is pressing in. There is no need to go further in an adult analysis; one has only to be a child therapist to know the element that constitutes the clinical weight of each of the cases we have to deal with, namely, the drive. There seems to be here, therefore, a reference to some ultimate given, something archaic, primal. Such a recourse, which my teaching invites you to renounce if you are to understand the unconscious, seems inevitable here.

Now, is what we are dealing with in the drive essentially organic? Is it thus that we should interpret what Freud says in a text belonging to *Jenseits des Lustprinzips*—that the drive, *Trieb*, represents the *Äusserung der Trägheit*, some manifestation of inertia in the organic life? Is it a simple notion, which might be completed with reference to some storing away of this inertia, namely, to fixation, *Fixierung*?

Not only do I not think so, but I think that a serious examination of Freud's elaboration of the notion of drive runs counter to it.

Drive (*pulsion*) is not thrust (*poussée*). *Trieb* is not *Drang*, if only for the following reason. In an article written in 1915 —that is, a year after the *Einführung zum Narzissmus*, you will see the importance of this reminder soon—entitled *Trieb und Triebschicksale*—one should avoid translating it by *avatar*, *Triebwandlungen* would be avatar, *Schicksal* is adventure, vicissitude—in this article, then, Freud says that it is important to distinguish four terms in the drive: *Drang*, thrust; *Quelle*, the source; *Objekt*, the object; *Ziel*, the aim. Of course, such a list may seem a quite natural one. My purpose is to prove to you that the whole text was written to show us that it is not as natural as that.

First of all, it is essential to remember that Freud himself tells us at the beginning of this article that the drive is a *Grundbegriff*, a fundamental concept. He adds, and in doing so shows himself to be a good epistemologist, that, from the moment when he, Freud, introduced the drive into science, one was faced with a choice between two possibilities—either this concept would be preserved, or it would be rejected. It would be preserved if it functioned, as one would now say—I would say if it traced its way in the real that it set out to penetrate. This is the case with all the other *Grundbegriffe* in the scientific domain.

What we see emerging here in Freud's mind are the fundamental concepts of physics. His masters in physiology are those who strive to bring to realization, for example, the integration of physiology with the fundamental concepts of modern physics, especially those connected with energy. How often, in the course of history, have the notions of energy and force been taken up and used again upon an increasingly totalized reality!

This is certainly what Freud foresaw. *The progress of knowledge*, he said, *can bear no* Starrheit, *no fascination with definitions*. Somewhere else, he says that the drive belongs to our myths. For my part, I will ignore this term myth—indeed, in the same text, in the first paragraph, Freud uses the word *Konvention*, convention, which is much closer to what we are talking about and to which I would apply the Benthamite term, *fiction*, which I have mapped for my followers. This term, I should say in passing, is much more preferable than that of *model*, which has been all too much abused. In any case, model is never a *Grundbegriff*, for, in a certain field, several models may function correlatively. This is not the case for a *Grundbegriff*, for a fundamental concept, nor for a fundamental fiction.

2

Now let us ask ourselves what appears first when we look more closely at the four terms laid down by Freud in relation to the drive. Let us say that these four terms cannot but appear disjointed.

First, *thrust* will be identified with a mere tendency to discharge. This tendency is what is produced by the fact of a stimulus, namely, the transmission of the accepted portion, at the level of the stimulus, of the additional energy, the celebrated Qn quantity of the *Entwurf*. But, on this matter, Freud makes, at the outset, a remark that has very far-reaching implications. Here, too, no doubt, there is stimulation, excitation, to use the term Freud uses at this level, *Reiz*, excitation. But the *Reiz* that is used when speaking of drive is different from any stimulation coming from the outside world, it is an internal *Reiz*. What does this mean?

In order to explicitate it, we have the notion of need, as it is manifested in the organism at several levels and first of all at the level of hunger and thirst. This is what Freud seems to mean when he distinguishes internal excitement from external excitement. Well! It has to be said that, at the very outset, Freud posits, quite categorically, that there is absolutely no question in *Trieb* of the pressure of a need such as *Hunger* or *Durst*, thirst.

What exactly does Freud mean by *Trieb*? Is he referring to something whose agency is exercised at the level of the organism in its totality? Does the real *qua* totality irrupt here? Are we concerned here with the living organism? No. It is always a question quite specifically of the Freudian field itself, in the most undifferentiated form that Freud gave it at the outset, which at this level, in the terms of the *Sketch* referred to above, that of the *Ich*, of the *Real-Ich*. The *Real-Ich* is conceived as supported, not by the organism as a whole, but by the nervous system. It has the character of a planned, objectified subject. I am stressing the surface characteristics of this field by treating it topologically, and in trying to show you how taking it in the form of a surface responds to all the needs of its handling.

This point is essential for, when we examine it more closely, we shall see that the *Triebreiz* is that by which certain elements of this field are, says Freud, *triebbesetzt*, invested as drive. This investment places us on the terrain of an energy—and not any energy—a potential energy, for—Freud articulated it in the most pressing way—the characteristic of the drive is to be a *konstante Kraft*, a constant force. He cannot conceive of it as a *momentane Stosskraft*.

What is meant by *momentane Stosskraft*? About this word *Moment*, we already have the example of a historical misunderstanding. During the siege of Paris in 1870, the Parisians made fun of Bismarck's *psychologische Moment*. This phrase struck them as being absurdly funny, for, until fairly recently, when they have had to get used to everything, the French have always been rather particular about the correct use of words. This quite new psychological moment struck them as being very funny indeed. All it meant was the psychological *factor*. But this *momentane Stosskraft* is not perhaps to be taken quite in the sense of factor, but rather in the sense of moment as used in the cinema. I think that this *Stosskraft*, or shock force, is simply a reference to the life force, to kinetic energy. In the drive, there is no question of kinetic energy; it is not a question of something that will be regulated with movement. The discharge in question is of a quite different nature, and is on a quite different plane.

The constancy of the thrust forbids any assimilation of the drive to a biological function, which always has a rhythm. The first thing Freud says about the drive is, if I may put it this way, that it has no day or night, no spring or autumn, no rise and fall. It is a constant force. All the same, one must take account of the texts, and also of experience.

3

At the other end of the chain, Freud refers to *Befriedigung*, satisfaction, which he writes out in full, but in inverted commas. What does he mean by satisfaction of the drive? *Well, that's simple enough*, you'll say. *The satisfaction of the drive is reaching one's* Ziel, *one's aim*. The wild animal emerges from its hole *querens quem devoret*, and when he has found what he has to eat, he is satisfied, he digests it. The very fact that a similar image may be invoked shows that one allows it to resonate in harmony with mythology, with, strictly speaking, the drive.

One objection immediately springs to mind — it is rather odd that nobody should have noticed it, all the time it has been there, an enigma, which, like all Freud's enigmas, was sustained as a wager to the end of his life without Freud deigning to offer any further explanation — he probably left the work to those who could do it. You will remember that the third of the four fundamental vicissitudes of the drive that Freud posits at the outset — it is curious that there are *four* vicissitudes as there are *four* elements of the drive — is sublimation. Well, in this article, Freud tells us repeatedly that sublimation is also satisfaction of the drive, whereas it is *zielgehemmt*, inhibited as to its aim — it does not attain it. Sublimation is nonetheless satisfaction of the drive, without repression.

In other words — for the moment, I am not fucking, I am talking to you. Well! I can have exactly the same satisfaction as if I were fucking. That's what it means. Indeed, it raises the question of whether in fact I am not fucking at this moment. Between these two terms—drive and satisfaction—there is set up an extreme antinomy that reminds us that the use of the function of the drive has for me no other purpose than to put in question what is meant by satisfaction.

All those here who are psycho-analysts must now feel to what extent I am introducing here the most essential level of accommodation. It is clear that those with whom we deal, the patients, are not satisfied, as one says, with what they are. And yet, we know that everything they are, everything they experience, even their symptoms, involves satisfaction. They satisfy something that no doubt runs counter to that with which they might be satisfied, or rather, perhaps, they give satisfaction *to* something. They are not content with their state, but all the same, being in a state that gives so little content, they are content. The whole question boils down to the following—*what* is contented here?

On the whole, and as a first approximation, I would say that to which they give satisfaction by the ways of displeasure is nevertheless—and this is commonly accepted—the law of pleasure. Let us say that, for this sort of satisfaction, they give themselves too much trouble. Up to a point, it is this *too much trouble* that is the sole justification of our intervention.

One cannot say, then, that the aim is not attained where satisfaction is concerned. It is. This is not a definitive ethical position. But, at a certain level, this is how we analysts approach the problem—though we know a little more than others about what is normal and abnormal. We know that the forms of arrangement that exist between what works well and what works badly constitute a continuous series. What we have before us in analysis is a system in which everything turns out all right, and which attains its own sort of satisfaction. If we interfere in this, it is in so far as we think that there are other ways, shorter ones for example. In any case, if I refer to the drive, it is in so far as it is at the level of the drive that the state of satisfaction is to be rectified.

This satisfaction is paradoxical. When we look at it more closely, we see that something new comes into play—the category of the impossible. In the foundations of the Freudian conceptions, this category is an absolutely radical one. The path of the subject—to use the term in relation to which, alone, satisfaction may be situated—the path of the subject passes between the two walls of the impossible.

This function of the impossible is not to be approached without prudence, like any function that is presented in a negative form. I would simply like to suggest to you that the best way of approaching these notions is not to take them by negation. This method would bring us here to the question of the possible, and the impossible is not necessarily the contrary of the possible, or, since the opposite of the possible is certainly the real, we would be lead to define the real as the impossible.

Personally, I see nothing against this, especially as, in Freud, it is in this form that the real, namely, the obstacle to the pleasure principle, appears. The real is the impact with the obstacle; it is the fact that things do not turn out all right straight away, as the hand that is held out to external objects wishes. But I think this is a quite illusory and limited view of Freud's thought on this point. The real is distinguished, as I said last time, by its separation from the field of the pleasure principle, by its desexualization, by the fact that its economy, later, admits something new, which is precisely the impossible.

But the impossible is also present in the other field, as an essential element. The pleasure principle is even characterized by the fact that the impossible is so present in it that it is never recognized in it as such. The idea that the function of the pleasure principle is to satisfy itself by hallucination is there to illustrate this—it is only an illustration. By snatching at its object, the drive learns in a sense that this is precisely not the way it will be satisfied. For if one distinguishes, at the outset of the dialectic of the drive, *Not* from *Bedürfnis*, need from the pressure of the drive—it is precisely because no object of any *Not*, need, can satisfy the drive.

Even when you stuff the mouth—the mouth that opens in the register of the drive—it is not the food that satisfies it, it is, as one says, the pleasure of the mouth. That is why, in analytic experience, the oral drive is encountered at the final term, in a situation in which it does no more than order the menu. This is done no doubt with the mouth, which is fundamental to the satisfaction—what goes out from the mouth comes back to the mouth, and is exhausted in that pleasure that I have just called, by reference to the usual terms, the pleasure of the mouth.

This is what Freud tells us. Let us look at what he says—*As far as the object in the drive is concerned, let it be clear that it is, strictly speaking, of no importance. It is a matter of total indifference.* One must never read Freud without one's ears cocked. When one reads such things, one really ought to prick up one's ears.

How should one conceive of the object of the drive, so that one can say that, in the drive, whatever it may be, it is indifferent? As far as the oral drive is concerned, for example, it is obvious that it is not a question of food, nor of the memory of food, nor the echo of food, nor the mother's care, but of something that is called the breast, and which seems to go of its own accord because it belongs to the same series. If Freud makes a remark to the effect that the object in the drive is of no importance, it is probably because the breast, in its function as object, is to be revised in its entirety.

To this breast in its function as object, *objet a* cause of desire, in the sense that I understand the term—we must give a function that will explain its place in the satisfaction of the drive. The best formula seems to me to be the following—that *la pulsion en fait le tour*.[1] I shall find other opportunities of applying it to other objects. *Tour* is to be understood here with the ambiguity it possesses in French, both *turn*, the limit around which one turns, and *trick*.

4

I have left the question of the source till last. If we wished at all costs to introduce vital regulation into the function of the drive, one would certainly say that examining the source is the right way to go about it.

Why? Why are the so-called erogenous zones recognized

---

[1] As Lacan explains, he is playing on the double meaning, in French, of the word *tour*—so the formula is strictly untranslatable. In terms of idiomatic usage, the pun is rather forced, since the expression *'faire le tour de quelque chose'* can only mean 'to walk, to drive, etc., round something', though outside this expression *'tour'* has also, of course, the sense of 'trick'. What the formula means, then, is a combination of (1) 'the drive moves around the object' and (2) 'the drive tricks the object' [Tr.].

only in those points that are differentiated for us by their rim-like structure? Why does one speak of the mouth and not of the oesophagus, or the stomach? They participate just as much in the oral function. But at the erogenous level we speak of the mouth, of the lips and the teeth, of what Homer calls the enclosure of the teeth.

The same goes for the anal drive. It is not enough to say that a certain vital function is integrated in a function of exchange with the world—excrement. There are other excremental functions, and there are other elements that participate in them other than the rim of the anus, which is however, specifically what, for us too, is defined as the source and departure of a certain drive.

Let me say that if there is anything resembling a drive it is a *montage*.

It is not a *montage* conceived in a perspective referring to finality. This perspective is the one that is established in modern theories of instinct, in which the presentation of an image derived from *montage* is quite striking. Such a *montage*, for example, is the specific form that will make the hen in the farm-yard run to ground if you place within a few yards of her the cardboard outline of a falcon, that is to say, something that sets off a more or less appropriate reaction, and where the trick is to show us that it is not necessarily an appropriate one. I am not speaking of this sort of *montage*.

The *montage* of the drive is a *montage* which, first, is presented as having neither head nor tail—in the sense in which one speaks of *montage* in a surrealist collage. If we bring together the paradoxes that we just defined at the level of *Drang*, at that of the object, at that of the aim of the drive, I think that the resulting image would show the working of a dynamo connected up to a gas-tap, a peacock's feather emerges, and tickles the belly of a pretty woman, who is just lying there looking beautiful. Indeed, the thing begins to become interesting from this very fact, that the drive defines, according to Freud, all the forms of which one may reverse such a mechanism. This does not mean that one turns the dynamo upside-down—one unrolls its wires, it is they that become the peacock's feather, the gas-tap goes into the lady's mouth, and the bird's rump emerges in the middle.

This is what he shows as a developed example. Read this text of Freud's between now and next time, and you will see that it constantly jumps, without transition, between the most heterogeneous images. All this occurs only by means of grammatical references, the artifice of which you will find easy to grasp next time.

Incidentally, how can one say, just like that, as Freud goes on to do, that exhibitionism is the contrary of voyeurism, or that masochism is the contrary of sadism? He posits this simply for grammatical reasons, for reasons concerning the inversion of the subject and the object, as if the grammatical object and subject were real functions. It is easy to show that this is not the case, and we have only to refer to our structure of language for this deduction to become impossible. But what, by means of this game, he conveys to us about the essence of the drive is what, next time, I will define for you as the trace of the act.

QUESTIONS AND ANSWERS

DR GREEN: *One point you have raised obviously seems quite crucial. This is the fact that the other qualities that specify the drive must be conceived as discontinuous elements. My question concerns the element of thrust that you have rather pushed to one side, in the course of your talk today, because, I think, it seemed to you one of the easiest ways of getting misled. But if, as you show, the drive is ultimately destined to the combinatory of the fact of discontinuity, it posits for itself the problem of the contradiction inherent in the energy of the system, which is conceived as a force that is both constant and subject to variation. It is this question that I would like you to develop in more detail if you can, in so far as it introduces the point of view that remains for me very important, and which I do not see very clearly in your teaching, namely, the economic point of view.*

LACAN: Yes, we shall come to it, and you will see from what angle. Indeed, it is easy to see how if you read my article. There is a reference that may put us on the right track, and which I did not wish to use, either because I did not have time, or because it eliminates itself—most of the time I play it by ear, in contact with the audience. It is a reference to a certain chapter in energetics.

In a limited system, there is a certain way of inscribing each defined point, as characterized in terms of potential energy between the closest points—one speaks of scale notation or index. One can now define each point by a certain derivation —you know that in infinitesimal calculus it is one of the ways of dimensioning infinitely small variations. For each point, then, there will be a derivation in relation to the slope immediately next to it, and this derivation will be noted for each point of the field. This derivation may be inscribed in the form of a vector and we can compose the set of vectors. There is, then, a law that seems odd at first sight, but which is certainly regarded as fundamental—that which, from a particular vector—which realizes the composition of these derivations connoted by each point of the field from the point of view of potential energy —that which, therefore, from a particular vector, crosses a certain surface—which is simply what I call the gap (*béance*), from the fact that it is defined by a rim-like structure—is, for the same surface, a constant. The variations of the system being what they may be, what is potential at the level of the integration, what is called the flux, is therefore constant.

What we seem to be dealing with, therefore, in the *Drang* of the drive is something that is, and is only, connotable in the relation to the *Quelle*, in so far as the *Quelle* inscribes in the economy of the drive this rim-like structure.

Physiological variations, deep variations, those that are inscribed in the totality of the organism, are subjected to all the rhythms, even to the very discharges that may occur as a result of the drive. On the other hand, what characterizes the *Drang*, the thrust of the drive, is the maintained constancy which, to take a fairly useful image, measures up to an opening that is, up to a certain individualized point, variable. That is to say, people have big mouths to a greater or lesser degree. Sometimes it might even be useful to take this into account, in the selection of analysts. But, anyway, that's something I shall be concerned with in another context.

This has not exhausted the question you asked, but it provides the beginning of a rational solution to the antinomy that you raise, and which is precisely what I left in suspense. For I stressed what Freud stresses—that, when the system functions in contact with the *Umwelt*, it is a question of discharge, and when it is a question of *Triebreiz*, there is a barrier. This is a point that does not receive enough attention. But what can that mean? There is no barrier, unless the investment is in the field itself. So, in fact, what we have to designate is this—in so far as the field itself involves this investment, there can be no question of the functioning of a barrier.

Dr MATHIS: *One question concerning the rim-like structure. When it is a question of the mouth and the anal rim, do you locate the eroticization at both extremities? Where do you place what may occur at the level of the oesophagus, at the gastric level, in sniffing, in vomiting, at the level of the trachea? Is there something profoundly different there from what you have articulated at the level of the lips?*

LACAN: I confined myself to the two rims concerned in the digestive track. I could also have told you that the rheumy rim of our eyelids, our ears, our navels, are also rims, and that all this is part of this function of eroticism. In the analytic tradition, we always refer to the strictly focused image of zones reduced to their function as rim. This does not in the least mean that, in our symptomatology, other zones do not come into play. But we consider that they come into play in that fall-out zone that I call desexualization and function of reality.

Let us take an example. It is in the function in which the sexual object moves towards the side of reality and presents itself as a parcel of meat that there emerges that form of desexualization that is so obvious that it is called in the case of the hysteric a reaction of disgust. This does not mean that we say that pleasure is located in these erogenous zones. Desire is concerned—thank God, we know only too well—with something quite different, and even with something quite different from the organism, while involving the organism at various levels. But what satisfaction is the central function of the drive intended to produce? It is precisely to the extent that adjoining, connected zones are excluded that others take on their erogenous function and become specific sources for the drive. You follow me?

Of course, other zones than these erogenous zones are concerned in the economy of desire. But note well what happens whenever they emerge. It was no accident that I chose the function of disgust. There are really two major aspects of desire as it may emerge in the fall of sexualization—on the one hand, disgust produced by the reduction of the sexual partner to a function of reality, whatever it may be, and, on the other hand, what I have called, in relation to the scopic function, *invidia*, envy. Envy is not the same thing as the scopic drive, nor is disgust the same thing as the oral drive.

6 May 1964

14

THE PARTIAL DRIVE
AND ITS CIRCUIT

Die ganze Sexualstrebung · Every drive is partial · Drive, sex and death · The supposed stages · Schaulust · Sado-masochism

τῷ τόξῳ ὄνομα βίος ἔργον δέ Θάνατς

Heraclitus. B 48.

When I read in the *Psychoanalytic Quarterly* an article like the one by Mr Edward Glover, entitled *Freudian or Neo-Freudian*, directed entirely against the constructions of Mr Alexander, I sense a sordid smell of stuffiness, at the sight of a construction like that of Mr Alexander being counter-attacked in the name of obsolete criteria. Good Heavens, I did not hesitate to attack it myself in the most categorical way fourteen years ago, at the 1950 Congress of Psychiatry, but, it is the construction of a man of great talent and when I see at what level this construction is discussed, I can pay myself the complement that through all the misadventures that my discourse encounters, here and certainly elsewhere, one can say that this discourse provides an obstacle to the experience of analysis being served up to you in a completely cretinous way.

At this point, I will resume my discourse on the drive. I was led to approach it after positing that the transference is what manifests in experience the enacting of the reality of the unconscious, in so far as that reality is sexuality. I find that I must pause here and ask myself what this very affirmation involves.

If we are sure that sexuality is present in action in the transference, it is in so far as at certain moments it is manifested in the open in the form of love. That is what it is about. Does love represent the summit, the culminating point, the indisputable factor, that makes sexuality present for us in the here and now of the transference?

Freud's text, not, certainly, any specific text, but the central import of those writings that deal with the drives and their vicissitudes, rejects such a view in the clearest possible way.

It was this text that I began to approach last time, when I was trying to make you feel in what a problematic form, bristling with questions, the introduction of the drive presents itself. I hope that many of you will have been able to refer to this text in the meantime, whether you are able to read it in German, which seems to me eminently desirable, or whether, as second best, you will be able to read it, always more or less improperly translated, in the two other languages of culture, English or French—I certainly give the worst marks to the French translation, but I will not waste time pointing out the veritable falsifications with which it swarms.

Even on a first reading, you would have been able to see that this article falls entirely into two parts—*first*, the deconstruction of the drive; *secondly*, the examination of *das Lieben*, the act of love. We shall now approach this second point.

I

Freud says quite specifically that love can in no way be regarded as the representative of what he puts in question in the term *die ganze Sexualstrebung*, that is to say, the tendency, the forms, the convergence of the striving of the sexual, in so far as it culminates in *Ganze*, in an apprehensible whole, that would sum up its essence and function.

Kommt aber auf damit nicht zuher, that's not at all how it happens, he cries, when answering this far-reaching suggestion. We analysts have rendered it by all sorts of misleading formulae. The whole point of the article is to show us that with regard to the biological finality of sexuality, namely, reproduction, the drives, as they present themselves in the process of psychical reality, are partial drives.

In their structure, in the tension they establish, the drives are linked to an economic factor. This economic factor depends on the conditions in which the function of the pleasure principle is exercised at a level that I will take up again, at the right time, in the term *Real-Ich*. Let me say at once that we can conceptualize the *Real-Ich* as the central nervous system in so far as it functions, not as a system of relations, but as a system intended to ensure a certain homeostasis of the internal tensions.

It is because of the reality of the homeostatic system that sexuality comes into play only in the form of partial drives. The drive is precisely that *montage* by which sexuality participates in the psychical life, in a way that must conform to the gap-like structure that is the structure of the unconscious.

Let us place ourselves at the two extremes of the analytic experience. The primal repressed is a signifier, and we can always regard what is built on this as constituting the symptom *qua* a scaffolding of signifiers. Repressed and symptom are homogeneous, and reducible to the functions of signifiers. Although their structure is built up step by step like any edifice, it is nevertheless, in the end, inscribable in synchronic terms.

At the other extreme, there is interpretation. Interpretation concerns the factor of a special temporal structure that I have tried to define in the term metonymy. As it draws to its end, interpretation is directed towards desire, with which, in a certain sense, it is identical. Desire, in fact, is interpretation itself.

In between, there is sexuality. If sexuality, in the form of the partial drives, had not manifested itself as dominating the whole economy of this interval, our experience would be reduced to a mantic, to which the neutral term psychical energy would then have been appropriate, but in which it would miss what constitutes in it the presence, the *Dasein*, of sexuality.

The legibility of sex in the interpretation of the unconscious mechanisms is always retroactive. It would merely be of the nature of interpretation if, at each moment of the history, we could be certain only that the partial drives intervened effectively in time and place. And not, as one tended to believe at the beginning of the analytic experience, in an erratic form. That infantile sexuality is not a wandering block of ice snatched from the great ice-bank of adult sexuality, intervening as an attraction over an immature subject—this was proved at once in analysis and with what, later, might seem a surprising significance.

In *Three Essays on the Theory of Sexuality*, Freud was able to posit sexuality as essentially polymorphous, aberrant. The spell of a supposed infantile innocence was broken. Because it was imposed so early, I would almost say too early, this sexuality made us pass too quickly over an examination of what it essentially represents. That is to say that, with regard to the agency of sexuality, all subjects are equal, from the child to the adult —that they deal only with that part of sexuality that passes into the networks of the constitution of the subject, into the networks of the signifier—that sexuality is realized only through the operation of the drives in so far as they are partial drives, partial with regard to the biological finality of sexuality.

The integration of sexuality into the dialectic of desire passes through the bringing into play of what, in the body, deserves to be designated by the term apparatus—if you understand by this that with which the body, with regard to sexuality, may fit itself up (*s'appareiller*) as opposed to that with which bodies may be paired off (*s'apparier*).

If all is confusion in the discussion of the sexual drives it is because one does not see that the drive represents no doubt, but *merely* represents, and partially at that, the curve of fulfilment of sexuality in the living being. Is it surprising that its final term should be death, when the presence of sex in the living being is bound up with death?

Today I have copied out on the blackboard a fragment of Heraclitus, which I found in the monumental work in which Diels has gathered together for us the scattered remains of the pre-Socratic period. *To the bow* (*Biós*), he writes, and this emerges for us as one of his lessons in wisdom which, before all the circuit of scientific elaboration, went straight to the target, *to the bow is given the name of life* (*Bíos*, the accent being this time on the first syllable) *and its work is death.*

What the drive integrates at the outset in its very existence is a dialectic of the bow, I would even say of archery. In this way we can situate its place in the psychical economy.

2

Freud now introduces us to the drive by one of the most traditional ways, using at every moment the resources of the language, and not hesitating to base himself on something that belongs only to certain linguistic systems, the three voices, active, passive and reflexive. But this is merely an envelope. We must see that this signifying reversion is something other, something other than what it dresses in. What is fundamental at the level of each drive is the movement outwards and back in which it is structured.

It is remarkable that Freud can designate these two poles simply by using something that is the verb. *Beschauen und beschaut werden,* to see and to be seen, *quälen* and *gequält werden,* to torment and to be tormented. This is because, from the outset, Freud takes it as understood that no part of this distance covered can be separated from its outwards-and-back movement, from its fundamental reversion, from the circular character of the path of the drive.

Similarly, it is remarkable that, in order to illustrate the

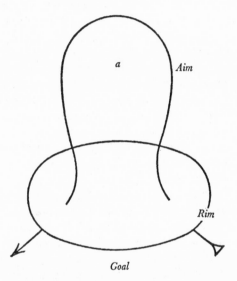

Goal

dimension of this *Verkehrung,* he should choose *Schaulust,* the pleasure of seeing, and what he cannot designate other than by the combination of two terms in *sado-masochism.* When he speaks of these two drives, and especially of masochism, he is careful to observe that there are not two stages in these drives, but three. One must distinguish the return into the circuit of the drive of that which appears—but *also does not appear*—in a third stage. Namely, the appearance of *ein neues Subjekt,* to be understood as follows—not in the sense that there is already one, namely the subject of the drive, but in that what is new is the appearance of a subject. This subject, which is properly the other, appears in so far as the drive has been able to show its circular course. It is only with its appearance at the level of the other that what there is of the function of the drive may be realized.

It is to this that I would now like to draw your attention. You see here, on the blackboard, a circuit formed by the curve of this rising and redescending arrow that crosses, *Drang* as it is in its origin, the surface constituted by what I defined last time as the rim, which is regarded in the theory as the source, the *Quelle*, that is to say, the so-called erogenous zone in the drive. The tension is always loop-shaped and cannot be separated from its return to the erogenous zone.

Here we can clear up the mystery of the *zielgehemmt*, of that form that the drive may assume, in attaining its satisfaction without attaining its aim—in so far as it would be defined by a biological function, by the realization of reproductive coupling. For the partial drive does not lie there. What is it?

Let us still suspend the answer, but let us concentrate on this term *but*, and on the two meanings it may present. In order to differentiate them, I have chosen to notate them here in a language in which they are particularly expressive, English. When you entrust someone with a mission, the *aim* is not what he brings back, but the itinerary he must take. The *aim* is the way taken. The French word *but* may be translated by another word in English, *goal*. In archery, the *goal* is not the *but* either, it is not the bird you shoot, it is having scored a hit and thereby attained your *but*.

If the drive may be satisfied without attaining what, from the point of view of a biological totalization of function, would be the satisfaction of its end of reproduction, it is because it is a partial drive, and its aim is simply this return into circuit.

This theory is present in Freud. He tells us somewhere that the ideal model for auto-eroticism would be a single mouth kissing itself—a brilliant, even dazzling metaphor, in this respect so typical of everything he writes, and which requires only to be completed by a question. In the drive, is not this mouth what might be called a mouth in the form of an arrow?—a mouth sewn up, in which, in analysis, we see indicating as clearly as possible, in certain silences, the pure agency of the oral drive, closing upon its own satisfaction.

In any case, what makes us distinguish this satisfaction from the mere auto-eroticism of the erogenous zone is the object that we confuse all too often with that upon which the drive closes —this object, which is in fact simply the presence of a hollow, a void, which can be occupied, Freud tells us, by any object, and whose agency we know only in the form of the lost object, the *petit a*. The *objet petit a* is not the origin of the oral drive. It is not introduced as the original food, it is introduced from the fact that no food will ever satisfy the oral drive, except by circumventing the eternally lacking object.

The question now confronting us is this—where is this circuit plugged in and, to begin with, is it spiral in form, that is to say, is the circuit of the oral drive continued by the anal drive, which would then be the following stage? Is it a case of dialectical progress being produced out of opposition? Even for people who are used to us, it is already to carry the question rather far, in the name of some kind of mystery of development, to regard the thing as already acquired, inscribed in the organism.

This conception seems to be sustained by the fact that as far as the emergence of sexuality in a so-called completed form is concerned, we are certainly dealing with an organic process. But there is no reason to extend this fact to the relation between the other partial drives. There is no relation of production between one of the partial drives and the next.

The passage from the oral drive to the anal drive can be produced not by a process of maturation, but by the intervention of something that does not belong to the field of the drive—by the intervention, the overthrow, of the demand of the Other. If we introduce the other drives with which the series may be formed, and the number of which is fairly short, it is quite clear that you would find it very difficult indeed to situate in relation to the drives that I have just named, in a historical succession, the *Schaulust*, or scopic drive, or even what I will later distinguish as the invocatory drive (*la pulsion invocante*), and to establish between them the slightest relation of deduction or genesis.

There is no natural metamorphosis of the oral drive into the anal drive. Whatever appearances may emerge to the contrary from the play of the symbol constituted, in other contexts, by the supposed anal object, namely, the faeces, in relation to the phallus in its negative effect, we can in no sense—experience shows us—consider that there is a continuity between the anal phase and the phallic phase, that there is a relation of natural metamorphosis.

We must consider the drive under the heading of the *konstante Kraft* that sustains it as a stationary tension. Let us take a look at the metaphors that Freud gives us to express these outlets. Take *Schub*, for example, which he immediately translates by the image that it bears in his mind, that of a spindle of lava, a material emission from the deflagration of energy that has occurred there in various successive stages, which complete, one after another, that form of return journey. Do we not see in the Freudian metaphor the embodiment of this fundamental structure—something that emerges from a rim, which redoubles its enclosed structure, following a course that returns, and of which nothing else ensures the consistency except the object, as something that must be circumvented.

This articulation leads us to make of the manifestation of the drive the mode of a headless subject, for everything is articulated in it in terms of tension, and has no relation to the subject other than one of topological community. I have been able to articulate the unconscious for you as being situated in the gaps that the distribution of the signifying investments sets up in the subject, and which figure in the algorithm in the form of a losange [$\lozenge$], which I place at the centre of any relation of the unconscious between reality and the subject. Well! It is in so far as something in the apparatus of the body is structured in the same way, it is because of the topological unity of the gaps in play, that the drive assumes its role in the functioning of the unconscious.

3

Let us now follow Freud when he talks to us about *Schaulust*, seeing, being seen. Is it the same thing? How can it even be sustained that it can be that, except by inscribing it in terms of signifiers? Or is there, then, some other mystery? There is a quite different one, and, in order to introduce you to it, I have only to point out that *Schaulust* is manifested in perversion. I stress that the drive is not perversion. What constitutes the enigmatic character of Freud's presentation derives precisely from the fact that he wishes to give us a radical structure—in which the subject is not yet placed. On the contrary, what defines perversion is precisely the way in which the subject is placed in it.

We must read Freud's text very attentively here. The value of Freud's texts on this matter, in which he is breaking new ground, is that like a good archaeologist, he leaves the work of the dig in place—so that, even if it is incomplete, we are able to discover what the excavated objects mean. When Mr Fenichel passes by the same ground, he does as one used to do, he gathers everything up, puts it in his pockets and in glass cases, without any kind of order, or at least in a completely arbitrary order, so that nothing can be found again.

What occurs in voyeurism? At the moment of the act of the voyeur, where is the subject, where is the object? I have told you that the subject is not there in the sense of seeing, at the level of the scopic drive. He is there as pervert and he is situated only at the culmination of the loop. As for the object—this is what my topology on the blackboard cannot show you, but can allow you to admit—the loop turns around itself, it is a missile, and it is with it, in perversion, that the target is reached.

The object, here, is the gaze—the gaze that is the subject, which attains it, which hits the bull's eye in target-shooting. I have only to remind you what I said of Sartre's analysis. Although this analysis brings out the agency of the gaze, it is not at the level of the other whose gaze surprises the subject looking through the keyhole. It is that the other surprises him, the subject, as entirely hidden gaze.

You grasp here the ambiguity of what is at issue when we speak of the scopic drive. The gaze is this object lost and suddenly refound in the conflagration of shame, by the introduction of the other. Up to that point, what is the subject trying to see? What he is trying to see, make no mistake, is the object as absence. What the voyeur is looking for and finds is merely a shadow, a shadow behind the curtain. There he will phantasize any magic of presence, the most graceful of girls, for example, even if on the other side there is only a hairy athlete. What he is looking for is not, as one says, the phallus—but precisely its absence, hence the pre-eminence of certain forms as objects of his search.

What one looks at is what cannot be seen. If, thanks to the

introduction of the other, the structure of the drive appears, it is really completed only in its reversed form, in its return form, which is the true active drive. In exhibitionism what is intended by the subject is what is realized in the other. The true aim of desire is the other, as constrained, beyond his involvement in the scene. It is not only the victim who is concerned in exhibitionism, it is the victim as referred to some other who is looking at him.

Thus in this text, we have the key, the nodus, of what has been so much an obstacle to the understanding of masochism. Freud articulated in the most categorical way that at the outset of the sado-masochistic drive, pain has nothing to do with it. It is a question of a *Herrschaft*, of *Bewältigung*, violence done to what?—to something that is so unspeakable that Freud arrives at the conclusion, and at the same time recoils from it, that its first model, in accordance with everything I have told you, is to be found in a violence that the subject commits, with a view to mastery, upon himself.

He recoils from it. And with good reason. The ascetic who flagellates himself does it for a third party. Now, this is not what he is trying to convey. He wishes only to designate the return, the insertion on one's own body, of the departure and the end of the drive.

At what moment, says Freud, *do we see the possibility of pain introduced into the sado-masochistic drive?*—the possibility of pain undergone by him who has become, at that moment, the subject of the drive. It is, he tells us, at the moment when the loop is closed, when it is from one pole to the other that there has been a reversal, when the other has come into play, when the subject has taken himself as the end, the terminus of the drive. At this moment, pain comes into play in so far as the subject experiences it from the other. He will become, will be able to become, in his theoretical deduction, a sadistic subject, in so far as the completed loop of the drive will have brought into play the action of the other. What is at issue in the drive is finally revealed here—the course of the drive is the only form of transgression that is permitted to the subject in relation to the pleasure principle.

The subject will realize that his desire is merely a vain detour with the aim of catching the *jouissance* of the other—in so far as the other intervenes, he will realize that there is a *jouissance* beyond the pleasure principle.

The forcing of the pleasure principle by the effect of the partial drive—it is by this that we may conceive that the partial, ambiguous drives are installed at the limit of an *Erhaltungstrieb*, of the maintenance of a homeostasis, of its capture by the veiled face that is that of sexuality.

It is in so far as the drive is evidence of the forcing of the pleasure principle that it provides us with evidence that beyond the *Real-Ich*, another reality intervenes, and we shall see by what return it is this other reality, in the last resort, that has given to this *Real-Ich* its structure and diversification.

QUESTIONS AND ANSWERS

J.-A. MILLER: *The question concerns the relation between the drive and the real, and the differences between the object of the drive, that of phantasy and that of desire.*

LACAN: The object of the drive is to be situated at the level of what I have metaphorically called a headless subjectification, a subjectification without subject, a bone, a structure, an outline, which represents one side of the topology. The other side is that which is responsible for the fact that a subject, through his relations with the signifier, is a subject-with-holes (*sujet troué*). These holes came from somewhere.

In his first constructions, his first networks of signifying crossroads to become stabilized, Freud was reaching towards something that, in the subject, is intended to maintain to the greatest possible degree what I have called homeostasis. This does not simply mean the crossing of a certain threshold of excitement, but also a distribution of ways. Freud even uses metaphors that assign a diameter to these ways, which permit the maintenance, the ever equal dispersal, of a certain investment.

Somewhere Freud says quite categorically that it is the pressure of what, in sexuality, has to be repressed in order to maintain the pleasure principle—namely, the libido—that has made possible the progress of the mental apparatus itself, as such and, for example, the establishment in the mental apparatus of that possibility of investment that we call *Aufmerksamkeit*, the possibility of attention. The determination of the functioning of the *Real-Ich*, which both satisfies the pleasure principle and, at the same time, is invested without defence by the upsurge of sexuality—this is what is responsible for its structure.

At this level, we are not even forced to take into account any subjectification of the subject. The subject is an apparatus. This apparatus is something lacunary, and it is in the lacuna that the subject establishes the function of a certain object, *qua* lost object. It is the status of the *objet a* in so far as it is present in the drive.

In the phantasy, the subject is frequently unperceived, but he is always there, whether in the dream or in any of the more or less developed forms of day-dreaming. The subject situates himself as determined by the phantasy.

The phantasy is the support of desire; it is not the object that is the support of desire. The subject sustains himself as desiring in relation to an ever more complex signifying ensemble. This is apparent enough in the form of the scenario it assumes, in which the subject, more or less recognizable, is somewhere, split, divided, generally double, in his relation to the object, which usually does not show its true face either.

Next time, I shall come back to what I have called the structure of perversion. Strictly speaking, it is an inverted effect of the phantasy. It is the subject who determines himself as object, in his encounter with the division of subjectivity.

I will show you—I must stop here today because of the time, I am very sorry to say—that the subject assuming this role of the object is precisely what sustains the reality of the situation of what is called the sado-masochistic drive, and which is only a single point, in the masochistic situation itself. It is in so far as the subject makes himself the object of another will that the sado-masochistic drive not only closes up, but constitutes itself.

It is only in a second stage, as Freud shows us in this text, that the sadistic desire is possible in relation to a phantasy. The sadistic desire exists in a crowd of configurations, and also in the neuroses, but it is not yet sadism in the strict sense.

I will ask you to look at my article *Kant avec Sade*, where you will see that the sadist himself occupies the place of the object, but without knowing it, to the benefit of another, for whose *jouissance* he exercises his action as sadistic pervert.

You see, then, several possibilities here for the function of the *objet a,* which is never found in the position of being the aim of desire. It is either pre-subjective, or the foundation of an identification of the subject, or the foundation of an identification disavowed by the subject. In this sense, sadism is merely the disavowal of masochism. This formula will make it possible to illuminate many things concerning the true nature of sadism.

But the object of desire, in the usual sense, is either a phantasy that is in reality the *support* of desire, or a lure.

On this subject of the lure, which poses at the same time all the previous quesions that you put forward just now concerning the relation of the subject to the real, the analysis that Freud gives of love enables us to make some progress.

The need Freud feels to refer to the relation of the *Ich* to the real in order to introduce the dialectic of love—whereas, strictly speaking, the neutral real is the desexualized real—is not introduced at the level of the drive. It is there that is to be found what, for us, will prove most valuable concerning how we should conceive of the function of love—namely, its fundamentally narcissistic structure.

There can be absolutely no doubt that there is a real. That the subject has a constructive relation with this real only within the narrow confines of the pleasure principle, of the pleasure principle unforced by the drive, this is—as we shall see next time—the point of emergence of the love object. The whole question is to discover how this love object may come to fulfill a role analogous with the object of desire—upon what equivocations does the possibility for the love object of becoming an object of desire rest?

Have I thrown some light on your question?

J.-A. MILLER: *Some light and some shadow.*

13 May 1964

15

FROM LOVE TO THE LIBIDO

The subject and the Other · The narcissistic field · Sexual difference ·
The field of the drive: making oneself . . . seen, heard, sucked, shitted ·
The myth of the lamella

Today I intend—this does not mean that I will have the time
to do so—to take you from love, at the threshold of which I left
things last time, to the libido.

I will say at the outset what will be the burden of this
elucidation by saying that the libido is not something fleeting
or fluid, it cannot be divided up, or accumulated, like magnet-
ism, in the centres of focusing offered it by the subject. The

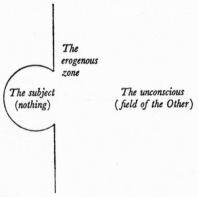

libido is to be conceived as an organ, in both senses of the term,
as organ-part of the organism and as organ-instrument.

I apologize if, as someone remarked last time, there are some
obscurities along the way I take you. I believe that obscurity is
characteristic of our field. Let us not forget that it is usual to
represent the unconscious as a cellar, even as a cave, by way of
allusion to Plato's cave. But it is not a good comparison. The
unconscious is much more like the bladder, and this bladder

can be seen only if one places a little light inside it. Why should one be surprised if it sometimes takes a little time for the light to come on?

In the subject who, alternately, reveals himself and conceals himself by means of the pulsation of the unconscious, we apprehend only partial drives. The *ganze Sexualstrebung*, the representation of the totality of the sexual drive, is not to be found there, Freud tells us. Following Freud, I will lead you along the path of this conclusion, and I would state quite clearly that everything I have learnt from my experience accords with it. I cannot expect everybody here to agree with it fully, since some of you do not have this experience, but your presence here is evidence of a certain trust in what we shall call—in the role in which I am in relation to you, that of the Other—good faith. This good faith is no doubt always a precarious assumption—for where, in the end, does this relation of the subject to the Other end?

What I, Lacan, following the traces of the Freudian excavation, am telling you is that the subject as such is uncertain because he is divided by the effects of language. Through the effects of speech, the subject always realizes himself more in the Other, but he is already pursuing there more than half of himself. He will simply find his desire ever more divided, pulverized, in the circumscribable metonymy of speech. The effects of language are always mixed with the fact, which is the basis of the analytic experience, that the subject is subject only from being subjected to the field of the Other, the subject proceeds from his synchronic subjection in the field of the Other. That is why he must get out, get himself out, and in the *getting-himself-out*, in the end, he will know that the real Other has, just as much as himself, to get himself out, to pull himself free. It is here that the need for good faith becomes imperative, a good faith based on the certainty that the same implication of difficulty in relation to the ways of desire is also in the Other.

The truth, in this sense, is that which runs after truth—and that is where I am running, where I am taking you, like Actaeon's hounds, after me. When I find the goddess's hiding place, I will no doubt be changed into a stag, and you can devour me, but we still have a little way to go yet.

I

Did I perhaps represent Freud to you last time as some such figure as Abraham, Isaac and Jacob? In his *Le Salut pour les juifs*, Léon Bloy depicts them as three equally old men who are there, according to one of the forms of Israel's vocation, squatting around some piece of canvas on the ground, engrossed in that eternal occupation of dealing in second-hand goods. They are sorting out the various objects on the canvas. Some things they put on one side, others on the other. On one side, Freud puts the partial drives and on the other love. He says—*They're not the same.*

The drives necessitate us in the sexual order—they come from the heart. To our great surprise, he tells us that love, on the other hand, comes from the belly, from the world of yum-yum.

It may come as a surprise, but it elucidates for us something fundamental to analytic experience, namely, that the genital drive, if it exists, is not at all articulated like the other drives —in spite of the love–hate ambivalence. In his premises, and in his own texts, Freud completely contradicts himself when he tells us that ambivalence may be regarded as one of the characteristics of the reversal of the *Verkehrung* of the drive. But when he examines it, he tells us quite clearly that ambivalence and reversion are not at all the same thing.

If, therefore, the genital drive does not exist, then it can get f . . . formed somewhere else, on the other side from the one in which the drive is to be found, on the left of my schema on the blackboard. You will have noticed already that it is on the right, in the field of the Other, that the genital drive has to find its form.

Well! This is precisely borne out by what we learn in the analytic experience, namely, that the genital drive is subjected to the circulation of the Oedipus complex, to the elementary and other structures of kinship. This is what is designated as the field of culture—somewhat inadequately, because this field is supposed to be based on a *no man's land* in which genitality as such subsists, whereas it is in fact dissolved, not re-assembled, for the *ganze Sexualstrebung* is nowhere apprehensible in the subject.

Yet because it is nowhere, it is nevertheless diffused, and it is this that Freud is trying to convey to us in this article.

Everything he says about love tends to emphasise the fact that, in order to conceive of love, we must necessarily refer to another sort of structure than that of the drive. He divides this structure into three, three levels—the level of the real, the level of the economic and the level of the biological.

To these levels correspond three oppositions. To the level of the real corresponds the that-which-interests/that-which-is-indifferent opposition. To the level of the economic, that-which-gives-pleasure/that-which-displeases. It is only at the level of the biological that the activity/passivity opposition presents itself, in its own form, the only valid one in its grammatical sense, the loving/being loved position.

We are invited by Freud to consider that love, in its essence, can be judged only as a sexual passion of the *gesamt Ich*. Now, in Freud, *gesamt Ich* is a *hapax*, which is to be understood in the sense suggested in his account of the pleasure principle. The *gesamt Ich* is the field that I have invited you to regard as a surface and a fairly limited surface so that the blackboard is able to represent it, and so that everything may be included in it on paper. I am referring to the network that is represented by arcs, lines linking points of convergence, of which the closed circle marks whatever is to be preserved in tensional homeostasis, in lower tension, in necessary diversion, in diffusion of excitement into innumerable channels—whenever it might be too intense in any one of them.

The filtering from stimulation to discharge is the apparatus, the dome, to be circumscribed on a sphere, in which is defined at first what he calls the stage of the *Real-Ich*. And it is to this that, later in his discourse, he attributes the qualification *autoerotisch*.

Analysts have concluded from this that—as it must be situated somewhere in what is called development, and since what Freud says is gospel—the infant must regard everything around him as indifferent. One wonders how things can go on, in a field of observers for whom articles of faith have such overwhelming value in relation to observation. For, after all, if there is one thing that cannot be said about the infant it is that he shows no interest in what enters his field of perception.

There can be no doubt that there are objects deriving from the earliest period of the neo-natal phase. *Autoerotisch* can in no way mean a lack of interest in them. If you read Freud on this, you will see that the second stage, the economic stage, consists precisely in that the second *Ich*—the second in a *de jure* sense, the second in logical sequence—is the *Lust-Ich*, which he calls *purifiziert*, the purified *Lust-Ich*, which is established in the field exterior to the dome in which I designate the first *Real-Ich* of Freud's explanation.

The *autoerotisch* consists in the fact—and Freud himself stresses this—that there would be no emergence of objects if there were no objects of use to me. This is the criterion of the emergence and distribution of objects.

Here, then, is constituted the *Lust-Ich*, and also the field of the *Unlust*, of the object as remainder, as alien. The object that one needs to know, and with good reason, is that which is defined in the field of *Unlust*, whereas the objects of the field of the *Lust-Ich* are lovable. The *hassen*, with its profound link with knowledge, is the other field.

At this level, there is no trace of drive functions, except those that are not true drives, and which Freud calls in his text the *Ichtriebe*. The level of the *Ich* is not that of the drive, and it is there—I would ask you to read the text very attentively—that Freud grounds love. Everything that is defined in this way at the level of the *Ich* assumes sexual value, passes from the *Erhaltungstrieb*, from preservation, to the *Sexualtrieb*, only in terms of the appropriation of each of these fields, its seizure, by one of the partial drives. Freud says quite clearly that *Vorhangung des Wesentlichen*, to bring out the essential here, it is in a purely passive, non-drive, way that the subject records the *äusseren Reize*, that which comes from the external world. Its activity comes only *durch seine eigene Triebe*, from its own drives. It is a question here of the diversity of the partial drives. In this way, we are brought to the third level that he introduces, that of activity/passivity.

Before noting the consequences of this, I would simply like to draw your attention to the classic character of this conception of love. Is there any need to stress that *se vouloir son bien*, to wish oneself one's own well being, is exactly the equivalent of what is traditionally called the physical theory of love, St Thomas's *velle bonum alicui*, which, for us, on account of the function of narcissism has exactly the same value. I have long stressed the specious character of this supposed altruism, which is pleased to preserve whose well being? — of him who, precisely, is necessary to us.

2

It is there, then, that Freud intends to set up the bases of love. It is only with activity/passivity that the sexual relation really comes into play.

Now, is the activity/passivity relation identical with the sexual relation? I would ask you to refer to a passage in the *Wolf-Man*, for example, or to various others scattered throughout the *Five Psycho-analyses*. There Freud explains in short that the polar reference activity/passivity is there in order to name, to cover, to metaphorize that which remains unfathomable in sexual difference. Nowhere does he ever say that, psychologically, the masculine/feminine relation is apprehensible otherwise than by the representative of the activity/passivity opposition. As such, the masculine/feminine opposition is never attained. This is sufficient indication of the importance of what is repeated here, in the form of a verb particularly appropriate in expressing what is at issue — this passivity/activity opposition is poured, moulded, injected. It is an arteriography, and even the masculine/feminine relations do no exhaust it.

Of course, it is well known that the activity/passivity opposition may account for many things in the domain of love. But what we are dealing with here is precisely this injection, one might say, of sado-masochism, which is not at all to be understood, as far as its properly sexual realization is concerned, as ready money.

Certainly, all the intervals of desire come into play in the sexual relation. *What value has my desire for you?* the eternal question that is posed in the dialogue of lovers. But the supposed value, for example, of *feminine masochism*, as it is called, should be subjected, parenthetically, to serious scrutiny. It belongs to a dialogue that may be defined, in many respects, as a masculine phantasy. There is every reason to believe that to sustain this phantasy would be an act of complicity on our part. In order not to deliver ourselves up completely to the results of Anglo-Saxon research, which is not worth very much on this subject, even if there is a certain amount of consent on the part of women in it, which means nothing—we analysts will confine ourselves, more legitimately, to the women in our own group. It is quite striking to see that the representatives of this sex in the analytic circle are particularly disposed to maintain the fundamental belief in feminine masochism. It may be that there is a veil here, concerning the interests of the sex, that should not be lifted too quickly. In any case, this is an excursion from our subject, but an excursion profoundly linked to it, as you will see, for we shall have to come back to a consideration of this link.

However, at this level, we can learn nothing from the field of love, that is to say, from the framework of narcissism, which, as Freud shows quite clearly in this article, is made up of the insertion of the *autoerotisch* in the organized interests of the ego.

Within this framework, there may well be a representation of the objects of the external world, choice and discernment, the possibility of knowledge, in short the whole field with which classical psychology concerned itself is included in it. But nothing—and that is why all psychology of the affections has, up to Freud, failed—nothing represents in it the Other, the radical Other, the Other as such.

This representation of the Other is lacking, specifically, between the two opposed worlds that sexuality designates for us in the masculine and the feminine. Carrying things as far as they will go, one might even say that the masculine ideal and the feminine ideal are represented in the psyche by something other than this activity/passivity opposition of which I spoke earlier. Strictly speaking, they spring from a term that I have not introduced, but of which one female psycho-analyst has pin-pointed the feminine sexual attitude—the term *masquerade*.

Masquerade is not that which comes into play in the display necessary, at the level of the animals, to coupling, and in any case display is usually to be seen on the side of the male. Masquerade has another meaning in the human domain, and that is precisely to play not at the imaginary, but at the symbolic, level.

It is on this basis that it now remains to us to show that sexuality as such comes into play, exercises its proper activity, through the mediation—paradoxical as that may seem—of the partial drives.

3

Everything Freud spells out about the partial drives shows us the movement that I outlined for you on the blackboard last time, that circular movement of the thrust that emerges through the erogenous rim only to return to it as its target, after having encircled something I call the *objet a*. I suggest —and a punctilious examination of this whole text is a test of the truth of what I propose—that it is in this way that the subject attains what is, strictly speaking, the dimension of the capital Other.

I suggest that there is a radical distinction between *loving oneself through the other*—which, in the narcissistic field of the object, allows no transcendence to the object included—and the circularity of the drive, in which the heterogeneity of the movement out and back shows a gap in its interval.

What have seeing and being seen in common? Let us take the *Schaulust*, the scopic drive. Freud certainly makes a distinction between *beschauen*, to look at an alien object, an object in the strict sense, and *beschaut werden*, being looked at by an alien person.

This is because an object and a person are not the same. At the end of the circle, let us say that they lose touch—or that the dotted line eludes us to some extent. Indeed, in order to link them together, it is at the base—where origin and point converge—that Freud must bring them together and try to forge a union between them—precisely at the point of return. He brings them together by saying that the root of the scopic drive is to be found entirely in the subject, in the fact that the subject sees himself.

But, because he is Freud, he does not fall into error here. It is not seeing oneself in the mirror, it is *Selbst ein Sexualglied beschauen*—*he looks at himself*, I would say, *in his sexual member*.

But, be careful! That's not right either. Because this statement is identified with its opposite—which is curious enough, and I am surprised that nobody has noticed the humorous side of it. This gives—*Sexualglied von eigener Person beschaut werden*. In a way, just as the number two delights at being odd, the sex, or widdler, delights at being looked at. Who has ever

really grasped the truly subject-making (*subjectivable*) character
of such a sentiment?

In fact, the articulation of the loop formed by the outward
and return movement of the drive is obtained very well by
changing only one of the terms in Freud's statement. I do not
change *eigenes Objekt*, the object in the strict sense, which is in
fact what the subject is reduced to and I do not change *von
fremder Person*, the other, of course, nor *beschaut*, but in place of
werden I put *machen*—what is involved in the drive is *making
oneself seen* (*se faire voir*). The activity of the drive is concentrated
in this *making oneself* (*se faire*), and it is by relating it to the *field*
of the other drives that we may be able to throw some light
upon it.

Unfortunately, I must move fairly quickly, and not only am I
cutting short, but I am filling in the gaps that Freud, surprisingly, left in his enumeration of the drives.

After *making oneself seen*, I will introduce another, *making
oneself heard*, of which Freud says nothing.

I must, very quickly, point out to you the difference between
making oneself heard and *making oneself seen*. In the field of the
unconscious the ears are the only orifice that cannot be closed.
Whereas *making oneself seen* is indicated by an arrow that really
comes back towards the subject, *making oneself heard* goes
towards the other. The reason for this is a structural one—it
was important that I should mention it in passing.

Let us turn to the oral drive. What is it? One speaks of
phantasies of devouring, *of being gobbled up*. Indeed, everyone
knows that this, verging on all the resonances of masochism, is
the altrified term of the oral drive. But why do we not get a
definite answer? Since we refer to the infant and the breast,
and since suckling is sucking, let us say that the oral drive is
getting sucked, it is the vampire.

Indeed, this throws some light on that singular object—which
I am trying to unstick in your minds from the food metaphor
—the breast. The breast is also something superimposed, who
sucks what?—the organism of the mother. Thus we see clearly
enough, at this level, the nature of the subject's claim to something that is separated from him, but belongs to him and which
he needs to complete himself.

At the level of the anal drive—you can now relax a bit—

things don't seem to work out like that at all. And yet, *se faire chier* has a meaning! When one says *here, on se fait rudement chier*, one has the *emmerdeur éternel* in mind.[1] It is quite wrong simply to identify the celebrated scybala with the function given it in the metabolism of obsessional neurosis. It is quite wrong to separate it from what it represents, a gift, as it happens, and from the relation it has with soiling, purification, catharsis. It is wrong not to see that it is from here that the function of oblativity emerges. In short, the object, here, is not very far from the domain that is called that of the soul.

What does this brief survey tell us? Does it not seem that the drive, in this turning inside out represented by its pocket, invaginating through the erogenous zone, is given the task of seeking something that, each time, responds in the Other? I will not go over the series again. Let us say that at the level of the *Schaulust*, it is the gaze. I point this out only to deal later with the effects on the Other of this movement of appeal.

4

I wish to note here the relation between the polarity of the drive cycle and something that is always at the centre. It is an organ, in the sense of an instrument, of the drive—in another sense, therefore, than that attributed to it earlier in the sphere of the induction of the *Ich*. We must now turn our attention to this ungraspable organ, this object that we can only circumvent, in short, this false organ.

The organ of the drive is situated in relation to the true organ. In order to make this clear to you and in order to show that this is the only pole that, in the domain of sexuality, is within our grasp, capable of being apprehended, I will take the liberty of setting a myth before you—and in doing so I shall take as my starting-point what is put into the mouth of Aristophanes on the subject of love in Plato's *Symposium*.

This usage presupposes of course that we give ourselves permission to use, in this judo with truth, the apparatus that I have always avoided using before my audiences.

[1] This sentence is strictly untranslatable on account of the play on words. *Se faire chier* means literally 'to get oneself shitted'. '*Tu me fais chier*' has the sense of 'you make me sick'. '*On se fait rudement chier*' means 'we were bored to death'. An '*emmerdeur*' (literally, a 'shitter') is a 'bore' [Tr.].

I have given my listeners ancient models, particularly those drawn from Plato, but I have merely given them the machinery to dig this field. I am not one of those who say—*Children, there is treasure buried here*—and leave them to get on with their digging. I have given them the plough share and the plough, namely, that the unconscious was made out of language, and at one point in time, approximately three and a half years ago, and three very good pieces of work have resulted from it. But we must now say—*You can only find the treasure in the way I tell you.*

There is something comical about this way. This is absolutely essential in understanding any of Plato's dialogues, and especially when one is dealing with the *Symposium*. This dialogue is even, one might say, a practical joke. The starting-point, on course, is Aristophanes' fable. This fable is a defiance to the centuries, for it traverses them without anyone trying to do better. I shall try.

In an attempt to establish what was said at the Congrès de Bonneval I managed to come up with something like the following—*I am going to talk to you about the lamella.*

If you want to stress its joky side, you can call it *l'hommelette*. This *hommelette*, as you will see, is easier to animate than primal man, in whose head one always had to place a homunculous to get it working.

Whenever the membranes of the egg in which the foetus emerges on its way to becoming a new-born are broken, imagine for a moment that something flies off, and that one can do it with an egg as easily as with a man, namely the *hommelette*, or the lamella.

The lamella is something extra-flat, which moves like the amoeba. It is just a little more complicated. But it goes everywhere. And as it is something—I will tell you shortly why —that is related to what the sexed being loses in sexuality, it is, like the amoeba in relation to sexed beings, immortal—because it survives any division, any scissiparous intervention. And it can run around.

Well! This is not very reassuring. But suppose it comes and envelopes your face while you are quietly asleep . . .

I can't see how we would not join battle with a being capable of these properties. But it would not be a very convenient battle. This lamella, this organ, whose characteristic is not to exist, but which is nevertheless an organ—I can give you more details as to its zoological place—is the libido.

It is the libido, *qua* pure life instinct, that is to say, immortal life, or irrepressible life, life that has need of no organ, simplified, indestructible life. It is precisely what is subtracted from the living being by virtue of the fact that it is subject to the cycle of sexed reproduction. And it is of this that all the forms of the *objet a* that can be enumerated are the representatives, the equivalents. The *objets a* are merely its representatives, its figures. The breast—as equivocal, as an element characteristic of the mammiferous organization, the placenta for example —certainly represents that part of himself that the individual loses at birth, and which may serve to symbolize the most profound lost object. I could make the same kind of reference for all the other objects.

The relation between the subject and the field of the Other becomes clearer. Take a look at what I have drawn in the lower part of the table. I will explain.

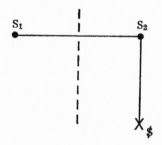

In the world of the *Real-Ich*, of the ego, of knowledge, everything may exist as now, including you and consciousness, without there being any need, whatever may be thought to the contrary, for anything in the way of a subject. If the subject is what I say it is, namely the subject determined by language and speech, it follows that the subject, *in initio*, begins in the locus of the Other, in so far as it is there that the first signifier emerges.

Now, what is a signifier? I have been drumming it into you long enough not to have to articulate it once again here. A signifier is that which represents a subject. For whom?—not for another subject, but for another signifier. In order to illustrate this axiom, suppose that in the desert you find a stone covered with hieroglyphics. You do not doubt for a moment that, behind them, there was a subject who wrote them. But it is an error to believe that each signifier is addressed to you—this is proved by the fact that you cannot understand any of it. On the other hand you define them as signifiers, by the fact that you are sure that each of these signifiers is related to each of the others. And it is this that is at issue with the relation between the subject and the field of the Other.

The subject is born in so far as the signifier emerges in the field of the Other. But, by this very fact, this subject—which, was previously nothing if not a subject coming into being —solidifies into a signifier.

The relation to the Other is precisely that which, for us, brings out what is represented by the lamella—not sexed polarity, the relation between masculine and feminine, but the relation between the living subject and that which he loses by having to pass, for his reproduction, through the sexual cycle.

In this way I explain the essential affinity of every drive with the zone of death, and reconcile the two sides of the drive —which, at one and the same time, makes present sexuality in the unconscious and represents, in its essence, death.

You will also understand that, if I have spoken to you of the unconscious as of something that opens and closes, it is because its essence is to mark that time by which, from the fact of being born with the signifier, the subject is born divided. The subject is this emergence which, just before, as subject, was nothing, but which, having scarcely appeared, solidifies into a signifier.

On this conjunction between the subject in the field of the drive and the subject as he appears in the field of the Other, on this effort to join oneself together, depends the fact that there is a support for the *ganze Sexualstrebung*. There is no other. Only there is the relation of the sexes represented at the level of the unconscious.

As for the rest, the sexual relation is handed over to the hazards of the field of the Other. It is handed over to the explanations that are given of it. It is handed over to the old woman of whom—it is not a pointless fable—Daphnis must learn what one must do to make love.

QUESTIONS AND ANSWERS

F. WAHL: *The question concerns the loss that the sexed living being is subjected to, then the activity/passivity articulation.*

LACAN: In fact, you have stressed one of the things lacking in what I have said. The lamella has a rim, it inserts itself into the erogenous zone, that is to say, in one of the orifices of the body, in so far as these orifices—all our experience shows this—are linked to the opening/closing of the gap of the unconscious.

The erogenous zones are linked to the unconscious because it is there that the presence of the living being becomes fixed. We have discovered that it is precisely the organ of the libido, the lamella, which links to the unconscious the so-called oral and anal drives, to which I would add the scopic drive and what one ought almost to call the invocatory drive, which has, as I told you in passing—nothing of what I say is mere joking—the privilege of not being able to close.

As to the relation between the drive and activity/passivity, I think I will be well enough understood if I say that at the level of the drive it is purely grammatical. It is support, artifice, which Freud uses in order to enable us to understand the outward-return movement of the drive. But I have repeated four or five times that we cannot reduce it purely and simply to a reciprocity. Today I have shown in the most articulated way possible that each of the three stages, *a, b, c,* with which Freud articulates each drive, must be replaced by the formula of *making oneself seen, heard* and the rest of the list I have given. This implies fundamentally activity, in which respect I come close to what Freud himself articulates when he distinguishes between the two fields, the field of the drives on the one hand, and the narcissistic field of love on the other, and stresses that at the level of love, there is a reciprocity of *loving* and *being loved,* and that, in the other field, it is a question of a pure activity *durch seine eigene Triebe,* for the subject. Do you follow me? In fact, it is obvious that, even in their supposedly passive phase, the exercise of a drive, a masochistic drive, for example, requires that the masochist give himself, if I may be permitted to put it in this way, a devil of a job.

29 May 1964

The Field of the Other
and back to the Transference

16

THE SUBJECT AND THE OTHER: ALIENATION

Sexual dynamics · Aphanisis · *The Piagetic error* · Vel · *Your money or your life!* · *The* why?

If psycho-analysis is to be constituted as the science of the unconscious, one must set out from the notion that the unconscious is structured like a language.

From this I have deduced a topology intended to account for the constitution of the subject.

At a time that I hope we have now put behind us, it was objected that in giving dominance to structure I was neglecting the dynamics so evident in our experience. It was even said that I went so far as to ignore the principle affirmed in Freudian doctrine that this dynamics is, in its essence, through and through, sexual.

I hope my seminar for this year, especially at the point at which it reached its culmen last time, has shown you that this dynamics is far from being ignored in my thinking.

I

I would remind you, for the benefit of those who were absent last time, that I added a quite new element to this dynamics, the use of which will become apparent later.

First, I stressed the division that I make by opposing, in relation to the entrance of the unconscious, the two fields of the subject and the Other. The Other is the locus in which is situated the chain of the signifier that governs whatever may be made present of the subject—it is the field of that living being in which the subject has to appear. And I said that it was on the side of this living being, called to subjectivity, that the drive is essentially manifested.

Every drive being, by its essence as drive, a partial drive, no drive represents—a notion that Freud raises for a moment when he asks himself whether it is love that realizes it—the totality of the *Sexualstrebung*, of the sexual tendency, as it might be conceived as making present in the psyche the function of *Fortpflanzung*, of reproduction, if this function entered the psyche at all.

Who would not accept this function on the biological plane? What I am saying, following Freud, who provides abundant evidence of it, is that this function is not represented as such in the psyche. In the psyche, there is nothing by which the subject may situate himself as a male or female being.

In his psyche, the subject situates only equivalents of the function of reproduction—activity and passivity, which by no means represent it in an exhaustive way. Freud even adds a touch of irony to this by stressing that this representation is not as constricting or as exhaustive as that—*durchgreifend aussch-lieblich*—the polarity of the male and the female being is represented only by the polarity of activity, which is manifested through the *Triebe*, and of passivity, which is passivity only in relation to the exterior, *gegen die äusseren Reize*.

Only this division—and it is here that I left off last time—makes necessary what was first revealed by analytic experience, namely, that the ways of what one must do as man or as woman are entirely abandoned to the drama, to the scenario, which is placed in the field of the Other—which, strictly speaking, is the Oedipus complex.

I stressed this last time, when I told you that the human being has always to learn from scratch from the Other what he has to do, as man or as woman. I referred to the old woman in the story of Daphnis and Chloe, which shows us that there is an ultimate field, the field of sexual fulfilment, in which, in the last resort, the innocent does not know the way.

Whether it is the drive, the partial drive, that orientates him to it, or whether the partial drive alone is the representative in the psyche of the consequences of sexuality, this is a sign that sexuality is represented in the psyche by a relation of the subject that is deduced from something other than sexuality itself. Sexuality is established in the field of the subject by a way that is that of lack.

Two lacks overlaps here. The first emerges from the central

defect around which the dialectic of the advent of the subject
to his own being in the relation to the Other turns—by the fact
that the subject depends on the signifier and that the signifier
is first of all in the field of the Other. This lack takes up the
other lack, which is the real, earlier lack, to be situated at the
advent of the living being, that is to say, at sexed reproduction.
The real lack is what the living being loses, that part of himself
qua living being, in reproducing himself through the way of sex.
This lack is real because it relates to something real, namely,
that the living being, by being subject to sex, has fallen under
the blow of individual death.

Aristophanes' myth pictures the pursuit of the complement
for us in a moving, and misleading, way, by articulating that it
is the other, one's sexual other half, that the living being seeks
in love. To this mythical representation of the mystery of love,
analytic experience substitutes the search by the subject, not of
the sexual complement, but of the part of himself, lost forever,
that is constituted by the fact that he is only a sexed living being,
and that he is no longer immortal.

You will now understand that—for the same reason that it
is through the lure that the sexed living being is induced into
his sexual realization—the drive, the partial drive, is profoundly a death drive and represents in itself the portion of
death in the sexed living being.

Thus defying, perhaps for the first time in history, a myth
that has acquired so much prestige, and which last time I placed
under the same heading as Plato places that of Aristophanes, I
substituted the myth intended to embody the missing part,
which I called the myth of the lamella.

This is new and it is important because it designates the
libido not as a field of forces, but as an organ.

The libido is the essential organ in understanding the nature
of the drive. This organ is unreal. Unreal is not imaginary.
The unreal is defined by articulating itself on the real in a way
that eludes us, and it is precisely this that requires that its
representation should be mythical, as I have made it. But the
fact that it is unreal does not prevent an organ from embodying
itself.

I will give you its materialization at once. One of the most
ancient forms in which this unreal organ is incarnated in the

body, is tattooing, scarification. The tattoo certainly has the function of being for the Other, of situating the subject in it, marking his place in the field of the group's relations, between each individual and all the others. And, at the same time, it obviously has an erotic function, which all those who have approached it in reality have perceived.

I have also shown that, in the profound relation of the drive, what is essential is that the movement by which the arrow that sets out towards the target fulfills its function only by really re-emerging from it, and returning on to the subject. In this sense, the pervert is he who, in short circuit, more directly than any other, succeeds in his aim, by integrating in the most profound way his function as subject with his existence as desire. Here the reversal of the drive is something quite different from the variation of ambivalence that makes the object oscillate from the field of hate to that of love and vice versa, depending on whether or not it benefits the well-being of the subject. It is not when the object in one's sights is not good that one becomes a masochist. It is not because her father disappointed her that Freud's female patient (known as 'the homosexual') becomes homosexual—she could have taken a lover. Whenever we are in the dialectic of the drive, something else takes charge. The dialectic of the drive is profoundly different both from that which belongs to the order of love and from that which belongs to the well-being of the subject.

That is why today I wish to stress the operation of the realization of the subject in his signifying dependence in the locus of the Other.

2

Everything emerges from the structure of the signifier. This structure is based on what I first called the function of the cut and which is now articulated, in the development of my discourse, as the topological function of the rim.

The relation of the subject to the Other is entirely produced in a process of gap. Without this, anything could be there. The relations between beings in the real, including all of you animated beings out there, might be produced in terms of inversely reciprocal relations. This is what psychology, and a whole area of sociology, is trying to do, and may succeed in doing as far as the mere animal kingdom is concerned, for the capture of the imaginary is enough to motivate all sorts of behaviour in the living being. Psycho-analysis reminds us that human psychology belongs to another dimension.

To maintain this dimension, philosophical analysis might have sufficed, but it has proved itself to be inadequate, for lack of any adequate definition of the unconscious. Psycho-analysis, then, reminds us that the facts of human psychology cannot be conceived in the absence of the function of the subject defined as the effect of the signifier.

Here the processes are to be articulated, of course, as circular between the subject and the Other—from the subject called to the Other, to the subject of that which he has himself seen appear in the field of the Other, from the Other coming back. This process is circular, but, of its nature, without reciprocity. Because it is circular, it is disymmetrical.

You will realize that today I am taking you on to the terrain of a logic whose essential importance I hope to stress.

The whole ambiguity of the sign derives from the fact that it represents something for someone. This someone may be many things, it may be the entire universe, in as much as we have known for some time that information circulates in it, as a negative of entropy. Any node in which signs are concentrated, in so far as they represent something, may be taken for a someone. What must be stressed at the outset is that a signifier is that which represents a subject for another signifier.

The signifier, producing itself in the field of the Other, makes manifest the subject of its signification. But it functions as a signifier only to reduce the subject in question to being no more than a signifier, to petrify the subject in the same movement in which it calls the subject to function, to speak, as subject. There, strictly speaking, is the temporal pulsation in which is established that which is the characteristic of the departure of the unconscious as such—the closing.

One analyst felt this at another level and tried to signify it in a term that was new, and which has never been exploited since in the field of analysis—*aphanisis*, disappearance. Ernest Jones, who invented it, mistook it for something rather absurd, the fear of seeing desire disappear. Now, *aphanisis* is to be situated in a more radical way at the level at which the subject manifests himself in this movement of disappearance that I have described as lethal. In a quite different way, I have called this movement the *fading* of the subject.

I wish to dwell on this for a moment in order to convey to you to what extent it is always possible to find oneself again in concrete experience, and even in observation, on condition that this key is used to lift the veil of blindness. I will show you this by means of an example.

The Piagetic error—for those who might think that this is a neologism, I would stress that I am referring to Monsieur Piaget—is an error that lies in the notion of what is called the *egocentric* discourse of the child, defined as he stage at which he lacks what this Alpine psychology calls reciprocity. Reciprocity is very far from the horizon of what we mean at that particular moment, and the notion of egocentric discourse is a misunderstanding. The child, in this discourse, which may be tape-recorded, does not speak for himself, as one says. No doubt, he does not address the other, if one uses here the theoretical distinction derived from the function of the *I* and the *you*. But there must be others there—it is while all these little fellows are there, indulging all together, for example, in little games of operations, as they are provided with in certain methods of so-called active education, it is there that they speak—they don't speak to a particular person, they just speak, if you'll pardon the expression, *à la can*tonade.[1]

This egocentric discourse is a case of *hail to the good listener*!

What we find once again here is the constitution of the subject in the field of the Other, as I have designated it for you in this little arrow on the blackboard. If he is apprehended at his birth in the field of the Other, the characteristic of the subject of the unconscious is that of being, beneath the signifier that develops its networks, its chains and its history, at an indeterminate place.

More than one dream element, indeed almost all, may be the point at which we will variously situate him in interpretation. If one thinks that one may make him say whatever one wishes, one has understood nothing—but one must admit that psycho-

[1] To speak 'à la cantonade' is to speak to nobody in particular, to the company at large. By stressing the first letters of the phrase, Lacan is punning on his own name [Tr.].

analysts do not explain themselves very well. Interpretation cannot be bent to any meaning. It designates only a single series of signifiers. But the subject may in effect occupy various places, depending on whether one places him under one or other of these signifiers.

I now come to the two operations that I intend to articulate today in the relation between the subject and the Other.

3

The rim process, the circular process, the relation in question is to be supported by the small losange that I used as algorithm in my graph precisely because it is necessary in integrating some of the finished products of this dialectic.

It is impossible not to integrate it, for example, in phantasy itself—it is $ ◇ a [barred S, punch, petit a]. It is impossible not to integrate it also in that radical node in which are conjoined demand and drive, designated by the $◇D [barred S, punch, capital D], which might be called the cry.

Let us keep with this little losange. It is a rim, a functioning rim. One has only to provide it with a vectorial direction, here anti-clockwise—this is governed by the fact that, at least in our writing, you read things from left to right.

Be careful! They are supports for your thought that are not without artifice, but there is no topology that does not have to be supported by some artifice—it is precisely the result of the fact that the subject depends on the signifier, in other words, on a certain impotence in your thinking.

The small V of the lower half of the losange, let us say here that it is the *vel* constituted by the first operation, where I wish to leave you for a moment.

Indeed, you may find that these things are all rather silly. But logic always is a bit silly. If one does not go to the root of the childish, one is inevitably precipitated into stupidity, as can be shown by innumerable examples, such as the supposed antinomies of reason, for example, the catalogue of all the catalogues that do not include themselves, and one arrives at an impasse, which, I can't think why, gives logicians vertigo. Yet the solution is very simple, it is that the signifier with which one designates the same signifier is evidently not the same signifier as the one with which one designates the other—this is obvious enough. The word *obsolete*, in so far as it may signify that the word *obsolete* is itself an *obsolete* word, is not the same word *obsolete* in each case. This ought to encourage us to develop this *vel* that I have introduced to you.

The subject is grounded in the *vel* of the first essential operation. To be sure, it is not at all without interest to develop it here, before so vast an audience, since it is a question of nothing less than that operation that we call *alienation*.

One has to admit that there is a lot of this alienation about nowadays. Whatever one does, one is always a bit more alienated, whether in economics, politics, psycho-pathology, aesthetics, and so on. It may be no bad thing to see what the root of this celebrated alienation really is.

Does it mean, as I seem to be saying, that the subject is condemned to seeing himself emerge, *in initio*, only in the field of the Other? Could it be that? Well, it isn't. Not at all—not at all — not at all.

Alienation consists in this *vel*, which—if you do not object to the word *condemned*, I will use it—condemns the subject to appearing only in that division which, it seems to me, I have just articulated sufficiently by saying that, if it appears on one side as meaning, produced by the signifier, it appears on the other as *aphanisis*.

There is a *vel* that is worth illustrating, in order to differentiate it from the other uses of the *vel*, of the *or*. There are two of them. You know, from your earliest lessons in logic, that there is the exclusive *vel*—I go *either* there *or* there—if I go there, I do not go there, I have to choose. There is another way of using *vel*—I go to one side or the other, I don't care, one's as good as the other. These two *vels* are not alike. Well, there is a third, and in order not to mislead you, I will tell you straight away what it is intended for.

Symbolic logic, which is very useful in bringing a little light into so tricky a domain, teaches us to distinguish the implications of the operation that we call joining. To speak as one speaks when it is a question of sets, adding two collections together is not identical to joining them. If in this circle, that on the left, there are five objects, and if, in the other, there are also five—adding them together makes ten. But some of them may belong to both circles. If there are two that belong to each of the two circles, joining them together will in this instance consist not in doubling their number—there will be in all only eight objects. I apologize if I am being naive in reminding you of this, but it is in order to give you the notion that this *vel* that I will try to articulate for you is supported only on the logical form of joining.

The *vel* of alienation is defined by a choice whose properties

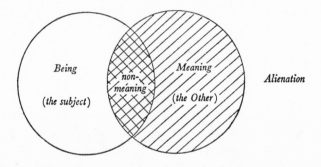

depend on this, that there is, in the joining, one element that, whatever the choice operating may be, has as its consequence a *neither one, nor the other*. The choice, then, is a matter of knowing whether one wishes to preserve one of the parts, the other disappearing in any case.

Let us illustrate this with what we are dealing with here, namely, the being of the subject, that which is there beneath the meaning. If we choose being, the subject disappears, it eludes us, it falls into non-meaning. If we choose meaning, the meaning survives only deprived of that part of non-meaning that is, strictly speaking, that which constitutes in the realization of the subject, the unconscious. In other words, it is of the nature of this meaning, as it emerges in the field of the Other, to be in a large part of its field, eclipsed by the disappearance of being, induced by the very function of the signifier.

This, as I have said, has a quite direct implication that passes all too often unperceived—when I tell you what it is, you will see that it is obvious, but for all that it is not usually noticed. One of the consequences is that interpretation is not limited to providing us with the significations of the way taken by the psyche that we have before us. This implication is no more than a prelude. Interpretation is directed not so much at the meaning as towards reducing the non-meaning of the signifiers, so that we may rediscover the determinants of the subject's entire behaviour.

I would ask you to refer to what my pupil Leclaire contributed, at the Congrès de Bonneval, by way of an application of my theses. You will see in his contribution that he isolated the sequence of the unicorn, not, as was thought in the discussion,

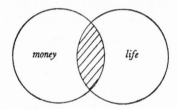

in its significatory dependence, but precisely in its irreducible and senseless character *qua* chain of signifiers.

One cannot emphasise too strongly the importance of some such thing as I have just described for you here. This alienating *or* is not an arbitrary invention, nor is it a matter of *how one sees things*. It is a part of language itself. This *or* exists. It is so much a part of language that one should distinguish it when one is dealing with linguistics. I will give you an example at once.

Your money or your life! If I choose the money, I lose both. If I choose life, I have life without the money, namely, a life deprived of something. I think I have made myself clear.

It is in Hegel that I have found a legitimate justification for the term alienating *vel*. What does Hegel mean by it? To cut a long story short, it concerns the production of the primary alienation, that by which man enters into the way of slavery. *Your freedom or your life!* If he chooses freedom, he loses both immediately—if he chooses life, he has life deprived of freedom.

There must be something special about this. This something

special we shall call the *lethal factor*. This factor is present in certain divisions shown us by the play of signifiers that we sometimes see at play at the heart of life itself—these are called chromosomes, and it sometimes happens that there is one among them that has a lethal function. We shall find a parallel to this function in a rather peculiar statement, by introducing death itself into one of these fields.

For example, *freedom or death!* There, because death comes into play, there occurs an effect with a rather different structure. This is because, in both cases, I will have both. Freedom, after all, as you know, is like the celebrated freedom to work, for which the French Revolution, it seems, was fought. It can also be the freedom to die of hunger—in fact, that's what it amounted to throughout the nineteenth century, which is why, since then, certain principles have had to be revised. You choose freedom. Well! You've got freedom to die. Curiously enough, in the conditions in which someone says to you, *freedom or death!*, the only proof of freedom that you can have in the conditions laid out before you is precisely to choose death, for there, you show that you have freedom of choice.

At this moment, which is also a Hegelian moment, for it is what is called the Terror, this quite different division is intended to make clear for you what is, in this field, the essence of the alienating *vel*, the lethal factor.

4

Given the time, I can do no more here than introduce the second operation. It completes the circularity of the relation of the subject to the Other, but an essential twist is revealed in it.

Whereas the first phase is based on the sub-structure of joining, the second is based on the sub-structure that is called intersection or product. It is situated precisely in that same lunula in which you find the form of the gap, the rim.

The intersection of two sets is constituted by the elements that belong to the two sets. It is here that the second operation in which the subject is led by this dialectic takes place. It is as essential to define the second operation as the first, because it is there that we shall see the emergence of the field of the transference. I shall call it—introducing my second new term here —*separation*.

Separare, to separate—I would point out at once the equivocation of the *se parare*, of the *se parer*, in all the fluctuating meanings it has in French. It means not only to dress oneself, but also to defend oneself, to provide oneself with what one needs to be on one's guard, and I will go further still, and Latinists will bear me out, to the *se parere*, the *s'engendrer*, the *to be engendered*, which is involved here. How, at this level, has the subject to procure himself? For that is the origin of the word that designates in Latin *to engender*. It is juridical, as indeed, curiously enough, are all the words in Indo-European that designate *to put into the world*. The word *parturition* itself originates in a word which, in its root, simply means to procure a child from the husband—a juridical and, it should be said, social operation.

Next time, I shall try to show how, like the function of the alienating *vel*, so different from the other *vels* defined so far, use is to be made of this notion of intersection. We shall see how it emerges from the superimposition of two lacks.

A lack is encountered by the subject in the Other, in the very intimation that the Other makes to him by his discourse. In the intervals of the discourse of the Other, there emerges in the experience of the child something that is radically mappable, namely, *He is saying this to me, but what does he want?*

In this interval intersecting the signifiers, which forms part of the very structure of the signifier, is the locus of what, in other registers of my exposition, I have called metonymy. It is there that what we call desire crawls, slips, escapes, like the ferret. The desire of the Other is apprehended by the subject in that which does not work, in the lacks of the discourse of the Other, and all the child's *whys* reveal not so much an avidity for the reason of things, as a testing of the adult, a *Why are you telling me this?* ever-resuscitated from its base, which is the enigma of the adult's desire.

Now, to reply to this hold, the subject, like Gribouille, brings the answer of the previous lack, of his own disappearance, which he situates here at the point of lack perceived in the Other. The first object he proposes for this parental desire whose object is unknown is his own loss—*Can he lose me?* The phantasy of one's death, of one's disappearance, is the first object that the subject has to bring into play in this dialectic, and he does indeed bring it into play—as we know from innumerable cases, such as in anorexia nervosa. We also know that the phantasy of one's death is usually manipulated by the child in his love relations with his parents.

One lack is superimposed upon the other. The dialectic of the objects of desire, in so far as it creates the link between the desire of the subject and the desire of the Other—I have been telling you for a long time now that it is one and the same—this dialectic now passes through the fact that the desire is not replied to directly. It is a lack engendered from the previous time that serves to reply to the lack raised by the following time.

I think I have sufficiently stressed the two elements that I have tried to present today, in this new and fundamental logical argument—non-reciprocity and the twist in the return.

QUESTIONS AND ANSWERS

J.-A. MILLER: *Do you not wish to show, all the same, that the alienation of a subject who has received the definition of being born in, constituted by, and ordered in a field that is exterior to him, is to be distinguished radically from the alienation of a consciousness-of-self? In short, are we to understand—Lacan against Hegel?*

LACAN: What you have just said is very good, it's exactly the opposite of what Green just said to me—he came up to me, shook my paw, at least morally, and said, *The death of structuralism, you are the son of Hegel.* I don't agree. I think that in saying Lacan *against* Hegel, you are much closer to the truth, though of course it is not at all a philosophical debate.

DR GREEN: *The sons kill the fathers!*

27 May 1964

17

THE SUBJECT AND THE OTHER: APHANISIS

The question of the Vorstellungsrepräsentanz · *Freedom · Representation and the Hegelian lure · Descartes' desire · Scepticism, certainty and the subject who is supposed to know · Small letters · The value of the Pavlovian experiment*

When I said, at the beginning of these talks — *I do not seek, I find*, I meant that, in Freud's field, one has only to bend down and pick up what is to be found. The real implication of the *nachträglich*, for example, has been ignored, though it was there all the time and had only to be picked up. I also remember the surprise of someone who was on the same track as I, seeing one day what could be done with the *einziger Zug*, the single stroke.

Today I would like to show you the importance, already designated by my schema last time, of what Freud calls, at the level of repression, the *Vorstellungsrepräsentanz*.

I

Vorstellung invoves a sort of defect that leads the German language to put unwarranted *ss*, which cannot be attached to the normal declension of the determinate, but which are necessary to it when forming composite words. There are therefore two terms — *Vorstellung, Repräsentanz*.

I spoke to you last time about the form of alienation, which I illustrated with several examples, and which I told you could be articulated in a *vel* of a very special nature. Today we might try to articulate it in some other ways. For example — *not* something . . . *without* something else. The dialectic of the slave is obviously *no freedom without life*, but there will be no life for him without freedom. From one to the other there is a necessary condition. This necessary condition becomes precisely the adequate reasons that, causes the loss of the original requirement.

Perhaps this is something like what also happens among some of my followers. There is no way of following me without passing through my signifiers, but to pass through my signifiers involves this feeling of alienation that incites them to seek, according to Freud's formula the small difference. Unfortunately, this small difference makes them lose the full significance of the direction I pointed out to them. Heavens, I am not so touchy, I leave everyone to go his own way in the direction that I point out —but I could have done without having to take note of what seemed to a particular individual so worthy of rectification in the translation that I had first given of this *Vorstellungsrepräsentanz*.

I had noted that Freud stresses the fact that repression bears on something that is of the order of representation that he calls the *Vorstellungsrepräsentanz*.

As soon as I introduced this remark several years ago— which was also a way of reading what Freud writes under the heading of *Verdrängung*, the article that follows the one on the unconscious in the series of texts collected together under the term *metapsychological*—I insisted on the fact that Freud emphasizes that it is not the affect that is repressed. The affect —and we shall see what this means in our theory—goes off somewhere else, as best it can. There will always be enough professors of psychology to justify with the patient that its meaning is to be found precisely where it is no longer in its place. So I inisited on the fact that what is repressed is not the represented of desire, the signification, but *the representative (le représentant)* —I translated literally—*of the representation (de la représentation)*.

Here the function of alienation intervenes for this or that individual, who, more or less animated by a care for the privileges of university authority, and anxious to enter the lists, claims to correct the translation that I have given. The *Vorstellungsrepräsentanz* is the *representative representative (le représentant représentatif)*, let us say.

This doesn't seem to amount to very much. But in a little book on psycho-somatics that has just appeared, one finds a whole passage arguing that there is some misunderstanding in something that must be called my theory of desire and, in a small note referring to some inaccessible passage taken from the text offered by two of my pupils, it is stressed that, following me, they make desire the representative representative of need. I'm not questioning whether in fact my pupils wrote that—we have been unable to find the passage in question—the important thing is that the only pertinent remark in this extremely slight book is as follows—*we would say rather that desire is the non-representative representative.*

Now, that is precisely what I mean, and say—for what I mean, I say—in translating *Vorstellungsrepräsentanz* by representative of the representation.

We can locate this *Vorstellungsrepräsentanz* in our schema of the original mechanisms of alienation in that first signifying coupling that enables us to conceive that the subject appears first in the Other, in so far as the first signifier, the unary signifier, emerges in the field of the Other and represents the subject for another signifier, which other signifier has as its effect the *aphanisis* of the subject. Hence the division of the subject—when the subject appears somewhere as meaning, he is manifested elsewhere as 'fading', as disappearance. There is, then, one might say, a matter of life and death between the unary signifier and the subject, *qua* binary signifier, cause of his disappearance. The *Vorstellungsrepräsentanz* is the binary signifier.

This signifier constitutes the central point of the *Urverdrängung*—of what, from having passed into the unconscious, will be, as Freud indicates in his theory, the point of *Anziehung*, the point of attraction, through which all the other repressions will be possible, all the other similar passages in the locus of the *Unterdrückt*, of what has passed underneath as signifier. This is what is involved in the term *Vorstellungsrepräsentanz*.

That by which the subject finds the return way of the *vel* of alienation is the operation I called, the other day, separation. By separation, the subject finds, one might say, the weak point of the primal dyad of the signifying articulation, in so far as it is alienating in essence. It is in the interval between these two signifiers that resides the desire offered to the mapping of the subject in the experience of the discourse of the Other, of the first Other he has to deal with, let us say, by way of illustration, the mother. It is in so far as his desire is beyond or falls short of what she says, of what she hints at, of what she brings out as meaning, it is in so far as his desire is unknown, it is in this point of lack, that the desire of the subject is constituted. The subject—by a process that is not without deception, which is not without presenting that fundamental twist by which what the subject rediscovers is not that which animates his movement of rediscovery—comes back, then, to the initial point, which is that of his lack as such, of the lack of his *aphanisis*.

We will come back in greater detail to the consequences that flow from it for the analytic treatment itself, and we shall see that this twist effect is essential in integrating the emergence phase of the transference. For the moment, I would like to dwell on what is essential in the function of desire, namely, that it is in as much as the subject plays his part in separation that the binary signifier, the *Vorstellungsrepräsentanz*, is *unterdrückt*, sunk underneath.

The thing is essential if we are to articulate properly—it immediately throws some light on very different regions—what is the sign of interpretation.

It might be useful in passing to bring out—however metaphysical it may seem, but in any case our technique often makes use, as if it were self-evident, of the expression *to free something* —it might be useful to remark that it is there that the whole business of this term freedom, which certainly merits the description of phantom, is played out. What the subject has to free himself of is the aphanisic effect of the binary signifier and, if we look at it more closely, we shall see that in fact it is a question of nothing else in the function of freedom.

It is not for nothing that having had to justify the term *vel* of alienation at the level of our experience, the two most obvious supports to occur to us were those two choices which, by their formula, structure, firstly, the position of the slave and, secondly, the position of the master. When the slave is confronted with the choice of his freedom or his life, he decides, *no freedom without life*—life remains forever deprived of freedom. And, when we stand back to look at things, we will see that the alienation of the master is structured in exactly the same way. For if Hegel shows us that the status of the master is established in the struggle to the death of pure prestige, it is because it is to bring his choice through death that the master also constitutes his fundamental alienation.

Certainly, one can say that the master is no more spared by

death than is his slave, that he will always die in the end, and that this is the limit of his freedom. But to say this is insufficient for this death is not the death that constitutes the alienating choice of the master, the death of the struggle to the death of pure prestige. The revelation of the essence of the master is manifested at the moment of terror, when it is to him that one says *freedom or death*, and then he has obviously only death to choose in order to have freedom. The supreme image of the master is that character in Claudelian tragedy, Sygne de Coûfontaine, of whom I have spoken at length in one of my seminars. It is she who wished to abandon nothing of her register, the register of the master, and the values to which she sacrifices bring her, over and above her sacrifice, no more than the need to renounce, in all its depths, her very being. It is in so far as, through the sacrifice of these values, she is forced to renounce her essence, her very being, her most intimate being, that she illustrates, in the end, how much radical alienation of freedom there is in the master himself.

2

Do I need to stress that we must understand *Repräsentanz* here in the sense in which things happens at the real level, where communication takes place in every human domain.

We mean by representatives what we understand when we use the phrase, for example, the representative of France. What do diplomats do when they address one another? They simply exercise, in relation to one another, that function of being pure representatives and, above all, their own signification must not intervene. When diplomats are addressing one another, they are supposed to represent something whose signification, while constantly changing, is, beyond their own persons, France, Britain, etc. In the very exchange of views, each must record only what the other transmits in his pure function as signifier, he must not take into account what the other is, *qua* presence, as a man who is likable to a greater or lesser degree. Interpsychology is an impurity in this exchange.

The term *Repräsentanz* is to be taken in this sense. The signifier has to be understood in this way, it is at the opposite pole from signification. Signification, on the other hand, comes into play in the *Vorstellung*.

It is with the *Vorstellung* that we are dealing in psychology, when the objects of the world are taken in charge, in some way, under the parenthesis of a subject in which a whole series of a, a', a", etc., unfolds. Here is situated the subjectivity on which the theory of knowledge is suspended. Of course, every representation requires a subject, but this subject is never a pure subject. If one believes that each subject is sustained in the world with his original—in both senses of the word (*originale ou originelle*)—*Weltanschauung*, then the path of truth passes—as a backward psychology or psycho-sociology is still showing us —through the inquiry, the totalization, the statistics of different *Weltanschauung*. And things might be thus, were there in the world subjects, each entrusted with the task of representing certain conceptions of the world.

Indeed, this is the essential flaw in philosophical idealism which, in any case, cannot be sustained and has never been radically sustained. There is no subject without, somewhere, *aphanisis* of the subject, and it is in this alienation, in this fundamental division, that the dialectic of the subject is established.

In order to answer the question I was asked last time concerning my adhesion to the Hegelian dialectic, is it not enough that I should answer that, because of the *vel*, the sensitive point, point of balance, there is an emergence of the subject at the level of meaning only from its *aphanisis* in the Other locus, which is that of the unconscious? Furthermore, this involves no mediation, and I promise, if I am provoked into doing so, to show that the effective experience that has been established in the perspective of an absolute knowledge never leads us to anything that may, in any way, illustrate the Hegelian vision of successive syntheses, nothing that provides even so much as a hint of the moment that Hegel in some obscure way links to this stage, and which someone has been pleased to illustrate by the title of *Dimanche de la vie*—when no opening remains in the heart of the subject.

I should indicate here where the Hegelian lure proceeds from. It is included in the approach of the Cartesian *I think*, in which I designated the inaugural point that introduces, in history, in our experience, in our necessity, the *vel* of alienation, which prevents us for ever from misunderstanding it. It is in the Cartesian approach that the *vel* was taken for the first time as the constituent of the dialectic of the subject, which now cannot be eliminated in his radical foundation.

This reference will be useful to me in characterizing the experience of the transference, so I shall be returning to it later in order to articulate certain of its features.

3

What distinguishes the Cartesian approach from the ancient search of the *episteme*, what distinguishes it from the scepticism that has been one of its terms, is what we shall try to articulate on the basis of the double function of alienation and separation.

What is Descartes looking for? He is looking for certainty. *I have*, he says, *an extreme desire to learn to distinguish the true from the false*—note the word *desire*—*in order to see clearly*—in what?— *in my actions, and to walk with assurance in this life.*

Is not this something quite different from the aim of knowledge? This approach is not that of a dialectician or a professor, still less that of a cavalier. It has been stressed that Descartes' biography is marked above all by his wanderings in the world, his encounters and, after all, his secret ambition— *Larvatus prodeo.* If I point this out, although I am one of those who regard concern for biography as secondary to the meaning of a work, it is because Descartes himself stresses that his biography, his approach, is essential to the communication of his method, of the way he has found to truth.

He makes it quite clear that what he has given is not—as Bacon tried to do some years earlier—the general means of conducting one's reason correctly, without abdicating it, for example, to experience. It is his own method, in so far as he set out in this direction with the desire to learn to distinguish the true from the false in order to see clearly—in what?—*in my actions.* This example, then, is a particular one, and Descartes goes so far as to add that if what was for me, at a particular moment, my way, does not seem right for others, that is their affair, that they should gather from my experience what they think is worth gathering. This forms part of the introduction by Descartes of his own way to science.

Does this mean that no knowledge is aimed at? Does it mean that knowledge weighs lightly in Descartes? Not at all, it is with this that he begins—there's enough knowledge around and to spare, there always has been, there still is. It is not I who have imposed this allusion here, but Descartes' own text. He was trained by the best teachers, he was a pupil of the Jesuits at the Collège de La Flèche and there was no lack of knowledge, or of sapience, there.

Shall I go so far as to say that it is not for nothing, that it is precisely a result of his Jesuit education, that he acquired his acute feeling of the superabundance of knowledge? Is there not at the heart of what is transmitted through a certain humanist wisdom something like a hidden *perinde ac cadaver*, which is not where it is usually placed, namely, in the supposed death that the rule of St Ignatius seems to require? Personally, I don't feel very close to it, and these Jesuits, as I myself see them, from the outside, always seem to me to be very much there, not to say full of life—they make their presence felt, and with a diversity that is far from suggesting that of death. No, the death referred to here is that which is hidden behind the very notion of humanism, at the heart of any humanist consideration. And even when an attempt is made to animate the term as in the phrase *the human sciences*, there is something that we shall call a skeleton in the cupboard.

It is here that Descartes finds a new way. His aim is not to refute uncertain knowledge. He is happy to let such knowledge run around quite freely, and with it all the rules of social life. Indeed, like everyone at this historical moment at the beginning of the seventeenth century, in that inaugural moment of the emergence of the subject, he has present all around him a profusion of libertines who serve as the other term of the *vel* of alienation. They are in reality Pyrrhonians, sceptics, and Pascal calls them by their name, except that he does not stress in a sufficiently free way its meaning and implications.

Scepticism does not mean the successive doubting, item by item, of all opinions or of all the pathways that accede to knowledge. It is holding the subjective position that *one can know nothing*. There is something here that deserves to be illustrated by the range, the substance, of those who have been its historical embodiments. I would show you that Montaigne is truly the one who has centred himself, not around scepticism but around the living moment of the *aphanisis* of the subject. And it is in this that he is fruitful, that he is an eternal guide, who goes

beyond whatever may be represented of the moment to be
defined as a historical turning-point. But this is not scepticism.
Scepticism is something that we no longer know. Scepticism is
an ethic. Scepticism is a mode of sustaining man in life, which
implies a position so difficult, so heroic, that we can no longer
even imagine it—precisely perhaps because of this passage
found by Descartes, which led the search for the path of certainty to this very point of the *vel* of alienation, to which there
is only one exit—the way of desire.

This desire for certainty led Descartes only to doubt—the
choice of this way led him to operate a rather strange separation.
I would simply like to touch on a few points, which will serve as
reference points in grasping an essential function, masked
though it may be, which is still vital, present and directive in
our method of investigating the unconscious.

4

Certainty, for Descartes, is not a moment that one may regard
as acquired, once it has been crossed. Each time and by each
person it has to be repeated. It is an ascesis. It is a point of
orientation that is particularly difficult to sustain in the in-
cisiveness that makes its value. It is, strictly speaking, the establishment of something separate.

When Descartes introduces the concept of a certainty that
holds entirely in the *I think* of cogitation, marked by this point
of non-exit that exists between the annihilation of knowledge
and scepticism, which are not the same thing—one might say
that his mistake is to believe that this is knowledge. To say that
he knows something of this certainty. Not to make of the *I think*
a mere point of fading. But it is because he has done something
quite different, which concerns the field, which he does not
name, in which all this knowledge wanders about—all this
knowledge which he had said should be placed in a radical
suspension. He puts the field of this knowledge at the level of
this vaster subject, the subject who is supposed to know, God.
You know that Descartes could not help reintroducing the presence of God. But in what a strange way!

It is here that the question of the eternal verities arises. In
order to assure himself that he is not confronted by a deceiving
God, he has to pass through the medium of a God—indeed, in

his register, it is a question not so much of a perfect, as of an infinite being. Does Descartes, then, remain caught, as everyone up to him did, on the need to guarantee all scientific research on the fact that actual science exists somewhere, in an existing being, called God?—that is to say, on the fact that God is supposed to know?

It may seem that I am taking you a long way from the field of our experience, and yet—I would remind you, both by way of an apology and in order to maintain your attention at the level of our experience—the subject who is supposed to know, in analysis, is the analyst.

Next time, we shall discuss, in terms of the function of the transference, how it is that we have no need of the idea of a perfect, infinite being—who would dream of attributing these qualities to his analyst?—to introduce the function of the subject who is supposed to know.

Let us go back to our Descartes, and to his subject who is supposed to know. How does he get rid of it? Well, as you know, by his voluntarism, by the primacy given to the will of God. This is certainly one of the most extraordinary sleights of hand that has ever been carried off in the history of the mind—the eternal verities are eternal because God wishes them to be.

I think you will appreciate the elegance of such a solution, which leaves a whole portion of the truths, in particular the eternal truths, in God's charge. Let us be quite clear about this, what Descartes means, and says, is that if two and two make four it is, quite simply, because God wishes it so. It is his business.

Now, it is true that it is his business and that two and two make four is not something that can be taken for granted without his presence.

I'm going to try to illustrate what I mean here. When Descartes speaks to us of his process, of his method, of clear ideas and confused ideas, simple ideas and complex ideas, he places the order to be followed between these two terms of his method. It is very possible after all that one plus one plus one plus one do not make four and I must tell you that what I am articulating the *vel* of alienation on is a good example of it. For, in the cardinal order, this would give more or less something like the following:

$$1 + (1 + (1 + (1 + (\ldots))))).$$

Whenever a new term is introduced, one always runs the risk of letting one or several of the others slip between one's fingers. In order to reach four, what matters is not the cardinal but the ordinal. There is a first mental operation to be carried out and then a second, then a third, then a fourth. If you do not do them in the right order, you fail. To know whether, in the last resort, it makes three, or four, or two, is of secondary importance. That's God's business.

What Descartes now introduces, and which is illustrated at once, for, at the same time as his discourse on method he introduces his geometry and his dioptrics, is this—he substitutes the small letters, *a, b, c*, etc., of his algebra for the capital letters. The capital letters, if you will, are the letters of the Hebrew alphabet with which God created the world and to each of which, as you know, there corresponds a number. The difference between Descartes' small letters and the capital letters is that Descartes' small letters do not have a number—they are interchangeable and only the order of the commutations will define their process.

To show you that the presence of the Other is already implied in number, I need only point out to you that the series of numbers can only be figured by introducing the zero, in a more or less masked way. Now, the zero is the presence of the subject who, at this level, totalizes. We cannot extract it from the dialectic of the subject and the Other. The apparent neutrality of this field conceals the presence of desire as such. I will illustrate this simply by a return effect. However, we should take a few more steps forward in the function of desire.

In effect, Descartes inaugurates the initial bases of a science in which God has nothing to do. For the characteristic of our science, and its difference with the ancient sciences, is that nobody even dares, without incurring ridicule, to wonder whether God knows anything about it, whether God leafs through modern treatises on mathematics to keep up to date.

I have gone far enough today, and I apologize for not going further. I will leave you at this point, and do no more than indicate for you the last aim of my discourse for this year— namely, to pose the question of the position of psycho-analysis in science. Can psycho-analysis be situated in our science, in so far as this science is considered as that in which God has nothing to do?

QUESTIONS AND ANSWERS

DR GREEN: *Is there not a way of articulating the question of the* Vorstellungsrepräsentanz *in what you said later—in particular, on the basis of the relation between the subject and the mirror, in so far as this relation refers the subject to the subject who is supposed to know, who is in the mirror?*

LACAN: Mmm . . . Well . . . I cannot follow you in this direction—because I think it's a short circuit.

The point at which the plug of the *Vorstellungsrepräsentanz* is connected—and this is of great importance to what I have said today—is the point that I told you was the virtual point of the function of freedom, in as much as the choice, the *vel*, is manifested there between the signifier and the subject. I illustrated it with an opening on what might be called the avatars of this freedom, which, in the final resort, is never, of course, discovered by any serious individual. I then passed on to Descartes, who is scarcely concerned with it at all, except in act. His own particular freedom takes the form of action, of the way in which he finds his certainty. This does not mean that he leaves it to us like a bank account.

Next time, I must return again to the locus of the *Vorstellungsrepräsentanz*, before I introduce, at the level of the transference, the terms that I was forced to introduce today concerning the function of the Other. They seem to be things very far removed from our domain. I am referring to the psychosomatic.

The psycho-somatic is something that is not a signifier, but which, nevertheless, is conceivable in so far as the signifying induction at the level of the subject has occurred in a way that does not bring into play the *aphanisis* of the subject.

In the small work I referred to earlier, and you can sample for yourselves how much useless chatter it contains, is to be found nevertheless an important little remark—though it claims to refute, not me, I, thank God, am not involved, but those who speak in my name—to the effect that desire is not representative of need. In this place, the *Vorstellungsrepräsentanz* will considerably limit the play of our interpretation for the reason that the subject, *qua aphanisis*, is not concerned in it. It is in so far as a need will come to be concerned in the function of desire that the psycho-somatic may be conceived as something other than the mere chatter that consists in saying that there is a psychical lining to whatever happens in the somatic field. We have known this for a long time now. If we speak of the psycho-somatic, it is in so far as desire must intervene in it. It is in so far as the link known as desire is preserved here, even if we can no longer take account of the *aphanisis* function of the subject.

I would like to convey to you, since I am on this terrain, what is in question in the conditioned reflex. It is not sufficiently stressed that the Pavlovian experiment is possible only in as much as the exercise of a biological function, that is to say, that to which we can attach the unifying, totalizing function of need, can be broken down. It can be broken down because more than one organ is involved in it. Once you have made your dog salivate at the sight of a piece of meat, your next job is to interrupt the process at the point of secretion, and to show that this point is articulable with something that functions as a signifier, since it is made by the experimenter. In other words, the Other is there.

But this proves absolutely nothing about the supposed psyche of the unfortunate animal. Even the supposed effects of neurosis that are obtained are not effects of neurosis, for one simple reason—they cannot be analysed by speech. The major interest of these conditioned reflexes is to show us what the animal may perceive. We use the signifier—which is not a signifier for the animal, but which, in order to see what possible differential there is at the level of its *perceptum*, which, however, does not at all mean that it will be the *percipiens* of that signifier in the subjective sense of the word. The main interest of these experiments is to show us that differential range of the animal at the level of a perception that cannot in any sense be a representation, for there is no other subject here than the subject of the experimenter. And this goes much further still. In fact, we interrogate the animal about our own perception. This way of limiting the scope of the Pavlovian experiments restores to them, at the same time, it can be seen, their very great importance.

Its effective, scientific benefits are those I have described, and they have no other practical use.

Ultimately, their interest may be to reveal the question that is posed to us by the fact that we discover in the animal that signifiers — which are ours, since it is we, the experimenters, who order them in perception — express among themselves a sort of equivalence.

I am not saying that I have resolved this question by formulating it.

Indeed, this sort of equivalence enables us to indicate the problem of the realism of number, in a form that is certainly not that referred to earlier, when I showed you what question is implied in all use of number, which means that arithmetic is a science that has been literally barred by the intrusion of algebrism. Here number intervenes as pure frequency, in what we can call, by putting things back in place, the Pavlovian signal. That is to say, an animal conditioned to a hundred visual stimuli a second reacts to a hundred auditory stimuli a second. A new question in thus introduced into experimentation. It is not yet a question, perhaps, of something to which we might give the full status of signifier, except for those of us who are counting the frequencies. But, all the same, the fact that the animal, without training, passes from a hundred frequencies in one register to a hundred frequencies in another, allows us perhaps to go a little further concerning the strictly perceptual structure.

I have taken advantage of the question asked to say things that I wanted to say and hadn't done so. Let's leave it at that.

3 June 1964

18

OF THE SUBJECT
WHO IS SUPPOSED TO KNOW,
OF THE FIRST DYAD,
AND OF THE GOOD

The trust placed in the analyst · Science itself · As soon as there is a subject who is supposed to know, there is transference · Belief · Alienation apprehended in the fort-da *· Alienation in pleasure*

The aim of my teaching has been and still is the training of analysts.

The training of analysts is a subject that is well to the forefront of analytic research. Nevertheless—I have already given you evidence of this—in the analytic literature, its principles are lost sight of.

It is clear, in the experience of all those who have passed through this training, that in the absence of adequate criteria, something that is of the order of ceremony is put in their place and—since for the psycho-analyst there is no beyond, no substantial beyond, by which to justify his conviction that he is qualified to exercise his function—the substitution, in this instance, can be interpreted in only one way—as simulation.

Yet what he obtains is of incalculable value—the trust of a subject as such, and the results that this involves by virtue of a certain technique. Now, he does not present himself as a god, he is not God for his patient. So what does this trust signify? Around what does it turn?

For him who places the trust, and who receives its reward, the question can no doubt be ignored. It cannot be for the psycho-analyst. The training of the psycho-analyst requires that he should know, in the process through which he guides his patient, what it is around which the movement turns. *He* must know, to him must be transmitted, through actual experience, what it is all *about*. This pivotal point is what I designate—in a way, which, I think, will seem to you sufficiently justified, but which, I hope, as we progress, will appear more and more clear to you, more and more necessary—it is what I designate under the term *the desire of the psycho-analyst*.

Last time, I showed you the point of application of the Cartesian approach, which, in its origin and in its end, is directed essentially not towards science, but towards its own certainty. It is at the heart of something that is not science in the sense in which, since Plato and before him, it has been the object of the meditation of philosophers, but Science *itself*.[1] The science in which we are caught up, which forms the context of the action of all of us in the time in which we are living, and which the psycho-analyst himself cannot escape, because it forms part of his conditions too, is Science *itself*.

It is in relation to this second science, Science *itself*, that we must situate psycho-analysis. We can do so only by articulating upon the phenomenon of the unconscious the revision that we have made of the foundation of the Cartesian subject. First, today, I shall say something about the phenomenology of the transference.

I

The transference is a phenomenon in which subject and psycho-analyst are both included. To divide it in terms of transference and counter-transference—however bold, however confident what is said on this theme may be—is never more than a way of avoiding the essence of the matter.

The transference is an essential phenomenon, bound up with desire as the nodal phenomenon of the human being—and it was discovered long before Freud. It was perfectly articulated—I took up a large part of a year devoted to the transference to showing this—with the most extreme rigour, in a text in which the subject of love is discussed, namely, Plato's *Symposium*.

It is possible that this text was written for the character of Socrates, who, nevertheless, is depicted in it in a particularly

[1] Lacan distinguishes between '*science*' and 'La *science*', in which the stress is placed on the article. I have translated 'La *science*' by 'Science *itself*' [Tr].

discreet way. The essential, initial moment that is of particular relevance to the question we must ask ourselves about the action of the analyst, is that in which it is said that Socrates never claimed to know anything, except on the subject of *Eros*, that is to say, desire. By this fact alone, and because, in the *Symposium*, he goes further than anywhere else in showing us the signification of comedy in his dialogues, carrying it even to the point of farce, Plato could not fail to show us, in the most precise way, the place of the transference.

As soon as the subject who is supposed to know exists somewhere—I have abbreviated it for you today at the top of the blackboard as *S.s.S.* (*sujet supposé savoir*) there is transference.

What does an organization of psycho-analysts mean when it confers certificates of ability, if not that it indicates to whom one may apply to represent this subject who is supposed to know?

Now, it is quite certain, as everyone knows, that no psycho-analyst can claim to represent, in however slight a way, a corpus of absolute knowledge. That is why, in a sense, it can be said that if there is someone to whom one can apply there can be only one such person. This *one* was Freud, while he was alive. The fact that Freud, on the subject of the unconscious, was legitimately the subject that one could presume to know, sets aside anything that had to do with the analytic relation, when it was initiated, by his patients, with him.

He was not only the subject who was supposed to know. He did know, and he gave us this knowledge in terms that may be said to be indestructible, in as much as, since they were first communicated, they support an interrogation which, up to the present day, has never been exhausted. No progress has been made, however small, that has not deviated whenever one of the terms around which Freud ordered the ways that he traced, and the paths of the unconscious, has been neglected. This shows us clearly enough what the function of the subject who is supposed to know is all about.

The function, and by the same token, the consequence, the prestige, I would say, of Freud are on the horizon of every position of the analyst. They constitute the drama of the social, communal organization of psycho-analysts.

Who can feel himself fully invested by this subject who is

supposed to know? This is not the question. The question is first, for each subject, where he takes his bearings from when applying to the subject who is supposed to know. Whenever this function may be, for the subject, embodied in some individual, whether or not an analyst, the transference, according to the definition I have given you of it, is established.

If things reach the point that this is already, on the part of the patient, determined for someone nameable, for a figure accessible to him, there will result from this, for whoever assumes responsibility for him in analysis, a quite special difficulty, concerning the enacting of the transference. And it can happen that even the most stupid analyst—I don't know whether this extreme term exists, it is a function that I designate here only in the way one designates that sort of mythical number in logic which is, for example, the greatest number that may be expressed in so many words—even the most stupid analyst realizes it, recognizes it and directs the analysis towards what remains for him the subject who is supposed to know. This is a mere detail, and almost an anecdote. Let us now begin the examination of what is really at issue.

The analyst, I said, occupies this place in as much as he is the object of the transference. Experience shows us that when the subject enters analysis, he is far from giving the analyst this place.

For the moment let us leave the Cartesian hypothesis that the psycho-analyst is a deceiver. This hypothesis is not to be excluded absolutely from the phenomenological context of certain entries into analysis. But psycho-analysis shows us that what, above all in the initial phase, most limits the confidence of the patient, his abandonment to the analytic rule, is the threat that the psycho-analyst may be deceived by him.

How often in our experience does it happen that we discover only very late some important biographical detail? Suppose, for example, that at a particular moment in his life, the subject contracted a venereal disease. *But why didn't you tell me earlier?* one might ask, if one is still naive enough. *Because, the analysand may reply, if I had told you earlier, you might have regarded it as responsible, in part at least, perhaps even wholly, for my disorders and I am not here for you to find an organic cause for them.*

This is an example that is unlimited in its implications, and which may be understood in a number of different ways—from the angle of social prejudice, of scientific discussion, of the confusion that remains around the very principle of analysis. I quote it here only as an illustration of the fact that the patient may think that the analyst may be misled if he gives him certain facts. He holds back certain facts so that the analyst may not go too quickly. I could give you other, better examples of this. Should not he who may be misled (*être trompé*) be *a fortiori* under suspicion of being capable, quite simply, of being mistaken (*se tromper*)?

Now, that certainly is the limit. It is around this *being mistaken* (*ce se tromper*) that the balance lies of that subtle, infinitesimal point that I wish to mark.

Given that analysis may, on the part of certain subjects, be put in question at its very outset, and suspected of being a lure —how is it that around this *being mistaken* something stops? Even the psycho-analyst put in question is credited at some point with a certain infallibility, which means that certain intentions, betrayed, perhaps, by some chance gesture, will sometimes be attributed even to the analyst put in question, *You did that to test me!*

The Socratic discussion introduced the following theme —that the recognition of the conditions for the good in itself would have something irresistible for man. This is the paradox of the teaching, if not of Socrates himself—what do we know about him other than through the Platonic comedy?—I will not even say Plato's comedy—for Plato develops in the terrain of the comic dialogue and leaves all the questions open—but of a certain exploitation of Platonism, which may be said to perpetuate itself in general derision. For, as we all know, the most perfect recognition of the conditions of the good will never prevent anyone from dashing into its opposite. So what is it all about, this trust placed in the analyst? How are we to know that he wishes this good, let alone for another? Let me explain.

Who does not know from experience that it is possible not to want to ejaculate? Who does not know from experience, knowing the recoil imposed on everyone, in so far as it involves terrible promises, by the approach of *jouissance* as such? Who does not know that one may not wish to think?—the entire universal college of professors is there as evidence.

But what does *not wanting to desire* mean? The whole of analytic experience—which merely gives form to what is for each individual at the very root of his experience—shows us that not to want to desire and to desire are the same thing.

To desire involves a defensive phase that makes it identical with not wanting to desire. Not wanting to desire is wanting not to desire. This discipline which, in order to find a way out of the impasse of the Socratic interrogation, was practised by people who were not only specifically philosophers, but, in their own way, some kind of practitioners of religion—the Stoics and the Epicureans. The subject knows that not to want to desire has in itself something as irrefutable as that Moebius strip that has no underside, that is to say, that in following it, one will come back mathematically to the surface that is supposed to be its other side.

It is at this point of meeting that the analyst is awaited. In so far as the analyst is supposed to know, he is also supposed to set out in search of unconscious desire. This is why I say—I will illustrate it for you next time with a small topological drawing that has already been on the blackboard—that desire is the axis, the pivot, the handle, the hammer, by which is applied the force-element, the inertia, that lies behind what is formulated at first, in the discourse of the patient, as demand, namely, the transference. The axis, the common point of this two-edged axe, is the desire of the analyst, which I designate here as an essential function. And let no one tell me that I do not name this desire, for it is precisely this point that can be articulated only in the relation of desire to desire.

This relation is internal. Man's desire is the desire of the Other.

Is there not, reproduced here, the element of alienation that I designated for you in the foundation of the subject as such? If it is merely at the level of the desire of the Other that man can recognize his desire, as desire of the Other, is there not something here that must appear to him to be an obstacle to his fading, which is a point at which his desire can never be recognized? This obstacle is never lifted, nor ever to be lifted, for analytic experience shows us that it is in seeing a whole chain come into play at the level of the desire of the Other that the subject's desire is constituted.

In the relation of desire to desire, something of alienation is preserved, not with the same elements—not with the S_1 and S_2 of the first dyad of signifiers, from which I deduced the formula of the alienation of the subject in my last but one lecture—but with, on the one hand, what has been constituted on the basis of primal repression, of the fall, of the *Unterdrückung*, of the binary signifier, and, on the other hand, what appears first as lack in what is signified by the dyad of signifiers, in the interval that links them, namely, the desire of the Other.

2

I will now re-articulate a number of formulae to be preserved as link points, without which thought will stumble and slip. Alienation is linked in an essential way to the function of the dyad of signifiers. It is, indeed, essentially different, whether there are two or three of them.

If we wish to grasp where the function of the subject resides in this signifying articulation, we must operate with two, because it is only with two that he can be cornered in alienation. As soon as there are three, the sliding becomes circular. When passed from the second to the third, it comes back to the first —but not from the second. The effect of *aphanisis* that is produced under one of the two signifiers is linked to the definition—let us say, to use the language of modern mathematics—of a set of signifiers. It is a set of elements such that, if there exist—as one says in the theory, with a capital E inverted for notation—only two, the phenomenon of alienation is produced, in other words, the signifier is that which represents the subject for the other signifier. Hence there results that, at the level of the other signifier, the subject fades away.

This is also why I pointed out to you the mistake that occurs in a certain translation of this *Vorstellungsrepräsentanz*, which is, as I told you, the signifying S_2 of the dyad.

I must articulate here what is involved and what, in the text of one of my pupils of whom I have spoken, was sensed, but expressed in a way that misses the point, and which may lead to error, because it specifically omits the fundamental character of the function of the subject. There is constant reference to the relation of the signifier and the signified, which has to do with what I will call the a,b,c, of the question. Of course, it had to happen that one day I would put on the blackboard something that had already been formulated at the roots of the Saussurian development, in order to show my starting point. But I immediately showed that it was effective and manageable only to include in it the function of the subject at the original stage. It is not a question of reducing the function of the subject to nomination, namely, to a label stuck on something. This would be to miss the whole essence of language. I must say that this text, which I described last time as providing proof of infatuation, also provides proof of crass ignorance, in letting it be understood that this is what is involved at the level of the Pavlovian experiment.

If there is something that is situated at the level of the experiment of the conditioned reflex, it is certainly not the association of a sign with a thing.

Whether or not Pavlov recognizes this, the characteristic of every experimental condition is strictly to *associate a signifier*, in so far as the experiment is instituted with the cut that may be made in the organic organization of a need—which is designated by a manifestation at the level of a cycle of interrupted needs, and which we find here again, at the level of the Pavlovian experiment, as being the cut of desire. And—rather as one says, *that's why your daughter is dumb*—that is why the animal will never learn to speak. At least in this way. Because, obviously, the animal is one step behind. The experiment may cause in him all sorts of disorders, all sorts of disturbances, but, not yet being a speaking creature, he is not called to put in question the desire of the experimenter, who, indeed, if one interrogated him, would be hard put to reply.

Nevertheless, when articulated in this way, this experiment is interesting, indeed is essential, in enabling us to situate our conception of the psycho-somatic effect. I will go so far as to formulate that, when there is no interval between S_1 and S_2, when the first dyad of signifiers become solidified, holophrased, we have the model for a whole series of cases—even though, in each case, the subject does not occupy the same place.

In as much, for example, as the child, the mentally-deficient child, takes the place, on the blackboard, at the bottom right, of this S, with regard to this something to which the mother reduces him, in being no more than the support of her desire in an obscure term, which is introduced into the education of the mentally-deficient child by the psychotic dimension. It is precisely what our colleague Maud Mannoni, in a book that has just come out and which I would recommend you to read, tries to indicate to those who, in one way or another, may be entrusted with the task of releasing its hold.[1]

It is certainly something of the same order that is involved in psychosis. This solidity, this mass seizure of the primitive signifying chain, is what forbids the dialectical opening that is manifested in the phenomenon of belief.

At the basis of paranoia itself, which nevertheless seems to us to be animated by belief, there reigns the phenomenon of

$$X \qquad \lozenge \qquad S_1$$

O. s, s', s'', s''',...   S (i (a, a', a'', a''',...))

$$S_2$$

O. s, s', s'', s''',... : *series of meanings.*

i(a, a', a'', a''',...) : *series of identifications.*

the *Unglauben*. This is not the *not believing in it*, but the absence of one of the terms of belief, of the term in which is designated the division of the subject. If, indeed, there is no belief that is full and entire, it is because there is no belief that does not presuppose in its basis that the ultimate dimension that it has to reveal is strictly correlative with the moment when its meaning is about to fade away.

There are all kinds of experiences that bear this out. One of them, concerning one of Casanova's misadventures, was told me in a very humourous way by Mannoni, who is with us today, and whose commentary on it is most amusing and revealing. At the end of a practical joke that succeeded to the point of moving the celestial forces and unleashing around him a storm which, in actual fact, terrified him, Casanova—who had been pursuing a cynical adventure with some silly goose

---

[1] *L'enfant arriéré et sa mère*, Paris, Éditions du Seuil, 1964; *The Retarded Child and the Mother*, trans. Alan Sheridan; London, Tavistock, 1973; New York, Pantheon Books, 1973.

of a girl, who was the object of the prank, which gathered round him a whole circle of idiots—Casanova, seeing his practical joke begin to work, become real, was so deeply affected—in a surprisingly comic way for a Casanova who defied earth and heaven at the level of his desire—that he was struck with impotence, as if he had really been stopped at the sight of God's face.

Take another look at the text I was talking about earlier. In this text, for example, the *fort-da* is presented as something rather old hat—it is almost as if this individual were apologizing for mentioning once again this *fort-da*, which everyone had wiped his feet on. It is treated as an example of primal symbolization, while apologizing for mentioning it as if it were something that had now passed into the public domain. Well! This is just as big a mistake, for it is not from a simple opposition of the *fort* and the *da* that it derives the inaugural force that its repetitive essence explains. To say that it is simply a question for the subject of instituting himself in a function of mastery is idiotic. In the two phonemes are embodied the very mechanisms of alienation—which are expressed, paradoxical as it may seem, at the level of the *fort*.

There can be no *fort* without *da* and, one might say, without *Dasein*. But, contrary to the whole tendency of the phenomenology of *Daseinanalyse*, there is no *Dasein* with the *fort*. That is to say, there is no choice. If the young subject can practise this game of *fort-da*, it is precisely because he does not practise it at all, for no subject can grasp this radical articulation. He practises it with the help of a small bobbin, that is to say, with the *objet a*. The function of the exercise with this object refers to an alienation, and not to some supposed mastery, which is difficult to imagine being increased in an endless repetition, whereas the endless repetition that is in question reveals the radical vacillation of the subject.

3

As usual, I must break off a train of thought in order to keep things within certain limits. However, I wish to say something, however briefly, about what I hope to discuss next time. I have illustrated the essential difference on the blackboard, in the form of two schemata.

In his text on the *Triebe* and the *Triebschicksale*, the drives and the vicissitudes of the drive, Freud places love at once at the level of the real, at the level of narcissism, at the level of the pleasure principle in its correlation with the reality principle, and deduces from this that the function of ambivalence is absolutely different from what occurs in the *Verkehrung*, in the circular movement. At the level at which love is in question, we have a schema, which, Freud tells us, is spread over two stages.

First there is an *Ich*, an *Ich* defined objectively by the combined functioning of the apparatus of the central nervous system and the condition of homeostasis, to preserve the tensions at the lowest possible level.

We can conceive that what there is outside this, if one can speak of an *outside*, is merely indifference. And, at this level, since it is a question of tension, indifference simply means non-existence. Freud tells us however that the rule of auto-eroticism is not the non-existence of objects, but the functioning of objects solely in relation to pleasure. In the zone of indifference a distinction is made between that which brings *Lust* and that which brings *Unlust*, pleasure or displeasure. In any case, did not the ambiguity of the term *Lustprinzip* become obvious to everyone long ago?—since some people also write it *Unlustprinzip*.

The next problem, then, is how this stage is to be represented—how are homeostasis and pleasure to be articulated? For, the fact that something brings pleasure is still too much for the equilibrium. What is the closest and most accurate schema that can be given of this hypothetical *Ich*, in which is motivated the first construction of an apparatus functioning as a psyche? I propose the following.

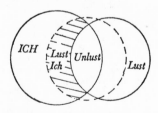

The proof by the objet **a**

You see, indicated by the capital letters ICH, the *Ich* as apparatus tending to a certain homeostasis—which cannot be the lowest because that would be death and, indeed, this was envisaged by Freud in a second stage. As for *Lust*, this is not a field strictly speaking, it is always an object, an object of pleasure, which, as such, is mirrored in the ego. This mirror-image, this bi-univocal correlate of the object, is here the puri-fied *Lust-Ich* of which Freud speaks, namely, that which, in the *Ich*, is satisfied with the object *qua Lust*.

Unlust, on the other hand, is what remains unassimilable, irreducible to the pleasure principle. It is out of this, Freud tells us, that the non-ego will be constituted. It is situated—note well—within the circle of the original ego, it bites into it, without the homeostatic functioning ever managing to re-absorb it. You see here the origin of what we shall find again later in the so-called functioning of the bad object.

You will notice especially that what structures the level of pleasure already gives the beginning of a possible articulation of alienation.

In the external zone, *Lust* says to itself, more or less—*Ah! the* Ich *is really something I must concern myself with*. And as soon as it does concern itself with it, the perfect tranquillity of the *Ich* disappears. The *Lust-Ich* stands out and, by the same token, *Unlust*, the foundation of the non-ego, falls back. This does not imply the disappearance of the apparatus, quite the contrary. You simply see being produced at a primitive level that breaking-off, that splitting-off, which I indicated in the dia-lectic of the subject with the Other, but here in the opposite direction.

This is expressed in the expression, *No good without evil, no good without pain*, which preserves in this good and in this evil a character of alternation, of a possible calibration, in which the articulation that I gave earlier of a dyad of signifiers will be reduced, and incorrectly. For, to return things at the level of good and evil, everyone knows that hedonism is unable to explain the mechanism of desire. This is because in passing over to the other register, to the alienating articulation, it is expressed quite differently. I almost blush to repeat here such catch-phrases as *beyond good and evil*, which idiots have been playing around with for so long without knowing exactly what they were doing. Nevertheless, we must articulate what occurs at the level of the alienating articulation thus—no evil without there resulting some good from it, and when the good is there, there is no good that holds with evil.

That is why, by situating itself purely and simply in the register of pleasure, ethics fails and why, quite legitimately, Kant objects to it that the sovereign good can in no way be conceived as some small good carried to infinity. For there is no possible law to be given of what might be the good in objects.

The sovereign good, if this confusing term must be retained, can be found again only at the level of the law, and in *Kant avec Sade*[1] I showed that this means that, at the level of desire, passivity, narcissism and ambivalence are the characteristics that govern the dialectic of pleasure at the level of the table on the left. Its term is, strictly speaking, what is called identification.

It is the recognition of the drive that enables us to construct, with the greatest certainty, the functioning that I call the functioning of the division of the subject, or alienation. And how has the drive itself been recognized? It has been recognized in this that, far from the dialectic of what occurs in the subject's unconscious being able to be limited to the reference to the field of *Lust*, to the images of beneficent, favourable objects, we have found a certain type of objects which, in the final resort, can serve no function. These are the *objets a*—the breasts, the faeces, the gaze, the voice. It is in this new term that resides the point that introduces the dialectic of the subject *qua* subject of the unconscious.

Next time, I shall continue to develop the theme of the subject of the transference.

QUESTIONS AND ANSWERS

M. Safouan: *I always find it difficult to understand the difference between the object in the drive and the object in desire. Now we are asked to see the difference between the id and the object in drive—I'm lost.*

Lacan: Look, it's simply a question of terminology. It is very kind of you to ask a question, even if it springs from a certain confusion, because this may help everybody else.

There are a lot of very pleasant things that we think we

[1] *Écrits*, Paris, Éditions du Seuil, 1966, pp. 765–90.

desire, in as much as we are healthy, but all we can say about them is this—we think we desire them. These things are on a quite transmissible level, it seems to me, but this is nothing to do with psycho-analytic theory.

The objects that are in the field of *Lust* have so fundamentally narcissistic a relation with the subject that in the last resort the mystery of the supposed regression of love in identification has its reason in the symmetry of these two fields, which I have designated as *Lust* and *Lust-Ich*. What one cannot keep outside, one always keeps an image of inside. Identification with the object of love is as silly as that. And I do not see why that should create so many difficulties, even to Freud himself. That, *mon cher*, is the object of love.

And, indeed, you see this very clearly when you speak of objects that do not have the individual value that attaches to the object of the drive. You then say, as Freud observed, *I love mutton stew*. It's precisely the same thing when you say, *I love Mrs X*, except that you say it to her, which makes all the difference. You say it to her for reasons that I will explain to you next time.

You love mutton stew. You're not sure you desiré it. Take the experience of the beautiful butcher's wife. She loves caviar, but she doesn't want any. That's why she desires it. You see, the object of desire is the cause of the desire, and this object that is the cause of desire is the object of the drive—that is to say, the object around which the drive turns. Since I am here in a dialogue with someone who has worked on my texts, I may express myself in some rather concentrated formulae. It is not that desire clings to the object of the drive—desire moves around it, in so far as it is agitated in the drive. But all desire is not necessarily agitated in the drive. There are empty desires or mad desires that are based on nothing more than the fact that the thing in question has been forbidden you. By virtue of the very fact that it has been forbidden you, you cannot do otherwise, for a time, than think about it. That, too, is desire. But whenever you are dealing with a good object, we designate it —it's a question of terminology, but a justified terminology —as an object of love. Next time, I will justify this by articulating the relation between love, the transference and desire.

10 June 1964

19

FROM INTERPRETATION
TO THE TRANSFERENCE

Field of the ego and field of the Other · Metaphor · Interpretation is not open to all meanings · Indetermination and determination of the subject · Love, transference, desire · The slave · The ego ideal and the petit a

As far as vocabulary is concerned, what I am going to introduce today will, unfortunately, not be very familiar to you.

We shall be dealing with the most ordinary terms, such as identification, idealization, projection, introjection. These are not easy terms to handle and it is not made any easier by the fact that they already have meanings.

What could be more ordinary than to identify? It even seems like the essential operation of thought. To idealize, that too might prove useful when the psychologistic position becomes more experimental. To project and to introject are seen by some people as reciprocal terms. Yet I pointed out long ago —perhaps this fact should be realized—that one of these terms refers to a field in which the symbolic is dominant, the other to a field in which the imaginary is dominant, which must mean that, in a certain dimension at least, they never meet.

The intuitive use of these terms, on the basis of the feeling that one has of understanding them, and of understanding them in an isolated way as revealing their dimension in the common understanding, is obviously at the source of all the misapprehensions and confusions. It is the common fate of anything to do with discourse. In common discourse, he who speaks, at least in his native language, expresses himself with such ease, with such evident familiarity, that it is to the most common user of a language, to the uneducated man, that one has recourse if one wishes to know the correct usage of a term.

As soon as he wishes to speak, man is orientated in the fundamental topology of language, which is very different from the simplistic realism in which he who thinks that he is at ease in the domain of science all too often confines himself. The natural use of such expressions—let us select some at random —as *in one's own heart* (*à part soi*), *for good or ill* (*bon gré mal gré*), *a business* (*une affaire*), which is different from *a thing to be done* (*une chose à faire*), implies the enveloping topology in which the subject recognizes himself when he speaks spontaneously.

If I can speak to psycho-analysts and try to locate to which implicit topology they are referring when using each of the terms I have just listed, it is obviously because, on the whole —however incapable they may often be, for lack of teaching, of articulating them—they frequently make adequate use of them, with the same spontaneity as the ordinary man uses ordinary speech. Of course, if they are determined to force the results of a case, and to understand where they do not understand, they will inevitably make a forced use of these results. In such instances, there will be few people to develop them.

Today, then, I'm referring to this tact in the psycho-analytic use of certain words, in order to be able to harmonize them with the evidence of a topology that I have already introduced here and which is, for example, embodied on the blackboard in the schema which shows you the field of the original *Ich*, the objectifiable *Ich*, in the last resort, in the nervous system, the *Ich* of the homeostatic field, in relation to which the field of *Lust*, of pleasure, is distinguished from the field of *Unlust*.

I have already pointed out that Freud distinguishes clearly between the level of the *Ich*, for example in the article on the *Triebe*, when stressing both that it is manifested as organized, which is a narcissistic sign, and that it is precisely to this extent that it is strictly articulated in the field of the real. In the real, it distinguishes, it privileges only that which is reflected in its field by an effect of *Lust*, as return to homeostasis.

But that which does not favour homeostasis and is maintained at all costs as *Unlust* bites still more into its field. Thus, what is of the order of *Unlust* is inscribed in the ego as non-ego, negation, splitting-off of the ego. The non-ego is not to be confused with what surrounds it, the vastness of the real. Non-ego is distinguised as a foreign body, *fremde Objekt*. It is there, situated in the lunula constituted by the two small Euler-type circles. Look at the blackboard. In the register of pleasure, then, we can make for ourselves an objectifiable foundation, just as the scientist is foreign to the object whose functioning he observes.

But we are not simply that, and even if we were, we would also have to be the subject who thinks. And in so far as we are the subject who thinks, we are implicated in a quite different way, in as much as we depend on the field of the Other, which was there long before we came into the world, and whose circulating structures determine us as subjects.

It is a question, then, of knowing in what field the different things with which we deal in the field of analysis occur. Some occur at the level of the first field, of the *Ich*, and others—which should be distinguished from the first, because if one confuses them, one is lost—in the other field, the field of the Other. I have already shown you the essential articulations of this other field in the two functions that I have defined and articulated as alienation and separation.

The rest of my discourse today presupposes that you have thought about these two functions since I introduced them to you—in other words, that you have tried to make them function at different levels, to put them to the test.

I have already tried to embody certain consequences of the very particular *vel* that constitutes alienation—the placing in suspense of the subject, its vacillation, the collapse of meaning—in such familiar forms as *your money or your life*, or *freedom or death*, which are reproduced from a *being or meaning*—terms that I do not propose without some reluctance. I would ask you not to be too hasty in overloading them with meanings, for if you do you will only succeed in sinking them. So I feel that it is incumbent upon me to warn you of this at the outset.

Nevertheless, I am introducing here what my discourse will try to articulate, if possible, next year. It is a question of something that ought to be entitled *the subjective positions*. For all this preparation, concerning the fundamentals of analysis, should normally serve to show—since nothing can be properly centred except the position of the subject—what the articulation of analysis, on the basis of desire, makes it possible to illustrate about these fundamentals.

Subjective positions, then, of what? If I relied on what is available, I would say—*the subjective positions of existence*, with all the advantages that this term may possess from being already much in the air. Unfortunately, this term would allow us a rigorous application only at the level of the neurotic—which, indeed, would be no small matter. That is why I will say *the subjective positions of being*. I am not committing myself in advance to my title, I may find a better one, but, in any case, that's what it's about.

I

Let us move on. In an article, to which I have already referred in order to correct what seemed to me its dangers, an attempt has been made, in an effort that is not without merit, to give form to certain notions I have introduced concerning the structure of language inherent in the unconscious. What emerged was a formula that consists, in short, in translating the formula that I gave of the metaphor. This formula was essential and usable, since it manifests the dimension in which the unconscious appears, in as much as the operation of signifying condensation is fundamental to it.

Of course, signifying condensation, with its metaphorical effect, can be observed quite openly in any poetic metaphor. That is why I took my example from *Booz endormi*. Go back to my article, *L'Instance de la lettre dans l'inconscient*, published in *La Psychanalyse*.[1] Of all poems, I have taken the one that, in French, may be said to echo in more people's memories than any other. Who did not learn when a child to recite *Booz endormi*! It isn't a bad example to be used by analysts, especially at the point I introduced it, that is to say, when introducing at the same time the paternal metaphor.

I won't go over again what I said, but my reason for introducing it now is obviously to show you what is contributed to the creation of meaning by the fact of designating the character who is in question, Booz—in that position both of divine father and instrument of God—by the metaphor—*Sa gerbe n'était pas avare ni haineuse* ('His sheaf was neither miserly nor spiteful'). The dimension of meaning opened up by this metaphor is nothing less than what appears to us in the final image, that of the golden sickle carelessly thrown into the field of

---

[1] And republished in *Écrits*, *op. cit.* A selection of the *Écrits*, including this article, appears in *Écrits: a selection*, trans. Alan Sheridan; London, Tavistock Publications; New York, Norton; 1977.

stars. It is the very dimension hidden in this poem. More hidden than you think, because it is not enough to refer to the sickle which Jupiter used to flood the world with the blood of Chronos. The dimension of castration that is involved here is, in the Biblical perspective, of a quite different order, and is at work there, present with all the echoes of history, including Booz's invocations to the Lord—*Comment surgira-t-il de moi, vieil homme, une descendance?* (How will there ever be offspring for such an old man as I.)

I don't know whether you have noticed—you would have been much more capable of doing so if this year I had done the seminar I intended doing on the Names-of-the-Father—but the Lord with the unpronounceable name is precisely he who sends children to barren women and old men. The fundamentally transbiological character of paternity, introduced by

$$F\left(\frac{S'}{S}\right)S \cong S\,(+)\,s \qquad\qquad \frac{S'}{S} \times \frac{S}{s} \to \frac{\dfrac{S'}{s}}{\dfrac{S}{S}}$$

Formula of the metaphor

*Transformed formula
in the article in question*

the tradition of the destiny of the chosen people, has something that is originally repressed there, and which always re-emerges in the ambiguity of lameness, the impediment and the symptom, of non-encounter, *dustuchia*, with the meaning that remains hidden.

This is a dimension that we find again and again and which, if we wish to formalize it, as the author I referred to just now tried to do, deserves to be handled with more prudence than is in fact the case—relying, in a way, on the formalism of fraction that results from marking the link that exists between the signifier and the signified by an intermediary bar. It is not absolutely illegitimate to consider that, at certain moments, this bar marks, in the relation of the signifier to the signified, the indication of a value that is strictly what is expressed in its use as fraction in the mathematical sense of the term. But, of course, it is not the only use. There is between the signifier and the signified, another relation which is that of the effect of meaning. Precisely at the point at which it is a question, in metaphor, of marking the effect of meaning, one can absolutely not, therefore, without taking certain precautions, and in as bold a way as has been done, manipulate this bar in a fractional transformation—which one could do if it were a question of a relation of proportion.

When it is a question of fractions, one may transform the product

$\dfrac{A}{B} \times \dfrac{C}{D}$ into a four-storeyed formula, as in the following: $\dfrac{\dfrac{A}{B}}{\dfrac{D}{C}}.$

It was thought to be very clever to do this with metaphor, arguing from the following—to that which carries the weight, in the unconscious, of an articulation of the last signifier to embody the metaphor with the new meaning created by its use, should correspond some kind of pinning out, from one to the other, of two signifiers in the unconscious.

Such a formula is quite definitely unsatisfactory. First, because one ought to know that there can be no relations between the signifier and itself, the peculiarity of the signifier being the fact that it is unable to signify itself, without producing some error in logic.

To be convinced of this, one has only to refer to the antinomies that have intervened as soon as an attempt has been made to produce an exhaustive logical formulation of mathematics. The catalogue of catalogues that do not contain themselves is obviously not the same catalogue that does not contain itself—when it is the one that is introduced in the definition and when it is the one that will be inscribed in the catalogue.

It is so much easier to realize that what is happening is that a substitutive signifier has been put in the place of another signifier to constitute the effect of metaphor. It refers the signifier that it has usurped elsewhere. If, in fact, one wished to preserve the possibility of a handling of a fractional type, one would place the signifier that has disappeared, the repressed signifier, below the principal bar, in the denominator, *unterdrückt*.

Consequently, it is false to say, as has been said, that interpretation is open to all meanings under the pretext that it is a question only of the connection of a signifier to a signifier, and consequently of an uncontrollable connection. Interpretation is not open to any meaning. This would be to concede to those who rise up against the character of uncertainty in analytic interpretation that, in effect, all interpretations are possible, which is patently absurd. The fact that I have said that the effect of interpretation is to isolate in the subject a kernel, a *kern*, to use Freud's own term, of *non-sense*, does not mean that interpretation is in itself nonsense.

Interpretation is a signification that is not just any signification. It comes here in the place of the *s* and reverses the relation by which the signifier has the effect, in language, of the signified. It has the effect of bringing out an irreducible signifier. One must interpret at the level of the *s*, which is not open to all

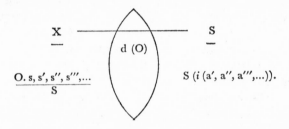

meanings, which cannot be just anything, which is a signification, though no doubt only an approximate one. What is there is rich and complex, when it is a question of the unconscious of the subject, and intended to bring out irreducible, *non-sensical*—composed of non-meanings—signifying elements. In this same article, Leclaire's work illustrates particularly well the crossing of significant interpretation towards signifying non-sense, when he proposes, on the subject of his obsessional neurotic patient, the so-called *Poordjeli* formula, which links the two syllables of the word *licorne* (unicorn), thus enabling him to introduce into his sequence a whole chain in which his desire is animated. Indeed, you will see in what he will publish later that things go much further still.

Interpretation is not open to all meanings. It is not just any interpretation. It is a significant interpretation, one that must not be missed. This does not mean that it is not this signification that is essential to the advent of the subject. What is essential is that he should see, beyond this signification, to what signifier —to what irreducible, traumatic, non-meaning—he is, as a subject, subjected.

This enables us to conceive what is materialized in the experience. I would ask you to take up one of Freud's great psycho-analytic cases, the greatest of all, the most sensational —because one sees in it, more clearly than anywhere else, where the problem of the conversion of phantasy and reality converge, namely, in something irreducible, *non-sensical*, that functions as an originally repressed signifier—I mean the case of the Wolf Man. In *The Wolf Man*, I would say, to give you the thread that will guide you through your reading, that the sudden appearance of the wolves in the window in the dream plays the function of the *s*, as representative of the loss of the subject.

It is not only that the subject is fascinated by the sight of these wolves, which number seven, and which, in fact, in his drawing of them perched on the tree number only five. It is that their fascinated gaze is the subject himself.

What does the whole case show? It shows that at each stage in the life of the subject, something always arrived to reshape the value of the determining index represented by this original signifier. Thus the dialectic of the subject's desire as constituting itself from the desire of the Other is correctly grasped. Remember the adventure of the father, the sister, the mother and the servant-woman Groucha. So many different stages that enrich the unconscious desire of the subject with something that is to be put, as signification constituted in the relation to the desire of the Other, in the numerator.

Note what happens then. I would ask you to consider the logical necessity of that moment in which the subject as X can be constituted only from the *Urverdrängung*, from the necessary fall of this first signifier. He is constituted around the *Urverdrängung*, but he cannot substitute anything for it as such —since this would require the representation of one signifier for another, whereas here there is only one, the first. In this X, we must consider two sides—that constituent moment that sees the collapse of significance, which we articulate in a place in its function at the level of the unconscious, but also the return effect, which operates from this relation that may be conceived on the basis of the fraction. It must be introduced only with prudence, but it is well indicated for us by the effects of language.

Everyone knows that if zero appears in the denominator, the value of the fraction no longer has meaning, but assumes by convention what mathematicians call an infinite value. In a way, this is one of the stages in the constitution of the subject. In so far as the primary signifier is pure non-sense, it becomes the bearer of the infinitization of the value of the subject, not open to all meanings, but abolishing them all, which is different. This explains why I have been unable to deal with the relation of alienation without introducing the word freedom. What, in effect, grounds, in the meaning and radical non-meaning of the subject, the function of freedom, is strictly speaking this signifier that kills all meanings.

This is why it is untrue to say that the signifier in the unconscious is open to all meanings. It constitutes the subject in his freedom in relation to all meanings, but this does not mean that it is not determined in it. For, in the numerator, in the place of the zero, the things that are inscribed are significations, dialectized significations in the relation of the desire of the Other, and they give a particular value to the relation of the subject to the unconscious.

It will be important, in what will follow in my seminar next year, to show how the experience of analysis forces us to seek a kind of formalization such that the mediation of this infinity of the subject with the finiteness of desire may occur only through the intervention of what Kant, on his entry into the gravitation of what is called philosophical thinking, introduced with so much freshness in the term *negative quantities*.

The freshness is important here, of course, because there is a difference between forcing philosophers to reflect on the fact that minus one (-1) is not zero and the fact that people soon lose interest in such talk and cease to listen. Nevertheless—and this is the only use of the reference to philosophical articulation —men survive only by being at each moment so forgetful of all their conquests, I am speaking of their subjective conquests. Of course, from the moment they forget them, they are nevertheless conquered, but it is rather they who are conquered by the effects of these conquests. And the fact of being conquered by something that one does not know sometimes has formidable consequences, the first of which is confusion.

Negative quantity, then, is the term that we shall find to designate one of the supports of what is called the castration complex, namely, the negative effect in which the phallus object enters into it.

This is no more than a foretaste, but I thought it worth saying.

2

However, we must move on to what is our main topic, namely, the transference. How can we take up the thread again? The transference is unthinkable unless one sets out from the subject who is supposed to know.

You will now have a better idea of what he is supposed to know. He is supposed to know that from which no one can escape, as soon as he formulates it—quite simply, signification.

Signification implies, of course—and that is why I first brought out the dimension of his desire—that he cannot refuse it.

This privileged point is the only one by which we can recognize the character of an absolute point with no knowledge. It is absolute precisely by virtue of being in no way knowledge, but the point of attachment that links his very desire to the resolution of that which is to be revealed.

The subject comes into play on the basis of this fundamental support—the subject is supposed to know, simply by virtue of being a subject of desire. Now what actually happens? What happens is what is called in its most common appearance the *transference effect*. This effect is love. It is clear that, like all love, it can be mapped, as Freud shows, only in the field of narcissism. To love is, essentially, to wish to be loved.

What emerges in the transference effect is opposed to revelation. Love intervenes in its function, revealed here as essential, in its function as deception. Love, no doubt, is a transference effect, but it is its resistance side. We are linked together in awaiting this transference effect in order to be able to interpret, and at the same time, we know that it closes the subject off from the effect of our interpretation. The alienation effect, in which is articulated, in the relation of the subject to the Other, the effect that we are, is here absolutely manifest.

We should point out here, then, something that is always avoided, which Freud articulates, and which is not an excuse, but the reason of the transference, namely, that nothing can be attained *in absentia, in effigie*. This means that the transference is not, of its nature, the shadow of something that was once alive. On the contrary, the subject, in so far as he is subjected to the desire of the analyst, desires to betray him for this subjection, by making the analyst love him, by offering of himself that essential duplicity that is love. The transference effect is that effect of deception in so far as it is repeated in the present here and now.

It is repetition of that which passed for such only because it possesses the same form. It is not ectopia. It is not a shadow of the former deceptions of love. It is isolation in the actuality of its pure functioning as deception.

That is why we can say that what is there, behind the love known as transference, is the affirmation of the link between the desire of the analyst and the desire of the patient. This is what Freud expressed in a kind of rapid sleight of hand when he said—*after all, it is only the desire of the patient*—this should reassure one's colleagues. It is the patient's desire, yes, but in its meeting with the analyst's desire.

I will not say that I have not yet named the analyst's desire, for how can one name a desire? One circumscribes a desire. There are many things in history that provide us with tracks and traces here.

Is it not strange, that echo that we found—though, of course, we are not going to stick our noses into this for long —between the ethic of analysis and the Stoic ethic? What does the Stoic ethic really amount to other than the recognition of the absolute authority of the desire of the Other, that *Thy will be done!* that is taken up again in the Christian register? But will I ever have the time to show you this?

We are solicited by a more radical articulation. The problem may be posed of the relation between the master's desire and the slave. Hegel declares it to be solved—this is not so at all.

Since I am ready to take my leave of you for this year —next time will be my last lecture—may I throw out a few points that may give you some idea of the direction in which we will travel later.

If it is true that the master situates himself only in an original relation to the assumption of death, I think that it is very difficult to attribute to him an apprehensible relation to desire. I'm speaking of the master in Hegel, not of the master of antiquity, of which we have one portrait, for example, in that of Alcibiades, whose relation to desire is visible enough. He asks Socrates for something, without knowing what it is, but which he calls *agalma*. Some of you will know the use that I made of this term some time ago. I will go back to this *agalma*, this mystery, which, in the mist that clouds Alcibiades' vision, represents something beyond all good.

How can one see anything other than a first adumbration of the technique of the mapping of the transference in the fact that Socrates replies to him, not what he said to him when he was young, *Look to your soul*, but something more suited to the florid, hardened man he now is, *Look to your desire, look to your onions*. As it happens, it is the height of irony on Plato's part to have embodied these *onions* in a man who is so futile and absurd, almost a buffoon. I think I was the first to remark that the lines Plato puts in his mouth concerning the nature of love are an indication of just such futility, verging on buffoonery, which makes of Agathon perhaps the least likely object to attract the desire of a master. Furthermore, the fact that he is called Agathon, that is to say, the name to which Plato gave the supreme value, adds an extra, perhaps involuntary, but incontestable, note of irony.

Thus, as soon as it comes into play in the story, the desire of the master seems, of its very nature, to be the most inappropriate term. On the other hand, when Socrates wishes to obtain his own answer, it is to the slave, who has no right to declare his own desire, that he turns. He can always be sure of obtaining the right reply from *him*. *The voice of reason is low*, Freud says somewhere, *but it always says the same thing*. I don't wish to draw a false parallel to the effect that Freud says exactly the same thing about unconscious desire. Its voice, too, is low, but its insistence is indestructible. Perhaps there is a relation between the two. It is in the direction of some kind of kinship that we should turn our eyes to the slave, when it is a question of mapping what the analyst's desire is.

3

But I would not like to leave you today without introducing, for next time, two remarks, two remarks that are grounded in the mapping that Freud made of the function of identification.

There are enigmas in identification, even for Freud himself. He seems to be surprised that the regression of love should take place so easily in terms of identification—even when, in texts written about the same time, he demonstrates that love and identification have an equivalence in a certain register and that narcissism and over-estimation of the object, *Verliebtheit*, is exactly the same thing in love.

At this point, Freud pauses—I would ask you to find for yourselves in the text the various *clues*, as the English say, the traces, the marks left on the trail. I think this is because he had not sufficiently distinguished something.

In the chapter of *Massenpsychologie und Ich-Analyse* devoted to identification, I stressed the second form of identification, in order to map in it, and to detach from it, the *einziger Zug*, the single stroke, the foundation, the kernel of the ego ideal. What is this single stroke? Is it a privileged object in the field of *Lust*? No.

The single stroke is not in the first field of narcissistic identification, to which Freud relates the first form of identification —which, very curiously indeed, he embodies in a sort of function, a sort of primal model which the father assumes, anterior even to the libidinous investment on the mother —a mythical stage, certainly. The single stroke, in so far as the subject clings to it, is in the field of desire, which cannot in any sense be constituted other than in the reign of the signifier, other than at the level in which there is a relation of the subject to the Other. It is the field of the Other that determines the function of the single stroke, in so far as it is from it that a major stage of identification is established in the topography then developed by Freud—namely, idealization, the ego ideal. I showed you the traces of this first signifier on the primitive bone on which the hunter makes a notch and counts the number of times he gets his target.

It is in the intersection by which the single signifier functions here in the field of *Lust*, that is to say, in the field of primary narcissistic identification, that is to be found the essential mainspring of the effects of the ego ideal. I have described elsewhere the sight in the mirror of the ego ideal, of that being that he first saw appearing in the form of the parent holding him up before the mirror. By clinging to the reference-point of him who looks at him in a mirror, the subject sees appearing, not his ego ideal, but his ideal ego, that point at which he desires to gratify himself in himself.

This is the function, the mainspring, the effective instrument constituted by the ego ideal. Not so long ago, a little girl said to me sweetly that it was about time somebody began to look after her so that she might seem lovable to herself. In saying this, she provided the innocent admission of the mainspring that comes into play in the first stage of the transference. The subject has a relation with his analyst the centre of which is at the level of the privileged signifier known as the ego ideal, in so far as from there he will feel himself both satisfactory and loved.

But there is another function, which institutes an identification of a strangely different kind, and which is introduced by the process of separation.

It is a question of this privileged object, discovered by analysis, of that object whose very reality is purely topological, of that object around which the drive moves, of that object that rises in a bump, like the wooden darning egg in the material which, in analysis, you are darning—the *objet a.*

This object supports that which, in the drive, is defined and specified by the fact that the coming into play of the signifier in the life of man enables him to bring out the meaning of sex. Namely, that for man, because he knows the signifiers, sex and its significations are always capable of making present the presence of death.

The distinction between the life drive and the death drive is true in as much as it manifests two aspects of the drive. But this is so only on condition that one sees all the sexual drives as articulated at the level of significations in the unconscious, in as much as what they bring out is death—death as signifier and nothing but signifier, for can it be said that there is a being-for-death? In what conditions, in what determinism, can death, the signifier, spring fully armed into treatment? This can be understood only by our way of articulating the relations.

Through the function of the *objet a*, the subject separates himself off, ceases to be linked to the vacillation of being, in the sense that it forms the essence of alienation. This function has been sufficiently indicated to us, for long enough, by enough traces. I have shown at one time or another that it is impossible to conceive of the phenomenology of verbal hallucination if we do not understand what the very term that we use to designate it means—that is to say, voices.

It is in so far as the object of the voice is present in it that the *percipiens* is present in it. Verbal hallucination is not a false *perceptum*, it is a deviated *percipiens*. The subject is immanent in his verbal hallucination. This possibility is there, which should make us ask the question as to what we are trying to achieve in analysis, concerning the accommodation of the *percipiens*.

Up till the advent of psycho-analysis, the path of knowledge was always traced in that of a purification of the subject, of the *percipiens*. Well! We would now say that we base the assurance of the subject in his encounter with the filth that may support him, with the *petit a* of which it would not be untrue to say that its presence is necessary.

Take Socrates. The inflexible purity of Socrates and his *atopia* are correlative. Intervening, at every moment, there is the demonic voice.

Could one maintain that the voice that guides Socrates is not Socrates himself? The relation between Socrates and his voice is no doubt an enigma, which indeed, tempted psychographers on several occasions in the early nineteenth century, and it is already a great merit on their part that they dared to broach the matter since nowadays one daren't touch it with a barge-pole.

It is a new trace to be interrogated in order to know what we mean when we speak of the subject of perception. Don't make me out to say what I'm not saying—the analyst must not hear voices. All the same, read a book by an analyst of good vintage, a Theodor Reik, a direct pupil and familiar of Freud, *Listening with the Third-Ear*—in actual fact, I do not approve of the formula, as if two were not enough to be deaf with. But he maintains that this third ear helps him to hear some voice or other that speaks to him in order to warn him of deceptions —he belongs to the good old days, the heroic days, when one was able to hear what was being said behind the deception of the patient.

Certainly, we have learnt a lot since then, because we know how to recognize in these circumventions, these cleavages, the *objet a*, which certainly has still scarcely emerged.

QUESTIONS AND ANSWERS

P. KAUFMANN: *Is there not some kind of connection between what you have said again, on the subject of Booz and Theodore Reik, and what you have said, elsewhere, concerning the father at the beginning of chapter seven of* The Interpretation of Dreams?

LACAN: It's quite clear, he is asleep—that's all there is to it. He is asleep so that we should sleep too, that is to say, so that we should understand only what there is to be understood.

I wanted to bring in the Jewish tradition, in order to take things up where Freud left them, because after all it is not for nothing that the pen fell from Freud's hands when he had reached the division of the subject, and that just previously he had written, in *Moses and Monotheism*, one of the most radical critiques of the Jewish tradition. However historically contestable his evidence or even his approach may be, the fact remains that to introduce into the heart of Jewish history the absolutely obvious radical distinction of the prophetic tradition in relation to another message, was certainly—as he seemed to be aware, or in any case as he wrote it—to make of the *collusion with truth* a function essential to our operation as analysts. And we can rely on truth, devote ourselves to it only in so far as we dethrone ourselves from a collusion with truth.

Since we are, in a sense, among friends here, and since, after all, there is more than one person here who is not completely out of touch with what is happening inside the psycho-analytic community, I can tell you something amusing. This morning I was listening to someone telling me about his life, of his disappointments, of all the inconveniences to be found in a normal scientific career, of being a director of studies, or in charge of a research group, or laboratory boss of a senior researcher whose ideas you must take account of if you wish to advance in your career. Such a situation, of course, is particularly detrimental from the point of view of the development of scientific thought. Well! I was thinking about what this person was saying and came to the conclusion that there is one field, that of psycho-analysis, in which, in fact—if anywhere—the subject is there only to seek his qualification for free search governed by a demand for truth, and may be regarded as authorized in this search only from the moment that he operates freely in it. Well! By a sort of strange effect of vertigo, it is in this very area of psycho-analysis that they are trying to reconstruct, to the maximum degree possible, the hierarchy of posts and titles to be found in the university, and to make their qualification to practise dependent on someone who is already qualified. This even goes further. When they have found their way, their mode of thinking, their very way of moving in the analytic field, on the basis of the teaching of a certain individual, it is through others, whom they regard as fools, that they will try to find the authorization, the express qualification that they are actually capable of practising analysis. I find that this is one more illustration of the difference and conjunctions, of the ambiguities, between the analytic field and the university field. If it is said that the analysts themselves form part of the problem of the unconscious, does it not strike you that we have here a fine illustration of it, and a good opportunity to analyse?

17 June 1964

To Conclude

20

IN YOU MORE THAN YOU

I love you, but, because inexplicably I love in you something more than
you—the objet petit a—*I mutilate you*

It now remains for me to conclude, for this year, the series of
seminars that I was forced to hold here owing to certain circumstances that have introduced into the course of my teaching
something which, after all, is accounted for by one of the fundamental notions that I have been examining here—that of
dustuchia, misfortune.

So I had to postpone dealing with a subject that I was pre-
paring to embark on with those who were following my course
on the Names-of-the-father, and to return here, before a rather
different audience, to the question that has been at issue from
the outset of this teaching, my teaching, namely, *what is the*
order of truth that our praxis engenders?

What makes us certain of our practice is something whose
basic concepts I think I have outlined for you here, under the
four headings of the unconscious, repetition, the transference
and the drive—a sketch of which, as you have seen, I was led
to include in my exploration of the transference.

Has that which our praxis engenders the right to map out for
itself necessities, even contradictory ones, from the standpoint
of truth? This question may be transposed in the esoteric formula: *how can we be sure that we are not imposters?*

I

It would not be too much to say that, in the putting in question
of analysis, in so far as it is always in suspense, not only in the
popular mind, but still more in the most private feelings of each
psycho-analyst, imposture looms overhead—as a contained,
excluded, ambiguous presence against which the psycho-
analyst barricades himself with a number of ceremonies,
forms and rituals.

If I am stressing the term imposture in my talk today, it is because it is certainly the first step by which one might approach the relation of psycho-analysis with religion and, through this, with science.

I would draw your attention here to a formula that had considerable historical value in the eighteenth century, when enlightenment man, who was also the man of pleasure, put in question religion as a fundamental imposture. I do not need to point out to you the road we have travelled since then. Who, nowadays, would dream of reducing the concerns of religion to such simplistic terms? It can be said that, throughout the world, and even where the struggle against it may be at its sharpest, religion nowadays enjoys universal respect.

This question also involves that of belief, which is presented by us in terms that are no doubt less simplistic. We have the practice of the fundamental alienation in which all belief is sustained, in that double subjective term by which, at the very moment when the signification of belief seems most profoundly to vanish, the being of the subject is revealed from what was strictly speaking the reality of that belief. It is not enough to overcome superstition, as one says, for its effects in the human being to be attenuated.

It is certainly this that makes it difficult for us to recognize what, in the sixteenth century, could have been the status of what was, strictly speaking, disbelief. In this sphere, we know that we are, in our time, incomparably and paradoxically disarmed. Our bulwark, the only one we have, and the religious have felt this in a quite admirable way, is, as Lamennais remarked on the subject of religion, that indifference that takes as its status precisely the position of science.

It is in as much as science elides, eludes, divides up a field determined in the dialectic of the alienation of the subject, it is in as much as science is situated at the precise point that I have defined as the point of separation, that it may also sustain the mode of existence of the scientist, of the man of science. This man of science could be approached in his style, his morals, his mode of discourse, in the way in which, through a series of precautions, he protects himself from a number of questions concerning the very status of the science of which he is the servant. This is one of the most important problems from the social point of view—less important, however, than that of the status to be given to the corpus of acquired scientific knowledge.

We will not appreciate the full implication of this corpus of science if we do not recognize that it is, in the subjective relation, the equivalent of what I have called here the *objet petit a*.

The ambiguity that persists in the question as to what in psycho-analysis is or is not reducible to science can be explained if we realize to what extent analysis implies, in effect, a beyond of science—in the modern sense of Science *itself*, whose status in the Cartesian departure I have tried to demonstrate. If measured against science understood in this sense, psycho-analysis might be reduced to the rank of something with whose forms and history it so often suggests an analogy—namely, a church and, therefore, a religion.

The only way to approach this problem is on the basis of the following—that, among the modes at man's disposal for posing the question of his existence in the world, and beyond, religion, as a mode of subsistence of the subject who interrogates himself, is to be distinguished by a dimension that is proper to it, and which is struck by a kind of oblivion. In every religion that deserves the name, there is in fact an essential dimension reserved for something operational, known as a sacrament.

Ask the faithful, or even the priests, what differentiates confirmation from baptism—for, indeed, if it is a sacrament, if it operates, it operates on something. Where it washes away sins, where it renews a certain pact—I would put a question-mark here—Is it a pact? Is it something else? What passes through this dimension?—in all the answers we get, we will always find this mark, by which is invoked the beyond of religion, operational and magical. We cannot evoke this operational dimension without realizing that within religion, and for strictly defined reasons—the separation and impotence of our reason, our finitude—it is this that is marked with oblivion.

It is in as much as psycho-analysis, in relation to the foundation of its status, finds itself in some way struck by a similar oblivion, that it manages to rediscover itself, marked, in ceremony, with what I will call the same empty face.

But psycho-analysis is not a religion. It proceeds from the same status as Science *itself*. It is engaged in the central lack in which the subject experiences himself as desire. It even has a medial, chance status, in the gap opened up at the centre of the dialectic of the subject and the Other. It has nothing to forget, for it implies no recognition of any substance on which it claims to operate, even that of sexuality.

On sexuality, in fact, it operates very little. It teaches us nothing new about the operation of sex. Not even a tiny piece of erotological technique has emerged from it, and there is more of this kind of thing to be found in any of the books that are constantly being reprinted, and which come to us from the depths of an Arab, Hindu, or Chinese tradition, even sometimes from our own. Psycho-analysis touches on sexuality only in as much as, in the form of the drive, it manifests itself in the defile of the signifier, in which is constituted the dialectic of the subject in the double stage of alienation and separation. Analysis has not kept, on the field of sexuality, what one might, mistakenly, have expected of it by way of promises—it has not kept such promises because it does not have to keep them. This is not its terrain.

On the other hand, in its own terrain, it is distinguished by such an extraordinary capacity for inconsequence and confusion that, sometime in the not too distant future, its entire literature will, I assure you, be classified among the works of what are known as the *fous littéraires*.

Certainly, one cannot but be struck by the extent to which an analyst may err in the correct interpretation of the very facts he advances—and recently I was struck once again on reading a book like *Basic Neurosis*, a book that is nevertheless so winning in the smart way it gathers together a number of very different observations that can certainly be borne out in practice. The particular fact that Bergler contributes concerning the function of the breast is truly wasted in a pointless discussion, of a rather fashionable kind, concerning the superiority of man over woman, and of woman over man, that is to say, concerning things which, by arousing the greatest possible emotion, are also, as far as the main question is concerned, what is of least interest.

Today, I must stress what, in the psycho-analytic movement, is to be referred to the function of what I isolate as the *objet a* —and it is not for nothing that I referred here to Bergler's book, which, because it lacks an adequate mapping of the proper function of the part-object, and of what is signified, for example, by the breast, which he deals with at length, is doomed although interesting in itself, to an aimless development that leads nowhere.

2

The *objet a* is that object which, in actual experience, in the operation and process sustained by the transference, is signalled to us by a special status.

One constantly has on one's lips, without quite knowing what one means, the term *the liquidation* of the transference. What, in fact, does the term mean? Exactly what assets are being liquidated? Or is it a question of some kind of operation in an alembic? Is it a question of— *It must go somewhere and empty itself somewhere*? If the transference is the enaction of the unconscious, does one mean that the transference might be a means of liquidating the unconscious? Do we no longer have any unconscious after an analysis? Or is it, to take up what I said before, the subject who is supposed to know who must be liquidated as such?

It would be odd all the same if this subject who is supposed to know, supposed to know something about you, and who, in fact, knows nothing, should be regarded as liquidated, at the very moment when, at the end of the analysis, he begins at last, about you at least, to know something. It is therefore at the moment what he takes on most substance, that the subject who is supposed to know ought to be supposed to have been vaporized. It can only be a question, then, if the term liquidation has any meaning, of the permanent liquidation of that deception by which the transference tends to be exercised in the direction of the closing up of the unconscious. I have already explained to you how it works, by referring to it the narcissistic relation by which the subject becomes an object worthy of love. From his reference to him who must love him, he tries to induce the Other into a mirage relation in which he convinces him of being worthy of love.

Freud designates for us its natural culmination in the function known as identification. The identification in question is not —and Freud articulates it with great subtlety, I would ask you to go back and read the two chapters in *Group Psychology and the*

Analysis of the Ego that I referred to last time, the first is called *Identification* and the second *Hypnosis and the State of being in Love* —the identification in question is not specular, immediate identification. It is its support. It supports the perspective chosen by the subject in the field of the Other, from which specular identification may be seen in a satisfactory light. The point of the ego ideal is that from which the subject will see himself, as one says, *as others see him*—which will enable him to support himself in a dual situation that is satisfactory for him from the point of view of love.

As a specular mirage, love is essentially deception. It is situated in the field established at the level of the pleasure reference, of that sole signifier necessary to introduce a perspective centred on the Ideal point, capital I, placed somewhere in the Other, from which the Other sees me, in the form I like to be seen.

Now, in this very convergence to which analysis is called by the element of deception that there is in the transference, something is encountered that is paradoxical— the discovery of the analyst. This discovery is understandable only at the other level, the level at which we have situated the relation of alienation.

This paradoxical, unique, specified object we call the *objet a*. I have no wish to rehash the whole thing again, but I will present it for you in a more syncopated way, stressing that the analysand says to his partner, to the analyst, what amounts to this—*I love you, but, because inexplicably I love in you something more than you—the* objet petit a—*I mutilate you.*

This is the meaning of that breast-complex, that *mammal-complex*, whose relation to the oral drive Bergler saw so clearly, except that the orality in question has nothing to do with food, and that the whole stress is placed on this effect of mutilation.

I give myself to you, the patient says again, *but this gift of my person*—as they say—*Oh, mystery! is changed inexplicably into a gift of shit*—a term that is also essential to our experience.

When this swerve is achieved, at the conclusion of the interpretative elucidation, we are able to understand retroactively that vertigo, for example, of the white page, which, for a particular character, who is gifted but stuck at the limits of the psychotic, is like the centre of the symptomatic barrage which blocks off for him every access to the Other. If, quite literally, he cannot touch this white page at which his ineffable intellectual effusions come to a stop, it is because he apprehends it only as a piece of lavatory paper.

How shall I describe for you the effect of this presence of the *objet a*, rediscovered always and everywhere, in the movement of the transference? I do not have much time today, but I will make use, by way of illustration, of a short fable, an apologue, which I happened to embark on the other day, with a smaller group of listeners. I will provide an end for it, so that if I apologize to them for repeating myself, they will see that what follows at least is new.

What happens when the subject begins to speak to the analyst?—to the analyst, that is to say, to the subject who is supposed to know, but of whom it is certain that he still knows nothing. It is to him that is offered something that will first, necessarily, take the form of demand. Everyone knows that it is this that has orientated all thinking on analysis in the direction of a recognition of the function of frustration. But what does the subject demand? That is the whole question, for the subject knows very well that, whatever his appetites may be, whatever his needs may be, none of them will find satisfaction in analysis, and that the most he can expect of it is to organize his menu.

In the fable I read, when I was a child, in these early forms of strip cartoon, the poor beggar at the restaurant door feasted himself on the smell of the roasting meat. On this occasion, the smell is the menu, that is to say, signifiers, since we are concerned with speech only. Well! There is this complication—and this is my fable—that the menu is written in Chinese, so the first step is to order a translation from the *patronne*. She translates—imperial pâté, spring rolls, etc. etc. It may well be, if it is the first time that you have come to a Chinese restaurant, that the translation does not tell you much more than the original, and in the end you say to the *patronne—Recommend something*. This means: *You should know what I desire in all this*.

But is so paradoxical a situation supposed, in the final resort, to end there? At this point, when you abdicate your choice to some divination of the *patronne*, whose importance you have exaggerated out of all proportion, would it not be more appropriate, if you felt like it, and if the opportunity presented itself, to tickle her tits a bit? For one goes to a Chinese restaurant not only to eat, but to eat in the dimensions of the exotic. If my fable means anything, it is in as much as alimentary desire has another meaning than alimentation. It is here the support and symbol of the sexual dimension, which is the only one to be rejected by the psyche. The drive in its relation to the part-object is subjacent here.

Well! Paradoxical, not to say free and easy, as this little apologue may seem, it is nevertheless precisely what is at issue in the reality of analysis. It is not enough that the analyst should support the function of Tiresias. He must also, as Apollinaire tells us, have breasts. I mean that the operation and manipulation of the transference are to be regulated in a way that maintains a distance between the point at which the subject sees himself as lovable—and that other point where the subject sees himself caused as a lack by a, and where a fills the gap constituted by the inaugural division of the subject.

The *petit a* never crosses this gap. Recollect what we learned about the gaze, the most characteristic term for apprehending the proper function of the *objet a*. This a is presented precisely, in the field of the mirage of the narcissistic function of desire, as the object that cannot be swallowed, as it were, which remains stuck in the gullet of the signifier. It is at this point of lack that the subject has to recognize himself.

It is for this reason that the function of the transference may be topologized in the form that I have already produced in my seminar on *Identification*—namely, the form that I have called on occasion the *internal eight*, that double curve that you see on the blackboard folding back upon itself, and whose essential property is that each of its halves, following one another, comes back to back at each point with the preceding half. Just suppose that a particular half of the curve is unfolded, then you will see it cover up the other.

That is not all. As it is a question here of a plane defined by the cut, you need only take a sheet of paper to get, with the help of a few small collages, an exact idea of the way in which what I am going to tell you may be conceived. It is very easy to imagine that, in short, the lobe constituted by this surface at its point of return covers another lobe, the two constituting themselves by a form of rim. Note that this in no way implies any contradiction, even in the most ordinary space—except that, in order to grasp its extent, one must abstract oneself from three-dimensional space, since it is a question here only of a topological reality that is limited to the function of a surface. You can thus conceive quite easily in the three dimensions that one of the parts of the plane, at the moment at which the other, by its rim, returns upon it, determines there a sort of intersection.

This intersection has a meaning outside our space. It is structurally definable, without reference to the three dimensions, by a certain relation of the surface to itself, in so far as, returning upon itself, it crosses itself at a point no doubt to be

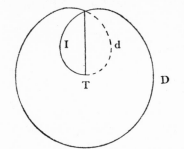

D: *line of demand.*

I: *line of 'identification' intersection .*

T: *point of the transference.*

d: *desire.*

determined. Well! This line of intersection is for us what may symbolize the function of identification.

In effect, by the very work that leads the subject, while telling himself in analysis, to orientate what he says in the direction of the resistance of the transference, of deception, deception of love as well as of aggression—something like closing up occurs and its value is marked in the very form of this spiral developing towards a centre. What I have depicted here by means of the rim comes back on to the plane constituted by the locus of the Other, from the place where the subject, realizing himself in his speech, is instituted at the level of the subject who is supposed to know. Any conception of analysis that is articulated —innocently or not, God only knows—to defining the end of the analysis as identification with the analyst, by that very fact makes an admission of its limits. Any analysis that one teaches as having to be terminated by identification with the analyst reveals, by the same token, that its true motive force is elided. There is a beyond to this identification, and this beyond is defined by the relation and the distance of the *objet petit a* to the idealizing capital I of identification.

I cannot enter into the details of what such an affirmation implies in the structure of practice. I will refer here to Freud's chapter on *Hypnosis and the State of being in Love*, which I mentioned earlier. In this chapter Freud makes an excellent distinction between hypnosis and the state of being in love, even in its most extreme forms, what he calls *Verliebtheit*. Here he provides the clearest doctrinal account to be read anywhere, if only one knows how to read it.

There is an essential difference between the object defined as narcissistic, the *i* (*a*), and the function of the *a*. Things are such that the only view of the schema that Freud gives of hypnosis,

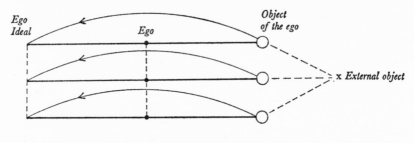

Freud's Schema

gives by the same token the formula of collective fascination, which was an increasing reality at the time when he wrote that article. He draws this schema exactly as I have represented it for you on the blackboard.

In it he designates what he calls the object—in which you must recognize what I call the *a*—the ego and the ego ideal. As for the curves, they are made to mark the conjunction of the *a* with the ego ideal. In this way Freud gives its status to hypnosis by superposing at the same place the *objet a* as such and this signifying mapping that is called the ego ideal.

I have given you the elements in order to understand it, adding that the *objet a* may be identical with the gaze. Well, Freud precisely indicates the nodal point of hypnosis when he formulates that the object is certainly an element that is difficult to grasp in it, but an incontestable one, namely, the gaze of the hypnotizer. Remember what I articulated for you about the function of the gaze, of its fundamental relations to the ink-blot, of the fact that there is already in the world something that looks before there is a view for it to see, that the ocellus of animal mimicry is indispensible as a presupposition to the fact that a subject may see and be fascinated, that the fascination of the ink-blot is anterior to the view that discovers it. You apprehend by the same token the function of the gaze in hypnosis, which may be fulfilled in fact by a crystal stopper, or anything, so long as it shines.

To define hypnosis as the confusion, at one point, of the ideal signifier in which the subject is mapped with the *a*, is the most assured structural definition that has been advanced.

Now, as everyone knows, it was by distinguishing itself from hypnosis that analysis became established. For the fundamental mainspring of the analytic operation is the maintenance of the distance between the I—identification—and the *a*.

In order to give you formulae-reference points, I will say—if the transference is that which separates demand from the drive, the analyst's desire is that which brings it back. And in this way, it isolates the *a*, places it at the greatest possible distance from the I that he, the analyst, is called upon by the subject to embody. It is from this idealization that the analyst has to fall in order to be the support of the separating *a*, in so far as his desire allows him, in an upside-down hypnosis, to embody the hypnotized patient.

This crossing of the plane of identification is possible. Anyone who has lived through the analytic experience with me to the end of the training analysis knows that what I am saying is true.

It is beyond the function of the *a* that the curve closes back upon itself, at a point where nothing is ever said as to the outcome of the analysis, that is, after the mapping of the subject in relation to the *a*, the experience of the fundamental phantasy becomes the drive. What, then, does he who has passed through the experience of this opaque relation to the origin, to the drive, become? How can a subject who has traversed the radical phantasy experience the drive? This is the beyond of analysis, and has never been approached. Up to now, it has been approachable only at the level of the analyst, in as much as it would be required of him to have specifically traversed the cycle of the analytic experience in its totality.

There is only one kind of psycho-analysis, the training analysis—which means a psycho-analysis that has looped this loop to its end. The loop must be run through several times. There is in effect no other way of accounting for the term *durcharbeiten*, of the necessity of elaboration, except to conceive how the loop must be run through more than once. I will not deal with this here because it introduces new difficulties, and because I cannot say everything, since I am dealing here only with the fundamentals of psycho-analysis.

The schema that I leave you, as a guide both to experience and to reading, shows you that the transference operates in the direction of bringing demand back to identification. It is in as much as the analyst's desire, which remains an *x*, tends in a direction that is the exact opposite of identification, that the crossing of the plane of identification is possible, through the mediation of the separation of the subject in experience. The experience of the subject is thus brought back to the plane at which, from the reality of the unconscious, the drive may be made present.

3

I have already indicated the interest to be found in situating, at the level of the subjective status determined as that of the *objet a*, what, for the past three hundred years, man has defined in science.

Perhaps the features that appear in our time so strikingly in the form of what are more or less correctly called the *mass media*, perhaps our very relation to the science that ever increasingly invades our field, perhaps all this is illuminated by the reference to those two objects, whose place I have indicated for you in a fundamental tetrad, namely, the voice—partly planeterized, even stratospherized, by our machinery—and the gaze, whose ever-encroaching character is no less suggestive, for, by so many spectacles, so many phantasies, it is not so much our vision that is solicited, as our gaze that is aroused. But I will leave these features to one side and stress something else that seems to me quite essential.

There is something profoundly masked in the critique of the

history that we have experienced. This, re-enacting the most monstrous and supposedly superseded forms of the holocaust, is the drama of Nazism.

I would hold that no meaning given to history, based on Hegeliano–Marxist premises, is capable of accounting for this resurgence—which only goes to show that the offering to obscure gods of an object of sacrifice is something to which few subjects can resist succumbing, as if under some monstrous spell.

Ignorance, indifference, an averting of the eyes may explain beneath what veil this mystery still remains hidden. But for whoever is capable of turning a courageous gaze towards this phenomenon—and, once again, there are certainly few who do not succumb to the fascination of the sacrifice in itself—the sacrifice signifies that, in the object of our desires, we try to find evidence for the presence of the desire of this Other that I call here *the dark God*.

It is the eternal meaning of the sacrifice, to which no one can resist, unless animated by that faith, so difficult to sustain, which, perhaps, one man alone has been able to formulate in a plausible way—namely, Spinoza, with his *Amor intellectualis Dei*.

What, quite wrongly, has been thought of in Spinoza as pantheism is simply the reduction of the field of God to the universality of the signifier, which produces a serene, exceptional detachment from human desire. In so far as Spinoza says—*desire is the essence of man*, and in so far as he institutes this desire in the radical dependence of the universality of the divine attributes, which is possible only through the function of the signifier, in so far as he does this, he obtains that unique position by which the philosopher—and it is no accident that it is a Jew detached from his tradition who embodies it—may be confused with a transcendent love.

This position is not tenable for us. Experience shows us that Kant is more true, and I have proved that his theory of consciousness, when he writes of practical reason, is sustained only by giving a specification of the moral law which, looked at more closely, is simply desire in its pure state, that very desire that culminates in the sacrifice, strictly speaking, of everything that is the object of love in one's human tenderness—I would say, not only in the rejection of the pathological object, but also in its sacrifice and murder. That is why I wrote *Kant avec Sade*.

This is the prime example of the eye-opening effect (*désillement*) that analysis makes possible in relation to the many efforts, even the most noble ones, of traditional ethics.

This is an extreme position, but one that enables us to grasp that man can adumbrate his situation in a field made up of rediscovered knowledge only if he has previously experienced the limit within which, like desire, he is bound. Love, which, it seems to some, I have down-graded, can be posited only in that beyond, where, at first, it renounces its object. This also enables us to understand that any shelter in which may be established a viable, temperate relation of one sex to the other necessitates the intervention—this is what psycho-analysis teaches us—of that medium known as the paternal metaphor.

The analyst's desire is not a pure desire. It is a desire to obtain absolute difference, a desire which intervenes when, confronted with the primary signifier, the subject is, for the first time, in a position to subject himself to it. There only may the signification of a limitless love emerge, because it is outside the limits of the law, where alone it may live.

24 June 1964

TRANSLATOR'S NOTE

This book is a translation of the first volume to be published of a series that will contain all Lacan's 'séminaires' since 1953, each volume representing the seminar for one academic year. *Les Quatre Concepts Fondamentaux de la Psychanalyse* is Book XI of that series, first delivered in 1964.

In his editor's note Jacques-Alain Miller alludes to the role of punctuation in the transcription of spoken language. In an attempt to render the inflexions of Lacan's speech, he has confined himself to the use of the comma, the full-stop, the dash and the paragraph. He is particularly anxious that this practice be maintained in the translation.

I am indebted to George Gross for suggestions made in the course of reading the translation in manuscript.

The short glossary below is not intended to provide adequate definitions of concepts. To do so would be quite alien to the nature of Lacan's work, which is peculiarly resistant to interpretation of a static, defining kind. Though rooted in Freudian psycho-analysis, Lacan's concepts have evolved over the years to meet the requirements of a constant reformulation of psycho-analytic theory. They are best understood, therefore, operationally, at work in a number of different contexts. However, some of the terms do call for comment, if only by way of introduction. This, with the assistance of Jacques-Alain Miller, I have attempted to provide. In certain cases, however, Lacan has preferred that a term be left entirely unglossed, on the grounds that any comment would prejudice its effective operation.

The first italicized word in brackets in each entry is Lacan's French word, the second, where necessary, Freud's German. It is assumed that the reader is familiar with the terminology of 'classical' Freudian psycho-analysis.

AGENCY (*instance, Instanz*). Lacan's use of the term '*instance*' goes well beyond Freud's '*Instanz*'. It represents, one might say, an exploitation of the linguistic possibilities of the French equivalent of Freud's German term. In the absence of any exact equivalent of Lacan's French term, one is thrown back to the term used by Freud's English translators, 'agency'. In Freud, the reference is most often to the three 'agencies' of the id, ego and superego. In Lacan, one must bear in mind the idea of an 'acting upon', even 'insistence', as in the title of the essay, 'L'instance de la lettre'.

COUNTERPART (*le semblable*). This notion of the 'specular ego' was first developed in the essay, 'The Mirror Stage'.

DEMAND (*demande*). See DESIRE.

DESIRE (*désir; Wunsch, Begierde, Lust*). The *Standard Edition* translates Freud's '*Wunsch*' as 'wish', which corresponds closely to the German word. Freud's French translators, however, have always used '*désir*', rather than '*voeu*', which corresponds to '*Wunsch*' and 'wish', but which is less widely used in current French. The crucial distinction between '*Wunsch*' and 'wish', on the one hand, and '*désir*', on the other, is that the German and English words are limited to individual, isolated acts of wishing, while the French has the much stronger implication of a continuous force. It is this implication that Lacan has elaborated and placed at the centre of his psycho-analytic theory, which is why I have rendered '*désir*' by 'desire'. Furthermore, Lacan has linked the concept of 'desire' with 'need' (*besoin*) and 'demand' (*demande*) in the following way.

The human individual sets out with a particular organism, with certain biological needs, which are satisfied by certain objects. What effect does the acquisition of language have on these needs? All speech is demand; it presupposes the Other to whom it is addressed, whose very signifiers it takes over in its formulation. By the same token, that which comes from the Other is treated not so much as a particular satisfaction of a need, but rather as a response to an appeal, a gift, a token of love. There is no adequation between the need and the demand that conveys it; indeed, it is the gap between them that constitutes desire, at once particular like the first and absolute like the second. Desire (fundamentally in the singular) is a perpetual effect of symbolic articulation. It is not an appetite: it is essentially excentric and insatiable. That is why Lacan co-ordinates it not with the object that would seem to satisfy it, but with the object that causes it (one is reminded of fetishism).

DRIVE (*pulsion*, *Trieb*). Lacan reinstates a distinction, already clear in Freud, between the wholly psychical *pulsion* (*Trieb*) and *instinct* (*Instink*), with its 'biological' connotations. As Lacan has pointed out, Freud's English translators blur this distinction by translating both terms as 'instinct'.

ENUNCIATION (*énonciation*). The distinction between '*énoncé*' and '*énonciation*' is a common one in contemporary French thinking. '*Énoncé*', which I translate as 'statement', refers to the actual words uttered, '*énonciation*' to the act of uttering them.

IMAGINARY, SYMBOLIC, REAL (*imaginaire*, *symbolique*, *réel*). Of these three terms, the 'imaginary' was the first to appear, well before the Rome Report of 1953. At the time, Lacan regarded the 'imago' as the proper study of psychology and identification as the fundamental psychical process. The imaginary was then the world, the register, the dimension of images, conscious or unconscious, perceived or imagined. In this respect, 'imaginary' is not simply the opposite of 'real': the image certainly belongs to reality and Lacan sought in animal ethology facts that brought out formative effects comparable to that described in 'the mirror stage'.

The notion of the 'symbolic' came to the forefront in the Rome Report. The symbols referred to here are not icons, stylized figurations, but signifiers, in the sense developed by Saussure and Jakobson, extended into a generalized definition: differential elements, in themselves without meaning, which acquire value only in their mutual relations, and forming a closed order—the question is whether this order is or is not complete. Henceforth it is the symbolic, not the imaginary, that is seen to be the determining order of the subject, and its effects are radical: the subject, in Lacan's sense, is himself an effect of the symbolic. Lévi-Strauss's formalization of the elementary structures of kinship and its use of Jakobson's binarism provided the basis for Lacan's conception of the symbolic—a conception, however, that goes well beyond its origins. According to Lacan, a distinction must be drawn between what belongs in experience to the order of the symbolic and what belongs to the imaginary. In particular, the relation between the subject, on the one hand, and the signifiers, speech, language, on the other, is frequently contrasted with the imaginary relation, that between the ego and its images. In each case, many problems derive from the relations between these two dimensions.

The 'real' emerges as a third term, linked to the symbolic and the imaginary: it stands for what is neither symbolic nor imaginary, and remains foreclosed from the analytic experience, which is an experience of speech. What is prior to the assumption of the symbolic, the real in its 'raw' state (in the case of the subject, for instance, the organism and its biological needs), may only be supposed, it is an algebraic x. This Lacanian concept of the 'real' is not to be confused with reality, which is perfectly knowable: the subject of desire knows no more than that, since for it reality is entirely phantasmatic.

The term 'real', which was at first of only minor importance, acting as a kind of safety rail, has gradually been developed, and its signification has been considerably altered. It began, naturally enough, by presenting, in relation to symbolic substitutions and imaginary variations, a function of constancy: 'the real is that which always returns to the same place'. It then became that before which the imaginary faltered, that over which the symbolic stumbles, that which is refractory, resistant. Hence the formula: 'the real is the impossible'. It is in this sense that the term begins to appear regularly, as an adjective, to describe that which is lacking in the symbolic order, the ineliminable residue of all articulation, the foreclosed element, which may be approached, but never grasped: the umbilical cord of the symbolic.

As distinguished by Lacan, these three dimensions are, as we say, profoundly heterogeneous. Yet the fact that the three terms have been linked together in a series raises the question as to what they have in common, a question to which Lacan has addressed himself in his most recent thinking on the subject of the Borromean knot (*Séminaire* 1974–75, entitled 'R.S.I.').

JOUISSANCE (*jouissance*). There is no adequate translation in English of this word. 'Enjoyment' conveys the sense, contained in *jouissance*, of enjoyment of rights, of property, etc. Unfortunately, in modern English, the word has lost the sexual connotations it still retains in French. (*Jouir* is slang for 'to come'.) 'Pleasure', on the other hand, is pre-empted by '*plaisir*'—and Lacan uses the two terms quite differently. 'Pleasure' obeys the law of homeostasis that Freud evokes in *Beyond the Pleasure Principle*, whereby, through discharge, the psyche seeks the lowest possible level of tension. '*Jouissance*' transgresses this law and, in that respect, it is *beyond* the pleasure principle.

KNOWLEDGE (*savoir, connaissance*). Where 'knowledge' renders '*connaissance*', I have added the French word in brackets. Most European languages make a distinction (e.g. Hegel's *Wissen* and *Kenntnis*) that is lost in English. In modern French thinking, different writers use the distinction in different ways. In Lacan, *connaissance* (with its inevitable concomitant, '*méconnaissance*') belongs to the imaginary register, while *savoir* belongs to the symbolic register.

LACK (*manque*). '*Manque*' is translated here as 'lack', except in the expression, created by Lacan, '*manque-à-être*', for which Lacan himself has proposed the English neologism 'want-to-be'.

LURE (*leurre*). The French word translates variously 'lure' (for hawks, fish), 'decoy' (for birds), bait (for fish) and the notion of 'allurement' and 'enticement'. In Lacan, the notion is related to '*méconnaissance*'.

MÉCONNAISSANCE. I have decided to retain the French word. The sense is of a 'failure to recognize', or 'misconstruction'. The concept is central to Lacan's thinking, since, for him, knowledge (*connaissance*) is inextricably bound up with *méconnaissance*.

NAME-OF-THE-FATHER (*nom-du-père*). This concept derives, in a sense, from the mythical, symbolic father of Freud's *Totem and Taboo*. In terms of Lacan's three orders, it refers not to the real father, nor to the imaginary father (the paternal imago), but to the symbolic father. Freud, says Lacan, was led irresistibly 'to link the appearance of the signifier of the Father, as the author of the Law, to death, even to the murder of the Father, thus showing that although this murder is the fruitful moment of the debt through which the subject binds himself for life to the Law, the symbolic Father, in so far as he signifies this Law, is certainly the dead Father' (*Écrits*, 'Of a question preliminary to any possible treatment of psychosis').

NEED (*besoin*). See DESIRE.

OBJET PETIT a. The '*a*' in question stands for '*autre*' (other), the concept having been developed out of the Freudian 'object' and Lacan's own exploitation of 'otherness'. The '*petit a*' (small 'a') differentiates the object from (while relating it to) the '*Autre*' or '*grand Autre*' (the capitalized 'Other'). However, Lacan refuses to comment on either term here, leaving the reader to develop an appreciation of the concepts in the course of their use. Furthermore, Lacan insists that '*objet petit a*' should remain untranslated, thus acquiring, as it were, the status of an algebraic sign.

OTHER (*Autre, grand Autre*). See OBJET PETIT a.

PLEASURE (*plaisir*). See JOUISSANCE.

REAL (*réel*). See IMAGINARY.

STATEMENT (*énoncé*). See ENUNCIATION.

SYMBOLIC (*symbolique*). See IMAGINARY.

WANT-TO-BE (*manque-à-être*). See LACK.

INDEX